THE PENITENTIARY IN CRISIS

SUNY Series in Deviance
and Social Control
RONALD A. FARRELL, Editor

THE PENITENTIARY IN CRISIS

From Accommodation to Riot in New Mexico

MARK COLVIN

With a Foreword by
Ben M. Crouch

STATE UNIVERSITY
OF NEW YORK PRESS

Published by
State University of New York Press, Albany

© *1992 State University of New York*

All rights reserved

Printed in the United States of America

For information, address State University of New York
Press, State University Plaza, Albany, N.Y. 12246

Production by Bernadine Dawes
Marketing by Terry Swierzowski

Library of Congress Cataloging-in-Publication Data

Colvin, Mark, 1947–
    The penitentiary in crisis : from accommodation to riot in New
Mexico / Mark Colvin : with a foreword by Ben M. Crouch.
        p. cm. — (SUNY series in deviance and social control)
    Includes bibliographical references and index.
    ISBN 0–7914–0929–5 (alk. paper) : $54.50. — ISBN 0–7914–0930–9
(pbk. : alk. paper) : $17.95
    1. New Mexico State Penitentiary. 2. Prison riots—New Mexico-
-Santa Fe. 3. Prison discipline—New Mexico—Santa Fe I. Title.
II. Series.
HV9475.N62N43 1992
365'.641—dc20
                                                                    91–3407
                                                                        CIP

10 9 8 7 6 5 4 3 2

This book is dedicated to
Roberto Samora,
Suzanne Colvin,
and the memory of
Michael Francke.

CONTENTS

FOREWORD

Through the 1970s, the Penitentiary of New Mexico (PNM) had a low national profile. Relatively small and isolated in the Southwest, PNM seemed to be outside the stream of turmoil that characterized many state prisons on both coasts and the midwest during the late 1960s and 1970s. The main prison outside Santa Fe gave every indication of being a generally orderly, rather progressive place, especially in the early 1970s. Yet PNM would undergo fundamental organizational change during that decade. While many of those changes ostensibly helped promote a peaceful prison, others began to move PNM slowly toward its destruction in a massive riot in February 1980.

In *The Penitentiary in Crisis,* Mark Colvin correctly focuses not on this tragic riot, but rather on the intricate course of external as well as internal change and conflict that influenced PNM for at least a decade prior to the riot. His effort is thus a major contribution to a growing, but still too sparse, case study literature on the transitions state prisons have undergone over the past two decades. Obviously, prison systems vary in many respects from state to state. They have different histories, population compositions, sizes, regional and economic conditions, and they have passed through 25 years of correctional change in America with varying degrees of conflict. They are at the same time, however, markedly similar. Wherever they are, all prisoners, officers and managers must live in a world where the ideal balance between accommodation and authority is always hampered by the inherent conflict among these players, sometimes including outside politicos. This book is a fascinating account of how conditions unique to PNM interact with the prison relationships and problems that are identifiable in any state prison.

Through the 1960s PNM was, like many other prisons of the time, stable and authoritarian. With the new decade, however, PNM began to experience important changes in policy and organization. These changes were encouraged in part by national efforts to improve the lot of the poor and powerless, including state prisoners. Impetus also came from a protest movement in northern New Mexico aimed at improving the state's treatment of some of its poorest citizens. Both trends fostered a new regime at PNM which embraced rehabilitation as the primary prison goal. New treatment and vocational programs soon followed. As had occurred in other prisons, the introduction of rehabilitation both altered the prisoner reward system and distressed veteran correctional officers. In PNM history, this was a period of accommodation during which prison managers allowed prisoners considerable freedom, while prisoners, in exchange, helped to maintain order.

In the mid-1970s this "pro-inmate" regime crumbled. Direct intervention by the New Mexico Governor led to the hiring at PNM of a new warden who could abide neither the loose security nor the rehabilitation programs he found there. The new warden's control orientation and the timing of his appointment coincided with a conservative political shift in New Mexico and in the country. His dismantling of the treatment orientation at PNM, supported by many correctional officers, led to an era of confrontation. This tightening of official control thwarted prisoners' rising expectations while it undermined the reward system that had for years helped keep prisoners in line.

The new warden was the first of a succession of managers appointed to run PNM through the late 1970s. As the Governor pressed for more direct control over corrections, PNM became a political football. Between 1976 and 1980, the prison system in New Mexico was characterized by political conflicts and organizational contradictions. The resulting lack of direction frustrated prisoners and staff alike, and tensions grew. Neither prison nor state officials seemed to appreciate how this administrative flux was affecting the critical, informal control systems defining safety and security in the cellblocks and dormitories of a prison. This turmoil was the prelude to a devastating riot.

In the early hours of February 2, 1980, inmates at PNM initiated a riot that for prisoner to prisoner violence is unrivaled in American prison history. By the end of the 36-hour riot, thirty-three prisoners had been killed; many prisoners and most of the correctional-officer hostages had been seriously injured. Gratuitous violence, including rape, torture, mutilation, and death by acetylene torch, was everywhere in evidence.

Immediately afterward, the New Mexico Attorney General appointed a team to investigate and report on the causes of this tragic event. A central figure of that team was Mark Colvin, who was then a sociology graduate student with considerable experience in prison work. This book is the result of years of work which began with that investigation. In it Colvin argues that, despite its fury, disorganization and apparent spontaneity, the riot can be understood as the brutal culmination of many elements of social change. From Mark Colvin's fine analysis of the interaction of these elements, it is difficult to escape the conclusion that the riot was at least in part the cost of political meddling, correctional inexperience and organizational naivete. The book therefore is, among other things, a compilation of lessons prison officials, politicians and students should not forget.

Ben M. Crouch
Texas A & M University
August, 1990

ACKNOWLEDGMENTS

This book is the result of years of association with many people who have given me insights, assistance, support, and encouragement. Many of the people who deserve credit for this study cannot be named. Hundreds of inmates, staff members, and officials from the Penitentiary of New Mexico, who consented to confidential interviews with the New Mexico Attorney General's Office and to off-the-record discussions and interviews with me, provided most of the information upon which this study is based. Their identities are held in confidence, though I will always remember them for their contribution.

This study would not have been possible without the enormous help of U.S. Senator Jeff Bingaman, who as New Mexico's attorney general in 1980 opened many doors to me by hiring me as a principal researcher for his probe into the 1980 New Mexico prison riot. As a member of the Attorney General's investigative team, I had access to all of the interviews and information collected during the probe. This huge information collection effort was conducted by the Attorney General's investigative team, whose other members included Reese Fullerton, David Brentlinger, Manny Aragon, Jim Wilson, Tim Orwig, Tess Monahan Fiddes, Ken Richards, Patrick Van Bargen, Carol Wantuchowicz, Patrick Whelan, Ray Gallagher, Jerrie Herrera, and Martha Wood. Michael Francke was coordinator for the first half of the inquiry; his tragic death in 1989 was a shock and profound loss not only to those of us who knew him but for anyone dedicated, as he was, to the improvement of corrections.

Ben M. Crouch provided the Attorney General's investigation with enormous assistance during the 1980 probe. He has continued to be a source of encouragement and support for my work.

My thanks to New Mexico Secretary of Corrections O.L. McCotter and PNM Warden Robert J. Tansy for providing me with up-dated information on the penitentiary.

Over the years, many other people have provided me with insights, assistance, and support. These include Raymon C. Forston, Tom Mayer, Robert M. Hunter, Robert Hanson, Del Elliott, Ed Greenberg, Bob Regoli, Martha Gimenez, John Pauly, Michael Neuschatz, Fred Templeton, Finn-Aage Esbensen, Linda Hill, Roberto Samora, Ruth Kay, Daniel O'Friel, Kitsy Schoen, Florence Slade, Lloyd McClendon, and the Espeset and Halbert clan.

I also owe thanks to John Stone, Chair of the Sociology and Anthropology Department, and to my other colleagues at George Mason University who afforded me the time and support necessary to finish this project. Mark Jacobs and Roger Lancaster gave me important guidance during the publishing process.

A special thanks to Suzanne Colvin who is a constant voice of encouragement and who read through and edited the early drafts of this book. Special thanks also to Thistle and Aram Neuschatz and to my parents, Emmett and Mary Lee Colvin.

Author's royalties for this book are donated directly to the American Friends Service Committee.

INTRODUCTION

Prisons in the United States today face a crisis, punctuated by violence, disorder, and overcrowding. This current crisis emerged in the 1970s when the ideological commitment to rehabilitation declined sharply, along with our nation's optimism about alleviating poverty and a host of other social ills (Cullen and Gilbert 1982). The liberal consensus of the post-World War II era gave consistent ideological support to correctional policies based on the notion of offender rehabilitation. The demise of this consensus has left corrections without a clear philosophy to guide its policies and programs.

The growth of the current prison crisis is also rooted in the series of shocks to the economy that first became apparent in the early 1970s and escalated in the 1980s (Box 1987). The recessions of 1974–75 and 1979–82 placed enormous strain on the penal system as the number of economically marginal members of U.S. society increased along with the prison population.

This erosion of liberal optimism and of the underlying economic structure of the U.S. provides the recent context for political decisions by agents of the state. The decision makers within state legislatures and bureaucracies respond to the political pressures created by these ideological and economic shifts. Yet, agents of the state also act with their own self-interests in mind (Evans, Rueschemeyer, and Skocpol 1985). Furthermore, these decision makers do not necessarily act in concert; they often contradict each others' decisions. Thus the outcome of state decisions may not reflect a concerted, thought out plan of action based on the interests of "The State." Rather, policy outcomes may reflect the myriad actions and miscalculations of decision makers who act in their perceived self-interest while responding to (or, at times, taking advantage of) the shifting ideological, economic, and political winds that blow, or at times blast, into the halls of state government. These decisions by agents of the state culminate in a product that often no one understands, intends, or claims responsibility for. Such is the process that produced the current crisis within our prison system. The decision making by the state, under the influence of the changing ideological and economic climate of the 1970s and 1980s, dramatically altered conditions of confinement and relations of control between the keepers and captives within our penal institutions.

The 1970s and 1980s were an important period of social, ideological, and economic change. As James B. Jacobs (1977: 2), in his social history of Stateville Penitentiary, has demonstrated, the history of a particular prison "reflects all of the major societal changes" of the period under study. Since 1975, the last year included in Jacobs' analysis, both society and prison organizations have undergone, yet again, enormous change and upheaval, the beginnings of which are captured in Jacobs' book.

Perhaps no prison in the United States better reflects the trend toward disorder, which has culminated in our current penal crisis, than the Penitentiary of New Mexico (PNM). This penitentiary experienced a drastic shift from order, before 1975, to growing disorder, beginning in 1976. It is remembered for the brutal 1980 riot during which thirty-three inmates were killed. This riot was a dramatic event in an organization that had already been facing growing disorder. The violence and disruptions continued at PNM long after the riot faded from public consciousness (Galan 1988). While the 1980 riot has been the subject of other works (Colvin 1982; Morris 1983; Office of the Attorney General 1980a, 1980b; Useem 1985; Useem and Kimball 1989) and is detailed in Chapter 6, the current book focuses on the larger organizational history of this penitentiary beginning in the 1960s and continuing into the 1980s. It is a period that encompasses the most significant changes in our ideologies, politics, and economy since the Great Depression.

The Penitentiary of New Mexico, built in 1956, emerged suddenly in 1968 from the "authoritarian regime" (Jacobs 1977) that characterized its early history. From 1968 to 1974, programs aimed at offender rehabilitation proliferated within the prison. The period can be seen as one in which inmates were predominantly controlled through accommodations, or incentives, connected to these programs. Escapes and violence were rare as the prison remained orderly. As the period came to a close, however, informal accommodations increased, including prison officials' tolerance of a growing trafficking into the prison of heroin. The resulting scandal, with its charges of corruption, led to a major organizational shake-up in 1975 that included the removal of PNM's top officials. The change in officials in late 1975 coincided with the ideological shift away from rehabilitation and with an economic downturn that led to large increases in inmate population.

The period from 1975 through 1977 was filled with confrontations at various levels of the New Mexico corrections bureaucracy. First, there was a confrontation between well-organized inmates and the new prison administration over a reduction in program opportunities and other accommodations. This conflict was reflected in organized inmate strikes and a major federal lawsuit initiated by inmates against the State of New Mexico. Second, there was a confrontation between various officials within the New Mexico corrections establishment over the direction of policies. The classic confrontation between "custody" and "treatment" was played out in the New Mexico corrections bureaucracy as officials struggled with each other for power and control over the future direction of the prison.

From 1978 to 1980, the prison organization and the corrections bureaucracy experienced a period of fragmentation. The confrontations of previous years gave way to administrative confusion and disorganization. The feuding top officials in New Mexico corrections provided little direction or leadership as the prison drifted toward increasingly arbitrary, inconsistent, and coercive tactics of control, which further incited inmate rage. Inmate relations also fragmented as the organized protests of the earlier period gave way to infighting and violence among inmates. The riot that erupted in 1980 reflected the disorganized relations among both agents of the state and inmates.

Since the 1980 riot, court-ordered reforms have been implemented and much of the poor living conditions and the overcrowding that had existed prior to 1980 have been eliminated. Yet PNM continued for several more years to experience the violence and escapes that characterized the disorder that led up to the 1980 riot (Galan 1988). The ideological, political, and administrative strife that had created instability after 1975 continued into the late 1980s.

A clear mission for corrections has yet to emerge in New Mexico and other states since the demise of the rehabilitative ideal in the mid-1970s. The mere warehousing of inmates is not a mission; it is not a means to any end that might give corrections departments a guiding direction. As Cullen and Gilbert (1982) argue, the rehabilitative ideal gives a legitimizing philosophy to the correctional enterprise. Any other approach becomes an absurdity as we spend more and more money to warehouse a seemingly never-ending stream of offenders in institutions that serve no apparent purpose but brutalization. Given this lack of direction, confused and contradictory policies continue to rule penal institutions. New Mexico, with the introduction of determinate sentencing in 1979, clearly moved away from the rehabilitative ideal. Yet its top correctional administrators have, in an on-again-off-again fashion, promoted rehabilitation.

This lack of policy direction has been fueled by a constant turnover of top administrators (see Appendix A). Complex organizations of all types are disrupted by the process of "administrative succession" (Gouldner 1954). Prisons are especially subject to instability when a new set of top administrators takes over and attempts to remold the organization in a new direction. In New Mexico, this often disruptive process of adminis-trative succession has been repeated on numerous occasions since 1975. As I write elsewhere (Colvin 1982: 456), "the [New Mexico] state correc-tions department was becoming *increasingly disorganized* as a result of the steady turnover in administrators. One warden and one secretary of cor-rections had administered the prison from 1970 to 1975, but after the 1975 shake-up, the prison [during the next four years] went through four wardens and [the department] through four secretaries."

New Mexico, which from 1966 to 1990 had a constitutional limit of one four-year successive term of office for its governor, was especially sus-ceptible to the disruptive consequences of administrative succession. Each new governor in the 1970s and 1980s had a new agenda for corrections and placed a new set of top administrators in charge to carry out this new agenda. And, at times, a governor simultaneously placed into key correc-tions department positions administrators who were at odds over the direction that correctional programs should take. From one four-year administration to the next, then, a new set of policies and a new set of cor-rections administrators had been put in place. PNM and other prisons throughout the United States have been increasingly unable to insulate their organizations from the political winds and whims emanating from their state capitol buildings and governors' mansions. The result has been continued disruption of policies and goals and a prison organization that is pulled in often contradictory directions.

The influence of the New Mexico Governor's Office on PNM has grown since the 1960s. The independence of PNM and its warden gradu-ally eroded after 1969 as it came under the purview of other executive agencies. To an increasing degree throughout the 1970s, these agencies, rather than PNM itself, acted on the Governor's behalf in presenting bud-gets and corrections initiatives to the state legislature. From the late 1960s to 1980, three agencies, the Corrections Commission, the Corrections Central Office, and the Governor's Council on Criminal Justice Planning, played larger roles. They supplanted PNM as lead agency for corrections. These three agencies along with PNM were eventually combined during a massive 1978 reorganization to form part of a new Criminal Justice Department; they immediately struggled for the lead role in developing correctional policies.

The major force behind the 1978 reorganization, Governor Jerry Apo-daca, left office in January 1979.His successor, Governor Bruce King (who had also served as governor from 1971 to 1975), dismantled key aspects of Apodaca's reorganized Criminal Justice Department. Governor King then gave simultaneous but vague messages of support for the leading role in corrections to the Corrections Commission, Corrections Central Office, and the former Governor's Council staff, three entities within the department that were actively pushing corrections in divergent and contradictory directions. As a result, the corrections administration became even more disorganized and fragmented as lines of authority and accountability dissolved. The confusing array of agencies that sprang up to oversee New Mexico corrections during the 1970s reflects the changing and, by 1979 and 1980, chaotic organizational context in which PNM operated.

The federal courts have attempted to provide direction, stability, and consistency in prison operations, as well as humane living conditions for inmates. But federal court intervention often becomes another confounding element in this confused direction of policies, especially, as has been the case in New Mexico, when agents of state governments ignore, fight, or attempt to undo court-mandated reforms.

A significant consequence of this confusion in policies is the failure to establish and maintain a consistent and effective strategy of control within the prison organization. There are obvious contradictions within a prison organization where an outnumbered staff, with limited resources, attempts to control the movement and behavior of captives who have no inherent reason to cooperate with their keepers (Silberman 1978). Such a situation is ripe for conflict. Strategies of control, which attempt to overcome these inherent contradictions, emerge and, for periods of time, are effective in holding the basic conflict between keepers and captives in a dormant state. Underlying the crisis we are witnessing in our prisons is the breakdown of control strategies that had placated and accommodated inmates and provided them with a self-interest in maintaining order.

A major focus of this book is to lay out the history of control strategies at one particular penitentiary. How did accommodative control strategies work? Why did they begin to break down? What internal organizational strains led to their demise? What forces external to the penitentiary hastened the breakdown of these controls? After these mechanisms of control broke down, the keepers had to devise new ways of keeping their charges in line. What were these new strategies of control? How did they affect relations between inmates and staff? How did they affect relations among inmates?

These questions focus on the dialectical interplay between the keepers and the captives. The prison contains within its walls opposing elements that make up its system. These elements tend to respond to and shape each other. As one shifts, the other shifts correspondingly, though not necessarily in ways that can be predicted. By applying Francis T. Cullen's (1983) concept of "structuring variables" to the prison setting, social control strategies by the prison administration can be seen to channel the behavior patterns of inmates. Shifts in control strategies thus may have unexpected and unintended consequences for the prison organization by altering the nature of relationships between staff and inmates and among inmates themselves. At times, these consequences can be explosive. The emerging crisis in the late 1970s at PNM can be understood as an outgrowth of such a shift in administrative control patterns. As is documented in the following chapters, when controls at PNM shifted from accommodative to coercive strategies, open confrontations between the keepers and captives emerged, and eventually solidarity among inmates gave way to fragmentation and infighting as inmate relations also became more coercive.

This book, then, draws attention to four interconnected tendencies that have disrupted prison organizations over the past two decades. First has been the lack of an effective legitimizing philosophy that gives direction to our correctional policies. As Christopher Adamson (1984) has demonstrated, correctional policies often shift with changes in the business cycle. Corresponding with the economic downturns of the 1970s and early 1980s, the demise in our consensus about rehabilitation has set corrections policies adrift. They are now dictated more by events growing out of the crisis than by any concerted, well-conceived plan of action. Second is the growing influence of politicians over correctional operations. The waning ideological commitment to rehabilitation and the growing influence of the "crime issue" in political campaigns have made prisons more subject than ever before to the whims of politicians. Third is the rapid turnover of top prison administrators who are unable to establish and carry through a consistent policy for corrections before they are dismissed by their politically appointed superiors. Disorganization in the corrections administration has been an obvious result of this repeated process of administrative succession. And fourth is the shift in control strategies over inmates. These four trends have had unexpected but nevertheless drastic consequences for the prison organization.

I bring personal experience to the study of prison organizations, particularly the Penitentiary of New Mexico. While completing my master's degree in sociology in the early 1970s, I served an internship as a correctional caseworker at the Federal Correctional Institution, Texarkana, Texas. I was exposed to highly trained professionals who understood the intricacies of inmate management and control. My mentor, O.C. Jenkins, an experienced caseworker at the federal prison, told me that you must always find an "honorable way out" for an inmate during a confrontation or dispute and to always make sure that each individual inmate is tied into your program through his perception that "he has something to lose by going against you and something to gain by going along with you." This bit of common sense, I discovered later, was actually an important key to control within prisons. During the completion of my master's degree I also studied prison organizational change and wrote a paper about administrative succession and disruption of prison organizations for a seminar in complex organizations.

After I graduated with my master's degree, I was told by a trusted advisor, my father, to experience the real world for a few years. I moved to Santa Fe, New Mexico, intent on working in corrections for a few years before continuing my graduate studies. My experience of the real world turned out to be somewhat more than I had anticipated. My move to Santa Fe coincided with the 1974 recession, which caused a doubling in the unemployment rate in New Mexico. For nine months in 1974, I worked sporadically in construction jobs and as a hospital orderly; but mostly I remained unemployed awaiting word on the many state jobs for which I had applied. This experience, no doubt, accounts for my focus on economic factors and unemployment in understanding social change. Finally, in late December 1974, I was called for a job interview at PNM.

During 1975, a year marked by important changes in the New Mexico prison organization, I worked at PNM as a counselor in education programs and as a parole officer in charge of coordinating a college release program between the prison and a local college. These two roles allowed me to observe PNM first-hand and, more importantly, to discuss the prison's history to that point with inmates, staff members, and officials.

In 1976, I became a corrections planner for the New Mexico Governor's Council on Criminal Justice Planning, which at that time was largely the "pass through" agency for federal funding of criminal justice programs. By 1977, however, the Governor's Council became the lead agency for New Mexico corrections policy as it spearheaded for then-Governor Jerry Apodaca a massive reorganization of state criminal justice agencies. In my capacity as corrections planner, I helped develop "Standards and Goals" for New Mexico corrections, assisted with the development of the "New Mexico Corrections Master Plan," wrote legislation based on the "Standards and Goals" and "Master Plan," reviewed budget requests from PNM, and assisted with the development of the Governor's reorganization plan. I thus observed and had a small role in the political process during this period of massive changes in New Mexico corrections.

In retrospect, many of the high hopes for corrections that were enunciated in the New Mexico Standards and Goals and the New Mexico Corrections Master Plan seem strangely irrelevant to the actual direction the prison organization took in the late 1970s. I began in 1978 to have a sense of despair and profound doubt about our capacity to determine the shape of New Mexico corrections. The Standards and Goals and Master Plan (which outlined progressive changes in corrections) were only effective to the extent that the Governor's Office gave them strong backing. By the time the Governor gave his full support to these initiatives, his term of office was close to expiration. In 1978, with new gubernatorial elections in a state that does not allow incumbent governors to succeed themselves, it became clear that initiatives begun in 1976 would not be completed. It also was becoming increasingly clear to me that the organizational structure of the prison was much more complex and resistant to planned, progressive change than I had imagined. Despite the Standards and Goals and good intentions of most top administrators in New Mexico corrections, PNM by 1978 was becoming increasingly unsafe, as violence became commonplace and conditions deteriorated.

I left my position in New Mexico corrections in late 1978 to continue my graduate studies, which focused on organizational change, the sociology of corrections, criminology, and political economy. I returned to graduate school with a new appreciation for the concept of "structural constraints" on human action.

A year and a half later, the riot at PNM occurred. Within a week of this event, in an attempt to update information for a graduate paper I had been writing on the organizational change at PNM from 1975 to 1978, I returned to Santa Fe. During my conversations with contacts in the correctional community (both staff members and former inmates), I was steered toward the office of New Mexico Attorney General Jeff Bingaman, who was preparing to undertake the official investigation of the riot. I gave Attorney General Bingaman the graduate paper based on my earlier observations of PNM; I discussed with him the possibility of my gathering more information. The following day, he offered me a role in the official investigation as a principal researcher into the long-term causes of the prison riot. I accepted.

The Attorney General made a decision very early in the investigation that was crucial for the inquiry. He had a choice of whether or not to involve the Attorney General's Office in the criminal investigations connected with the takeover and killings during the riot. He chose not to be part of these criminal investigations, which were then handled by the Santa Fe County District Attorney's Office. This decision allowed me and the other investigators involved with the Attorney General's probe to conduct confidential interviews with inmates, staff members, and officials and to guarantee the anonymity essential for encouraging respondents to give information during interviews. Respondents were asked not to mention their names during the taped interviews; and interview transcripts did not identify respondents. In addition, inmate respondents were asked not to mention the names of other inmates since ours was not a criminal investigation. This final condition was necessary to avoid any possibility of our inmate respondents' being labeled as "snitches" or informants, a particularly sensitive issue following the riot. This procedure meant that our respondents could not be called into court based on anything they might have told interviewers involved in the Attorney General's probe.

A total of 302 respondents were interviewed during all phases of the New Mexico Attorney General's investigation. These included current and former correctional officers, inmates, and state and corrections officials. Each interview lasted from two to four hours. In addition to these interviews, former prisoners and current and former staff members, who had been reliable sources of information for me in the past, provided important insights and information during the investigation. We also had access to the hundreds of other interviews that had been conducted by the New Mexico State Police during and immediately after the riot. Unless otherwise noted, quotes used in this book are drawn from the confidential interviews conducted during the New Mexico Attorney General's 1980 investigation of PNM. Throughout, I maintain confidentiality by identifying quotes only by the category of respondent: inmate, correctional officer (CO), or official.

The Attorney General's investigation consisted of two phases. First, we reconstructed the events during the riot itself (Office of the Attorney General 1980a). In this phase, 169 interviews were conducted. During this phase of interviewing, I asked preliminary questions of respondents about conditions leading up to the riot. These inquiries produced some useful information about conditions and the organizational structure of the prison, but more importantly became the basis for developing a comprehensive interview schedule, used during the second phase of the inquiry to conduct 133 interviews that focused on the long-term history of PNM (Office of the Attorney General 1980b).[1] This latter set of interviews included 34 correctional officers and 57 inmates who were selected through a random sample that was stratified by length of association with the prison.

I had primary responsibility during phase two of the Attorney General's probe for researching the long-term history of PNM and the conditions that led up to the 1980 riot. I conducted interviews and prepared the initial drafts of the phase two report. The research for this phase of the Attorney General's probe, however, was truly a team effort. The other investigators, report writers, and transcribers included Reese Fullerton (coordinator of phase two of the inquiry), David Brentlinger, Manny Aragon, Jim Wilson, Tim Orwig, Tess Monahan Fiddes, Ken Richards, Patrick Van Bargen, Carol Wantuchowicz, Patrick Whelan, Ray Gallagher, Jerrie Herrera, and Martha Wood. Michael Francke coordinated the inquiry during phase one.

I was the only social scientist and the only person who had worked in prisons to be employed on a full-time basis for the Attorney General's investigation. Ben M. Crouch, a professor of sociology at Texas A&M University, who has made extensive studies of prisons, provided me and the investigation staff with enormous assistance. Many of the insights in this study were the direct result of discussions, which often went late into the night, with Ben Crouch, who came to Santa Fe on several occasions during the investigation to assist with developing interview schedules, reviewing our reports, giving guidance to the investigators and the Citizens' Commission overseeing the probe, and generally helping to keep the inquiry on track. Ben Crouch's visits were especially helpful for me, since they allowed me to bounce ideas off an experienced prison researcher.

In September 1980, the final report of the Attorney General was released and I returned to graduate school to finish my doctoral studies. In 1982, I published my initial interpretation of the causes of the 1980 riot in *Social Problems* (Colvin 1982). The Attorney General's report and the *Social Problems* article do not provide the type of detailed social history that I think is necessary for a complete understanding of the organizational changes that led to the period of crisis in New Mexico corrections—a crisis that was punctuated by the 1980 riot. The current book draws upon these earlier works and the thousands of pages of interview transcripts from the New Mexico Attorney General's investigation. It also draws upon my own observations as a correctional employee and upon confidential interviews and discussions with scores of former prisoners, staff members, and corrections officials. These are people with whom I have developed mutual trust and who have been reliable sources of information throughout my association with New Mexico corrections.

Given my experience and academic training, I strongly believe that a sociological perspective, focusing on the prison organization and the structural changes that have occurred there, provides the most coherent explanation of the current prison crisis. The most immediate cause of prison disorder is the change in relations among inmates. This change cannot be understood without exploring the evolution of the organizational structure of prisons.

Both a prison administration's control structure and an inmate social structure contribute to the organization of prisons. The administration's control structure is comprised of the formal and informal relations of power and authority instituted and maintained by the prison staff to control inmate behavior. The inmate social structure involves relations of power, status, and economic exchange among inmates (Bowker 1977; Clemmer 1940; Davidson 1974; Kalinich 1980; Sykes 1958; Thomas and Petersen 1977). I deliberately use the term "inmate social structure," rather than "inmate subculture," to emphasize the relations of power among inmates rather than the supposedly isolated system of inmate roles, values, mores, and beliefs first emphasized by Clemmer (1940) and later by other researchers (cf., Bowker 1977). These authorities tend to perceive more of a subcultural than a social structural phenomenon when observing inmate relations. I have found the idea of an isolated inmate subculture to have little relevance in contemporary prisons. The structure of inmate relations, however, is extremely important for understanding the prison organization.

The prison administration's control structure greatly influences the pattern of inmate relations. Changes in the control structure have a potentially enormous impact on the inmate social structure. Thus, much attention is focused in the analysis on shifts in control strategies and their effect on inmate social relations.

These changes in the administration's control structure and the inmate social structure must be placed in a larger social context of historical and political trends outside the prison. As Jacobs (1977) makes clear in his case study of Stateville Penitentiary, changes within prisons are affected by and reflect changes in the larger society. While the current analysis attempts to go beyond Jacobs' "mass society" explanation by incorporating it within a "class society" perspective, it follows Jacobs' pioneering approach by connecting external with internal factors in understanding shifts in prison organizations. From the late 1960s to the 1980s, the U.S. experienced enormous ideological, economic, and political shifts that had direct consequences for control relations within prisons. A major focus of the current book is tracing the interaction between these important external and internal changes that affected the organizational development of PNM.

Before laying out the social history of this penitentiary, certain theoretical questions must first be considered. What forces and events of the larger society, external to prison organizations, have affected prisons in the last several decades? And what internal forces of change within the prison itself shape the prison organization? We consider these questions at a more theoretical level in the next chapter before exploring them through the concrete example of the organizational changes that took place at the Penitentiary of New Mexico.

THEORETICAL
CONSIDERATIONS

The prison organization is shaped by both internal and external forces and events. A complete understanding of change within a prison organization requires an exploration of these internal and external dynamics. This chapter lays out the broader theoretical issues, focusing first on the forces of the larger society that have affected prisons in general and second on the dynamics of organizational change within prisons.

THE PENITENTIARY IN "MASS SOCIETY" AND "CLASS SOCIETY"

The internal organization of the prison is greatly influenced by forces in the larger society. James B. Jacobs (1977) and John Irwin (1980) in their important prison studies broke new ground in exploring the connections between the internal organization of prisons and the events and trends outside prison walls. Following these pioneering works, I attempt to situate the Penitentiary of New Mexico (PNM) within a specific historical context that includes important patterns and shifts in political, economic, and ideological structures of U.S. society. In later chapters, this general theoretical discussion will be applied to the specific case history of PNM.

Jacobs (1977) argues that prison organizational change in recent decades can be understood as an outgrowth of an emerging "mass society," in which governing groups are more tightly bound by the rule of law, and rights to citizenship (including those for prisoners) expand through corporate forms of rational management. In this section, I argue that while the mass society perspective accurately describes an important movement during the post-World War II period, it does not adequately account for its origin or explain countertrends to it that have emerged since the mid-1970s. A conceptualization of larger social trends that also incorporates a "class society" perspective yields a more complete understanding of the contemporary United States and the place of prisons within it.

The "mass society" perspective of larger social trends

Jacobs (1983: 17) correctly maintains that "[p]risons do not exist in a vacuum: they are part of a political, social, economic, and moral order." Jacobs' *Stateville* (1977) is the most important attempt to date at situating changes in prison organizations within larger societal trends. I outline Jacobs' basic argument below.

Following the theoretical work of Edward Shils (1975), Jacobs views the U.S. as moving toward a mass society, in which marginal groups on the periphery are continually being brought into the center of society's institutions and value system through a process of inclusion and expansion of rights to citizenship (Jacobs 1977: 6). With rapid industrialization and urbanization, a mass society that promotes egalitarian values develops. In response to these values, a new national (or "center") elite, composed of leaders from large-scale (core-sector) industries, major universities, national print and electronic media, and the federal government, promotes legal and bureaucratic constraints upon governing groups in both the center and periphery of society. Thus, "Shils points to a heightened sensitivity on the part of the elite to the dignity and humanity of the masses" (Jacobs 1977: 6). According to Jacobs, the granting of rights to prisoners and the construction of legal forms of accountability over prison administrators are specific manifestations of this trend toward mass society.

This theory of a movement toward rational forms of governance, which includes expansion of legally defined rights and obligations, concentrates mainly on the activities of governing groups as the movers of societal trends. In Jacobs' (1977) study of Stateville Penitentiary, the primary focus is on the top administrators' struggle to build an accountable, more enlightened, bureaucratic order, based on a "corporate model," to replace a declining and fractured authoritarian regime, which had been disrupted by forces outside the prison walls.

According to this view, conflict in prisons, and indeed in the society as a whole, arises during the period of transition from one state of equilibrium, based on particularistic rule through personal dominance, to an emerging state of equilibrium, based on the generalized rule of law and bureaucratic dominance. Thus the prison faces a time of turmoil as it moves from a period of equilibrium based on authoritarian rule to a new period of equilibrium based on a corporate model of bureaucratic rule.

For Jacobs, the period of equilibrium at Stateville Penitentiary from 1936 to 1961 was based largely on the personal dominance of Warden Joseph E. Ragen, whose authoritarian regime was never challenged by outside interest groups or by his nominal superiors in the Illinois Department of Corrections. During this period, Stateville Penitentiary was an organization on the periphery of the emerging mass society. It remained untouched by the value system supporting the expansion of citizenship rights, legal obligations, and restraints on officials.

However, beginning in the 1960s, external forces emanating from mass society disrupted the equilibrium at Stateville. The extension of legal rights and obligations to all sectors of society was, according to mass society theory, a growing phenomenon arising out of the continuation of mass urbanization and industrialization. A new national order, reflecting the emergence of egalitarian values, was steadily and increasingly challenging old patterns of authoritarian rule in the periphery, i.e., in rural, agricultural economies, political machines in cities, and other relatively isolated social systems. These forces from the center precipitated a disruption of the long-standing equilibrium in social relations in communities and organizations on the periphery, including state penitentiaries like Stateville.

At Stateville, "the prison became less able to dominate its relations with the outside" (Jacobs 1977: 52). Outside interest groups demanding rights for prisoners and access to the prison were backed by institutions, such as the federal courts, that were influenced by the value system emanating from the "center." The disruption of equilibrium was also exacerbated by the entry into Stateville of members of Chicago's inner-city gangs who brought their street wars into the prison. Increasingly, outside society invaded the prison. According to Jacobs' analysis, this disruption would continue until the penitentiary, like other peripheral organizations, became fully integrated into the emerging mass society. This would only occur when new bureaucratic structures arose that protected inmates' rights and bound the prison administration to the rule of law.

This movement toward a corporate-bureaucratic, rational-legal administration is not, according to Jacobs, unilinear; Jacobs (1977: 10) points to "various countertrends and internal inconsistencies and limits in the movement toward increased bureaucratization." He focuses much of his discussion on the "tension between the rehabilitative ideal, which prescribed the individualization of treatment, and the rule of law, which demanded universalistic criteria of decision making," as a primary internal inconsistency in the movement toward a corporate-bureaucratic model (1977: 206). The corporate-bureaucratic model that Jacobs discusses reflects the "justice model," which was popular among some liberals during the mid-1970s when they rejected rehabilitation as a goal of corrections and opted for legal, due process reforms (Cullen and Gilbert 1982). Other limits that Jacobs mentions are the increasing prisoner populations and the fiscal crisis (which were only beginning to emerge at the time of his writing).

Moving beyond Jacobs' analysis, the fiscal crisis, prison overcrowding, and the ideological shift away from rehabilitation emerged from even deeper limitations and contradictions of U.S. society. Incorporating mass society theory's insights within a class society perspective gives greater understanding of the recent direction of penal policies and prison conditions. The trajectory toward a realization of mass society in which rights of citizenship are extended to all members has been undermined by countertrends, limits, and contradictions that were not fully apparent when Jacobs was writing in the mid-1970s. These limits and contradictions are not merely conflicts between ideal models of governance. More fundamentally, these limits on the extension of rights spring from basic contradictions in the political economy of modern capitalism.

An important limit to the extension of rights was reached in the late 1960s when the movement for legal and civil rights was transformed into an effort to gain economic rights through Dr. Martin Luther King's organization of the Poor People's March (Hampton 1990). Shortly following this period, the larger society began to retreat from the extension of rights, and has increasingly shown signs of polarization in economic conditions between classes (Katz 1989), of which the deterioration of prisons is but an aspect.

The "rational," corporate-liberal approaches to corrections that Jacobs presents as a model grew out of a specific social-historical context that was characterized by a long wave of economic expansion following World War II. By 1975, this expansion ended along with the liberal optimism it spawned. The "justice model" of the mid-1970s represented liberalism in retreat, and paved the way for the hard-line conservative approaches that dominate today (Cullen and Gilbert 1982). Federal courts to some extent have provided a counter to the hard-line factions in state legislatures and governor's mansions. But since the mid-1970s, corporate-liberal approaches for solving the social problems of poverty and crime have been increasingly abandoned throughout the United States. This important ideological change has been spurred by shifts in our economic and political order. These changes underlie the current prison crisis.

A "class society" perspective of larger social trends

The value system that emerged during the post-World War II period supporting an expansion of rights did not inevitably flow out of urbanization and industrialization. The idea of expanding rights of citizenship, which indeed has been an important ideological trend since World War II, emerged initially in response to workers' movements in the 1930s and 1940s. It was through the limited successes of these movements that certain rights have been granted, often as concessions designed to restore order.

Jacobs (1977: 6) agrees with Shils' assessment of "a heightened sensitivity on the part of the [center] elite to the dignity and humanity of the masses." Adherence to a value system supporting greater equality, according to the mass society perspective, caused these center, or national, elites to shape social institutions around bureaucratic, corporate models in which rights and obligations are clearly spelled out. It is more historically accurate, however, to view the limited expansion of rights that did occur as emanating less from the actions and values of center elites and more from those arising from popular social movements (e.g., McElvaine's [1984] history of the New Deal and Great Depression).[1] Center elites (composed largely of the leaders of major, core-sector industries as well as officials in the federal government) were hit earlier with confrontations from social movements than were governing groups on the periphery. The labor movement, which periodically from the 1890s until the late 1940s encountered violent opposition from owners and managers of major industries, eventually gained important concessions that restored labor peace. The granting to organized labor of legal protection for collective bargaining and regular cost of living adjustments in wages were important extensions of rights. These concessions, which emerged in the 1930s and late 1940s, set important precedents that shaped post-World War II industrial relations and the prevailing corporate-liberal ideology that dominated until the mid-1970s (Brody 1980; Davis 1986). This ideology is primarily what mass society theorists are capturing in their description of values that emanate from the "center."

This corporate-liberal ideology, which reflected the compromise that ended the labor wars, influenced later responses to social movements that emerged in the 1960s. Limited concessions became an important tool for restoring order and maintaining control. Only after a half century of continued labor violence and attempts at controlling workers through coercive means was labor granted significant concessions. Leaders of major core-sector industries (an important element of the "center elite" referred to by mass society theorists) were not acting for the most part on an impulse emanating from their adherence to an egalitarian value system. Rather, they were responding to the pragmatic needs of the moment in which continual labor strife threatened their opportunities, following World War II, to accumulate wealth on an unprecedented scale. They needed to extend to labor certain rights and establish a structure of bureaucratic rule to ensure labor peace and their continued control of production (Brody 1980; Lichtenstein 1982).

The compromises with labor and the establishment of a bureaucratic, corporate structure became the model for creating order and stability in other organizations. This model did not merely arise from a new value system based on an emerging "mass society"; it emerged only after many long years of labor strife and workers' movements. And, importantly, it was a model that rested on continued expansion of the U.S. economy, an expansion that became more precarious after 1974 (Davis 1986).

Mass society theory tends to focus on the conflict in values between the center and the periphery. While such conflict is an important element of a capitalist society such as that of the U.S., which has had a history of uneven regional economic development, a more basic class conflict is assumed in the class society perspective to be the underlying dynamic.

The most fundamental antagonism in capitalist societies revolves around the extraction of surplus labor. David F. Greenberg (1981: 14) defines surplus labor as "labor [or its products] above and beyond what is needed to 'reproduce' the laborer from day to day and from generation to generation...the form in which it is appropriated varies greatly [from society to society]." Greenberg (1981: 28) goes on to explain: "In the capitalist mode of production, workers sell their labor power to capitalists in return for wages. The difference between the value that workers receive in the form of wages and the value they produce is surplus value—the specific form that surplus labor takes in the capitalist mode of production—and is appropriated by the capitalist. This is the source of profits." As capitalists compete to expropriate higher levels of surplus value from workers, wealth, used to produce further wealth, increases in a process known as capital accumulation. This process gives the capitalist mode of production its dynamic impetus and constant drive for expansion. Capital accumulation thus involves inherent conflicts between capital and labor over the appropriation of surplus value and between the capitalist class and petty commodity producers over expansion of capitalist markets into precapitalist economic structures. The basic dynamics and operations of capitalism induce antagonisms. Historically, these conflicts are effectively contained, or explode to the surface, depending on specific structures of social control.

Such structures (which can be economic, political, and ideological) are instituted by capitalists and governing groups in an attempt to manage conflict. These structures may involve concessions, such as wage increases to allay worker discontent, or coercion, such as dismissal from work for engaging in union activities. The antagonistic relations that arise from exploitation in the accumulation process may be conceptualized (metaphorically) as a centrifugal force that pushes society toward disintegration. This is a constant force operating within the capitalist system that promotes periodic disruptions and necessitates the establishment (if historical conditions permit) of specific control structures. These structures can be seen (again metaphorically) as a centripetal force that pulls the society toward integration. When effectively implemented, they obscure the underlying antagonism that is at the bottom of social relations in class societies. Equilibrium arises only to the extent that this antagonism can be obscured, contained, or controlled. Rather than seeing equilibrium as the normal state of society which is periodically disrupted by external forces, the class society perspective sees normalcy in open conflict, which for periods of varying duration is made dormant through structures of social control.

Disruption of these control structures does not arise only from external sources but more importantly from internal contradictions that periodically undermine or tear apart the social controls that provide order. External sources of disruption become the catalyst for disorder only to the extent that these external forces bring to the surface underlying conflicts already present within a particular organization or social system. Social controls that have kept these conflicts contained can indeed be disrupted by external forces, but it is the underlying conflict within the organization or social system itself that is at the root of open disruption.

For example, the underlying conflict between capital and labor can be obscured and contained, as it was in the 1950s, through wage concessions or other accommodations. Severe economic crises can undermine the ability of capitalists to maintain such accommodations. This external crisis in the economy can lead to the disruption of important concessions that were effectively holding back the antagonism between workers and management, and were thus providing key elements of social control. The ensuing conflict arises as an open expression of an already existing internal contradiction between opposing forces within the enterprise.

Similarly, an underlying contradiction exists within the prison organization. Inmates are in prison against their will; the staff can and will use force to keep them in prison. Yet such a forceful confrontation is rare. Social controls within the prison usually keep this underlying organizational contradiction dormant, allowing a state of seeming equilibrium to exist. External forces, such as intervention by the courts or social movements by disenfranchised groups which begin to affect prisoners' consciousness, can disrupt these social controls and allow the underlying antagonism between the keepers and captives to break out in more open forms of conflict.

In the prison, as in capitalist enterprises, social controls can also break down under the force of internal sources of change. Concessions to workers or to prisoners may lose their effectiveness as these organizational subordinates begin to expect and demand further concessions in exchange for their continued cooperation in achieving organizational ends. These demands may collide with the strained resources available to the managers of these organizations. Under this internal source of strain, controls may break down, again leading to open antagonism between the opposing camps within the organization.

John Irwin in *Prisons in Turmoil* (1980) tends to view prisons from a conflict perspective. Irwin explicitly rejects the view of the prison, promoted by Sykes (1958), as a self-contained "social system" that seeks a state of equilibrium. Instead the prison is seen to contain opposing groups that reflect and are influenced by opposing groups external to the prison. The internal conflict between prison administrators and prisoners becomes more acute as social movements affect the consciousness of prisoners. Indeed, Irwin cites the Black and Chicano power movements as important sources of militancy among California prisoners in the 1960s. This politicization of prisoners undermined the effective control networks, based on rehabilitation programs and indeterminate sentencing, that prevailed in California prisons in the 1950s and 1960s. The ensuing crisis in prison management that these movements induced led to the institution by prison administrators of coercive controls that attempted to "divide and conquer" prisoner groups. These coercive controls and the growing influence of ethnically based prison gangs with ties to urban street gangs led to conflicts and violence among inmates, which undermined the political solidarity among prisoners that had emerged in the late 1960s. As social controls were continually disrupted the prison moved into a state of even greater turmoil.

The external forces that Irwin cites—militant movements by Blacks and Hispanics and later the importation of street gangs—are also cited by Jacobs as having profound effects on the internal organization of the prison. However, the growing militancy of minority groups in the 1960s, and gang violence, both within and outside prisons, in the 1970s and 1980s, have even deeper roots in the dynamics of modern capitalist society.

Capitalist development and surplus populations

Modern capitalist society can be conceptualized as a *social formation* (Greenberg 1981) composed of two modes of production: capitalist and petty commodity production. In petty commodity production, the direct producer obtains means for subsistence by selling, on a very localized market, commodities that he or she owns and has independently produced with the possible help of family members, apprentices, tenant workers, and only a few, if any, wage laborers. In contrast, capitalism is characterized by larger scale (partially socialized and interdependent) production of commodities by direct producers who are separated from ownership and control over the means and ends of production and must, therefore, sell their labor power for wages in order to obtain means for subsistence.

Limited by its less productive technical means and division of labor, petty commodity production is geared toward smaller-scaled, simple reproduction of the family unit. However, market competition between producers engenders an expansionary thrust in which direct producers are compelled to introduce innovations in technology and expand the division of labor, to avoid being increasingly separated from the means and ends of production as they lose out in this competition. Thus petty commodity producers predominate in areas where profits are low or precarious (such as small family farming enterprises), and competition subjects petty commodity producers to the constant threat of losing their source of livelihood and being forced to sell their labor power to capitalists. Capitalism's expansionary impetus constantly and increasingly encroaches upon petty commodity producers and forces them to be engulfed by capitalist relations of production.

Where mass society theorists see an expansion of values from the center to the periphery, the class society perspective also sees a more fundamental, direct economic intrusion from center, or core, oligopolies into traditionally rural, agricultural systems organized around petty commodity production. These encroachments of the capitalist mode of production force people to leave rural areas in search of jobs. Many of these people are able to find work and even prosper; others fall into urban poverty to become part of the "surplus population" (Braverman 1974; Spitzer 1975).

Surplus populations are largely a product of capitalist development. Throughout the history of capitalism, technological innovations, changes in production relations, and expanding markets (especially in agriculture) have increasingly pushed masses of people from rural areas into cities. The last great "setting free" in the U.S. of agricultural workers and tenant farmers (many of whom were Black and Hispanic) occurred after World War II, with the technological revolution in agriculture and the rapid expansion of capitalist firms into the less developed, or peripheral, areas of the South and Southwest. More recently, shifts in agricultural production relations in the Third World, especially in the Caribbean and Latin America, have added to the numbers of this surplus population as poor people from these areas enter the U.S., both legally and illegally, searching for work. In addition, continual technological innovation in industry and the flight of domestic corporations to cheap labor markets abroad are growing sources of the surplus population in the U.S. Thus the growth and expansion of capitalism entails the relative growth of surplus populations (Lynch 1988; Lynch and Groves 1989).

The surplus population includes those members of capitalist society who are economically redundant and marginal to its productive relations (Braverman 1974). Though marginal to capitalist production, they nonetheless play an important role in the maintenance of capitalist relations. This role has changed in correspondence with variations in labor market structures, from non-union to unionized labor markets.

In non-unionized labor market structures, surplus populations create an excess supply of labor-power and thus foster intensified job competition, which serves to enhance the position of management in bargaining for (or forcing upon workers) cheaper labor costs. These factors also reinforce the discipline of labor at the point of production by undermining any attempts at collective organizing by workers. With large surplus populations actively competing for jobs, workers who organize or demand higher wages are easily replaced. This threat of replacement, and consequent pauperization, is the most fundamental of coercive controls in capitalist workplaces. Surplus populations thus provide an essential weapon, external to the production process, for capitalist exploitation in non-union labor markets.

These competitive, non-union labor markets cannot employ all, or even a great proportion, of the surplus population. Following the logic of labor supply and demand, wages under conditions of maximum employment would rise to a point where many enterprises in a competitive economy would become bankrupt, thus reproducing redundant labor. While this structural limit to their actual employment exists, surplus populations must nonetheless be forced into the role of job competitors.

Steven Spitzer (1975) argues that while surplus populations play an essential role in capitalist relations, they are, at the same time, "problem populations" that potentially create social disorder. Thus, state policies are required for their control. An array of control mechanisms over surplus populations have evolved with the development of capitalism. Some controls attempt to gain compliance through concessions and accommodations. Piven and Cloward (1971) argue that welfare concessions are a primary tool for "regulating the poor." Controls can also be coercive. Rusche and Kirchheimer (1939) were early proponents of the view that prisons (in addition to crime control) act as mechanisms to control the unemployed and regulate labor markets.

Rusche and Kirchheimer also argue that rates of imprisonment and prison conditions correspond to labor market conditions. With higher unemployment, more people are sent to prison. And, with worsening conditions of life for the poor during periods of high unemployment, conditions of life in prisons also deteriorate.[2]

There is no conscious effort to increase the use of prisons during periods of high unemployment, or to create worsened conditions in prisons. While many subtle mechanisms produce these consequences (Milovanovic 1983), some not-so-subtle ones also play an important role. As John Hagan (1989: 7) points out, "many sentencing guidelines and criminal codes designate unemployment as a legitimate criterion in determining pre-trial release status and the post-conviction use of probation."

Judges are likely to base these decisions (when other factors such as prior criminal record and seriousness of offense are about equal) on judgments of individuals' stability. One important indicator a judge often uses to determine "stability" is whether or not an individual has steady employment. During periods of high unemployment, a judge is more likely to observe a greater number of "unstable" individuals and send them off to prison. This apparent individual attribute is largely a reflection of the structural condition of the economy. Also, conditions in prisons tend to deteriorate not by conscious design but because government revenues drop while prison populations grow during an economic downturn. The tendency toward higher imprisonment rates under worsening penal conditions when unemployment is high reflects the connections between labor markets and prisons.

Rusche and Kirchheimer also imply that penal policies shift with the business cycle from harsh practices with limited opportunities for rehabilitation to more enlightened practices that promote rehabilitation. Prisons act (again not consciously) as a mechanism for holding excess workers off the job market during periods of high unemployment. Periods of low unemployment create greater demand for workers entering the labor market. Thus, during economic booms, rehabilitation programs and prison industries serve to draw more people into the labor market as viable job competitors.

Many of Rusche and Kirchheimer's ideas are supported empirically. Using a set of time-series analyses, Ivan Jankovic (1980) found a significant positive relationship between levels of unemployment and imprisonment in the U.S. from 1926 to 1974, even when controlling for levels of population, crime, and arrests.

James Inverarity and Daniel McCarthy (1988: 274), citing evidence from their time-series analysis of 1948–1984 data on U.S. unemployment and state prison admissions, conclude, "Rusche and Kirchheimer appear to be substantially correct about the relationship between labor markets and criminal sanctions in capitalist society. Our results confirm a variety of previous investigations that link rates of unemployment directly to prison admissions."

Christopher Adamson (1984) examined six periods of U.S history from 1790 to 1914 to demonstrate the correspondence between business conditions and labor supply and shifts in penal policies. Generally, Adamson found that during periods of economic downturn, criminal populations are viewed as "threats" and are more subject to severe penal sanctions. During periods of economic upturn, criminal populations are seen as exploitable economic resources, whose treatment as prisoners is generally aimed at reform and reintegration into society's labor force. As comparative examples, Adamson (1984: 454) discusses "boom and bust" periods in the early 1800s:

> The economic upswing during Jackson's presidency [1829–37] led to a penological outlook which combined reformative treatment with productive industry. During the recession of 1818–22 and the depression of 1837–43, when prison industries were brought to the point of financial collapse, penologists had serious doubts about both the reformative and productive potential of prison labor. And unlike the Jacksonian reformers, they viewed captive criminal populations more as a dangerous threat to social order than as an economic resource to be exploited.

The rise and fall of the "rehabilitative ideal" in the nineteenth century closely paralleled the rise and fall of economic conditions. A similar rise and fall of the rehabilitative ideal occurred from 1945 to 1980 in correspondence with shifts in political and economic conditions. It is these shifts that underlie the emergence and decline of the ideology portrayed in mass society theory and the recent trends and countertrends in U.S. prisons.

The rise of corporate liberalism, 1945–1974

The labor shortage and economic mobilization during World War II swelled the ranks of labor unions. But workers' wartime grievances against management could not be effectively addressed by organized labor because of its no-strike pledge during the war. Thus the end of the war "released a wave of pent-up frustration" among the now much larger and better organized labor movement (Lichtenstein 1982: 222). This change in labor union strength coincided with two other important conditions affecting major core industries at the center of the U.S. economy. First, World War II provided unprecedented windfall profits for these more monopolized core firms. Second, pent-up consumer demand (arising from wartime commodity shortages), the core sector's ability to set noncompetitive prices (which had risen sharply following the war), and an emerging international market meant that the core sector was poised to accumulate capital at an expanding rate unparalleled in the history of capitalism. The "labor problem" was the only obstacle to the core sector's control of this expansion. The strike wave beginning in the late fall of 1945 "was bigger than any previous strike wave in American history" (Davis 1986: 86). Labor was demanding not only a greater share of economic growth but also a significant role in production and management decisions. Unions were solidly organized as never before. At the same time, core industries facing these militant workers had unprecedented economic resources. Thus core capitalists, by the late 1940s, responded to organized worker opposition by granting economic concessions and establishing bureaucratic mechanisms that allowed management to retain complete control over the production process (Brody 1980; Davis 1986). These concessions led to a new "corporate model" of management that greatly expanded bureaucratic controls over workers and supervisors in many core sector firms (Edwards 1979).

These important concessions to organized labor, which began in response to militant labor organizing during the 1930s but greatly expanded following World War II, altered the labor market dynamics through which these core sector firms operated. Non-union labor markets (still prevalent in the more competitive periphery-sector of capital) operated through the dynamics of labor supply and demand and thus relied on surplus populations actively competing for jobs. These labor markets were replaced in many core-sector firms by an internal system of labor control that included wage incentives, job promotion ladders, and bureaucratic rules. Except for some entry level positions, this more unionized, internal labor market removed these core-sector firms from the external labor market forces of classical capitalism, and thus from the effects of job competition by surplus populations (Edwards 1979; Gordon, Edwards, and Reich 1982). As Mike Davis (1986: 112) writes:

> In tandem with the seniority system and internal promotion within the plant, the wage system thus established for the core economy, and for the core only, became relatively immune to the cyclical layoffs and the tides of the labor reserve army [i.e., of the surplus population].

Importantly, these concessions contributed greatly to the decline during the 1950s of labor militancy.[3] A lesson in the use of concessionary controls and accommodative strategies for dealing with disruptive groups was thus imprinted on the most powerful group in the U.S., the owners and executives of the leading core firms. This first major granting of rights laid the groundwork for future confrontations with militant social movements and became the basis for a corporate-liberal ideology, which would blossom in the 1960s, supporting the extension of rights of citizenship. The precedent set by these important concessions to organized labor would be applied to the poor people's movements of the 1960s (Piven and Cloward 1977). The traditional "iron fist" would now be augmented, and at times replaced, with the "velvet glove" (Institute for the Study of Labor and Economic Crisis 1982).[4]

This corporate-liberal ideology, similar to the value system described by mass society theorists as emanating from the center, was shaped by earlier struggles between capital and labor and gave important justification for the compromises and concessions that ended labor strife. The mass society described by Shils and Jacobs is largely a theoretical depiction of the "New Deal order" (Fraser and Gerstle 1989) that emerged in the late 1940s and dominated until the early 1970s. In this new order, leading core industries and a now tamed organized labor bureaucracy provided a new model of social control.[5]

These late 1940s' actions by organized labor and the subsequent concessions from management altered the relationship between these core-sector industries and the surplus population. The latter no longer provided for these core firms a source of job competition that controlled wage demands and disciplined workers. Wages and the labor process were now controlled largely through bureaucratic mechanisms internal to these firms, at least during the period from the 1950s until the early 1970s.

While the surplus population no longer provided an external source of job competition in these core industries' labor markets, this population did present a recurring (and always potential) political threat to the order and legitimacy of the capitalist system. During the Great Depression, militant movements by the unemployed were taking shape and radical proposals for "sharing the wealth" were gaining widespread support (McElvaine 1984). Later, in the 1960s, the Civil Rights movement spawned welfare rights, Black Power, La Raza, and poor people's movements that included radicalized members of the urban poor (Hampton 1990; Piven and Cloward 1977). The 1960s' civil disorders and ghetto riots hammered home to influential industrialists and federal officials the extent and ferocity of discontent among the poor.

Thus propelled by militant poor people's movements (Piven and Cloward 1977), the federal government expanded concessions such as welfare (Berkowitz and McQuaid 1980; E.S. Greenberg 1979). The rapid growth of welfare concessions from the 1930s through the early 1970s, and the emphasis on accommodative strategies for controlling discontented groups (Janowitz 1969), became major responses to these political threats.

Welfare concessions included not only higher benefit levels, though this was a major concession, but the 1960s' "War on Poverty" programs also embraced attempts at political accommodation through strategies of power sharing. In its original conception, community action programs of the War on Poverty directly involved poor people in neighborhood-controlled boards, which had a major voice in program decisions (Chafe 1986; Hodgson 1976; Lemann 1988). The direct connection between activists in poverty areas and federal agencies served a twofold purpose. First, directly inspired by the theoretical insights of Cloward and Ohlin (1960), empowerment of local poverty groups was seen as an important component in building the neighborhood cohesion that was essential for reducing crime and raising communities out of poverty. Second, through the federal programs, more radical activists in these poverty areas could either be supplanted by less militant leadership or co-opted by channeling their activities toward less disruptive behavior. Since surplus populations no longer functioned to regulate the labor market for major core industries, programs that raised the levels of subsistence for the poor presented no threat to the core sector's labor market arrangements. In fact, the welfare and political accommodations might provide a positive benefit to center elites by restoring peace to urban areas that were rocked by riots and open defiance.

Many of the innovations contained in the original War on Poverty were soon rescinded, however, as local politicians, connected to businessmen in more competitive periphery-sector industries, were able to shift resources away from these neighborhood boards. These federally sponsored, community-action boards were perceived by local elites as a direct political threat. "Community action was designed to let poor people substantially determine their own poverty-fighting strategies, which might be anything, including organizing opposition to the local power structure" (Lemann 1989: 56). Also, businesses in the periphery sector of capital, which still relied very heavily on active job competition by surplus populations to maintain a low-wage labor market, were threatened by programs that offered alternative opportunities for survival to these businesses' low-paying jobs. As for the rioting and militancy of the urban poor, these were seen by local political and business leaders as a problem that the police, not welfare and anti-poverty agencies, were best equipped to handle. Thus local political organizations, such as Mayor Richard Daley's machine in Chicago, successfully lobbied Congress and the Johnson Administration for key changes in poverty programs that significantly reduced the influence of community groups. Federal anti-poverty funds would increasingly pass through local and state government agencies, under the control of these local elites, rather than being granted directly to neighborhood-controlled groups in poverty areas (Katz 1986; Lemann 1988; Rose 1972).

This conflict between federal and local officials over aspects of the War on Poverty had as its background the divergent labor markets of the core and periphery sectors of the capitalist economy. Since surplus populations played different roles in these labor markets, each sector had a stake in the outcomes of public policies aimed at the poor. These divergent labor market dynamics were at the bottom of ideological conflicts between the center and the periphery over the extension of rights; they framed the debate between respective liberal and conservative approaches to domestic public policy in the 1960s and 1970s.

Changes in approaches to the "crime problem," which took on new meaning with the urban riots of the 1960s, also reflect the divergence in labor market arrangements between the core and periphery sectors of capital. While the iron fist remained the ultimate weapon for combating crime, this war on crime was seen as an aspect of the war on poverty by important elements of the Kennedy and Johnson Administrations.

The President's Commission on Law Enforcement and the Administration of Justice (which included academics from major universities and core-industry-supported foundations) was the Johnson Administration's attempt to respond to the "crime issue," first raised in 1964 by presidential candidate Barry Goldwater and later by groups and politicians, such as George Wallace, who tapped discontent about civil rights legislation, Black progress, and civil unrest by invoking "law and order" and the "fear of crime" (Chafe 1986). In response, the President's Commission on Law Enforcement developed recommendations that paralleled the War on Poverty effort (Feeley and Sarat 1980). Indeed, the report of the President's Commission (1967: 6) said, "warring on poverty, inadequate housing and unemployment is warring on crime."

The federal government's push for more liberal approaches to the crime problem resulted in the enactment of the Safe Streets and Crime Control Act of 1968, featuring a large-scale grant-in-aid program to state and local units of government. The federal government would oversee the development of state and metropolitan comprehensive plans for dealing with crime, and fund innovative programs and demonstration projects arising from these plans. At the federal level, the major push would be toward community crime prevention and rehabilitation programs. The final version of the act, however, reflected the attitudes of Congressmen, responsive to local business and political leaders, who "questioned the wisdom of direct categorical grants, having found that they frequently (under Johnson's Great Society programs) supported insurgent political organizations and frequently spawned Washington-directed bureaucratic nightmares, both of which challenged established political groups in their own constituencies" (Feeley and Sarat 1980: 42). Thus the federal role in the war on crime, like its role in the war on poverty, was watered down to accommodate powerful local elites.

Much of the federal funding provided by the Law Enforcement Assistance Administration (LEAA) paid for law enforcement hardware and personnel in an effort to crack down on crime, reflecting the more coercive policy approaches favored by local officials and businessmen attached to the labor market dynamics contained in the periphery sector. Nonetheless, some key liberal approaches for dealing with crime at state and local levels could be launched through LEAA's funding of innovative rehabilitation and treatment programs in both communities and prisons. In addition, the federal prison system (under more direct influence of center elites) expanded programs aimed at rehabilitation and treatment during the 1960s. It became a major model for liberal approaches to corrections. The coercive function of incarceration in maintaining a labor market in which surplus populations must be forced into actively competing for jobs lost importance for the more unionized, core sector of capital, which had predominant influence over the federal executive branch during the post-World War II period. It is no accident that during the economic expansionary wave of the 1950s and 1960s, "rehabilitation" replaced "punishment" as the official corrections ideology, starting in the federal government and key industrial states containing the more unionized labor markets of core sector firms. In the late 1960s, largely through the influence of federal funding agencies and transplanted corrections officials from the federal government and states with more unionized labor markets, the periphery regions of the U.S. (southwestern, southern, and Rocky Mountain) began to adopt liberal, rehabilitative approaches to corrections.

The adoption of these more liberal programs coincided with a strong dip in the unemployment rate in these periphery states during the late 1960s. As discussed above, low unemployment often coincides with the adoption of rehabilitative approaches to corrections. This low level of unemployment, coupled with federal grants and the model rehabilitation programs in unionized states and the federal prison system, provided the impetus in the late 1960s for the most widespread adoption of rehabilitation programs, focusing on inmate education, in state prisons in U.S. history. States, like New Mexico, that had traditionally taken a law and order approach to crime, reflecting local labor market dynamics, were included in this spread of rehabilitation programs. Indeed, researchers who undertook a major survey of prison programs in the early 1970s described U.S. prisons as "transforming themselves into educational institutions.... This appears to be a significant development" (Reagen and Stoughton 1976: 92).

The fall of corporate liberalism, 1975–1980s

By the mid-1970s, liberal approaches to corrections were quickly abandoned in states containing more periphery industries, and were greatly eroded in other states containing core industries. Four important factors contributed to this shift: 1) unemployment increased dramatically after the 1974–75 recession; 2) labor market dynamics began to change with the erosion at the national level of unionized labor and the simultaneous rise of non-unionized service-sector jobs; 3) the federal role in funding innovative programs diminished during the mid-1970s as LEAA and anti-poverty programs were curtailed and finally dismantled; and 4) the poor, whose political organizing in the 1960s led to major concessionary responses from the federal government, became increasingly disorganized and depoliticized after the early 1970s. All of these factors contributed to a decline after the mid-1970s in liberal ideology. They are related to a retrenchment in welfare concessions (Katz 1989; Piven and Cloward 1982), to the decline of the rehabilitative ideal, which had informed penal policies since the 1950s (Cullen and Gilbert 1982), and to the largest growth in rates of imprisonment in U.S. history (Shover and Einstadter 1988: 77-79; *Washington Post* 9/11/89).

The first factor contributing to these changes was the shift in economic conditions (cf., Harrison and Bluestone 1988). "The growing European and Japanese challenge to American superiority...strained the nation's resources and began generating a string of economic woes, many of which to this day remain unsolved" (Fraser and Gerstle 1989: xix). The recession of 1974 accompanied the largest jump in unemployment since the Great Depression. This recession ended a long wave of economic expansion that had spurred liberal optimism in the 1950s and 1960s (Gordon, Edwards and Reich 1982; Mandel 1978). In a continuation of trends observed by Adamson (1984), Jankovic (1980), and Inverarity and McCarthy (1988) in the nineteenth and twentieth centuries, an increase in unemployment led to greater numbers of people being incarcerated and coincided with a decline in policymakers' faith in rehabilitation. This recession was followed by even worse economic downturns in the late 1970s, early 1980s, and early 1990s.

The second factor related to these policy shifts away from liberal approaches to corrections is the change in labor market dynamics. By the mid-1970s, unionized labor markets were declining rapidly, and continued a steep decline through the 1980s. Consequently, the direct political clout of organized labor, an important element of corporate liberalism, was also waning. The post-World War II compromise between labor and management, along with corporate liberalism's cornerstone of collective bargaining, unraveled in the late 1970s as industry began a large-scale attack on union prerogatives (Davis 1986). Simultaneously, low-paying, non-unionized labor markets were expanding (Harrison and Bluestone 1988). Labor market dynamics, even in many core industries, were shifting back to their pre-World War II configuration, when surplus populations played a direct role in regulating labor markets through job competition. Thus an important structural base for center elites' support of liberal policies was eroding after the early 1970s. The value system described by mass society theory was thus in decline. This shift in labor market dynamics and ideology corresponds with a shift away from concessionary to more coercive controls of the poor.[6]

The third factor contributing to the decline of liberal policies was the drop in federal funding for rehabilitation and poverty programs. Feeley and Sarat (1980) document the decline of federal crime control efforts, which coincided with the general fall of the "New Deal order" (Fraser and Gerstle 1989). After 1975, grants for innovative programs dried up. Many important rehabilitation programs in communities and prisons had been funded through LEAA. As these funds were no longer available, many of these programs ended when local and state governments discontinued their funding. During its last years of existence, LEAA attempted to design and implement "Criminal Justice Standards and Goals" for adoption by states. The Standards and Goals still enunciated a corporate-liberal approach to crime control that emphasized bureaucratic accountability and inmate rights; and rehabilitation was still promoted as a major purpose of corrections. Liberal segments of some state governments (including New Mexico) attempted to use the Standards and Goals to influence state correctional policies. But they ran into growing conservative elements in both state bureaucracies and legislatures that had opposing goals for penal policies. Without the federal funding as an inducement, these liberal elements in state correctional agencies had very little to back them up. Support for liberal corrections policies waned at the state level, especially in less unionized states on the periphery. Promotion of liberal policies on the part of the federal government after the mid-1970s was largely restricted to federal judges, many of whom had been appointed during the 1960s and who responded positively to lawsuits filed by inmates (Crouch and Marquart 1989). The result of this shift in the federal role was a period of conflict over the purposes and goals of corrections, a conflict that continues into the 1990s. But the general trend has been a steep decline of the liberal position, which had found its greatest support at the federal level during the late 1960s.

The fourth factor contributing to the shift away from liberal policies is the increasingly disorganized nature of disruptions by the poor. The ideological climate affecting state policies is influenced by the disruptiveness of surplus populations. These disruptions can contribute either to a liberal ideological climate or to a more conservative ideological climate depending on the nature of the disruptions. Organized political movements by surplus populations tend to contribute to the creation of a more liberal climate, which promotes the granting of concessions to quell organized discontent. Enhanced organization allows for a concerted response to be mounted against repressive actions by the state and promotes growing sympathy and support for those who are repressed. In contrast, disorganized violence, rioting, and crime tend to elicit repressive measures and a more reactionary, conservative ideological climate. Disorganized disruption leaves the surplus population open to increased state repression, which gains popular support as politicians exploit the public's growing fear of crime (Davis 1988). As the organized political protests and activities of the Civil Rights, Black Power, and Chicano Power movements of the 1960s gave way to increasingly disorganized activities such as violent crime, gang wars, and drug use in the 1970s and 1980s, the ideological climate of the U.S. shifted from liberal to conservative.

The trend on the streets of the U.S. from organized protests in the 1960s to disorganized and atomized disruptions in the late 1970s parallels a similar movement among inmates in U.S. prisons (Irwin 1980). After the Civil Rights movement had successfully secured some political and legal concessions, efforts began to shift toward gaining economic rights when Dr. Martin Luther King organized the Poor People's March. These demands for economic justice began to hit the limits of the capitalist system's ability to accommodate organized poor people's movements. The combination of co-optation through government programs, harassment by the FBI and police, the assassinations of Dr. King, Robert Kennedy, and Black Panther leader Fred Hampton, and the sheer exhaustion of those fighting for social and economic justice fragmented the organizing campaigns of poor people, who became increasingly depoliticized in the 1970s and 1980s (Chafe 1986). Simultaneously, prisoners also lost their political consciousness and solidarity. Part of this parallel phenomenon was due to direct influences from the street into the prison. Another important reason for these parallel movements, however, was the shift in the way the poor both outside and inside prisons were being controlled. Government policies in the 1970s and 1980s tended to isolate and divide poor people, both in prisons (Irwin 1980; Stastny and Tyrnauer 1982) and in the streets (Piven and Cloward 1977, 1982). By the late 1970s, concessionary controls had been increasingly supplanted by coercive controls, both outside and inside U.S. prisons (Colvin 1981, 1982). The violence and disorganization in inner-city areas parallels the disorder in many of our prisons. Both reflect a structural change since the early 1970s in the social, political, and economic position of the surplus population in the United States.

The conservative trend of the late 1970s and early 1980s, which drastically altered corrections policies, coincided with rising levels of unemployment and underemployment, a major shift from unionized to non-unionized labor markets, reductions in federal funding for anti-poverty and rehabilitation programs, and increasing disorganization of the poor. These underlying trends affected the political and ideological climate which, in turn, led to policy shifts for dealing with the poor both in and out of prison. These economic changes and political and ideological conflicts are the external forces that buffeted prison organizations during the 1970s and 1980s.

Understanding external sources of change

In contrast to Jacobs' implication that prisons are moving toward a new equilibrium based on a corporate model of accountability arising from mass society, it is more accurate to see U.S. prisons in a precarious state of instability that reflects economic, political, and ideological contradictions arising from class society. After World War II, the U.S. experienced a long wave of economic expansion that fostered liberal optimism and accommodative controls over labor and other discontented groups. These accommodative controls were extended into the prison during the 1960s in the form of rehabilitation programs. By the mid-1970s, as the long wave of economic expansion fell flat, the structure of liberal, corporate capitalism, based on these accommodative controls, began to dissolve with the rise of economic contradictions. Increasingly, this structure has been replaced with coercive controls inside prisons, in workplaces, and generally throughout U.S. society. In the process, the corporate model of bureaucratic accountability has been undermined; conditions for prisoners, the poor, and many subordinates of capitalist enterprises have worsened; and a tendency toward atomized and violent disruptions both in the streets and in prisons has increased. By itself, mass society theory cannot adequately explain these trends. It must be incorporated into a theoretical conception that takes into account class antagonisms and the political, ideological, and economic contradictions arising from them. This broader theoretical approach is necessary for understanding the recent deterioration in prison conditions that corresponds to worsening conditions of labor in the United States.

Prisons are thus greatly influenced by forces from the larger society. Yet prisons contain unique sets of human relationships that also shape their organizational structures and processes. The dynamic interplay between external and internal forces gives rise to specific patterns of relationships within prisons. The internal social structure of the prison exists within the context of often shifting goals and policies set for prisons through dynamics of the larger society. However, internal forces within the prison itself also have direct influences on the direction of the organization. It is on these internal forces within prisons that we now focus our attention.

CONTROL, COMPLIANCE, AND CHANGE
WITHIN THE PRISON ORGANIZATION

More significant for the prison's day-to-day operations than the official goals, emanating from the larger society, of punishment, deterrence, and rehabilitation are the primary objectives of the prison organization: custody and the promotion of order within its walls. As Sykes (1958: 18, 21–22) writes:

> The prison exists as a dramatic symbol of society's desire to segregate the criminal.... One escape from the maximum security prison is sufficient to arouse public opinion to a fever pitch and an organization which stands or falls on a single case moves with understandable caution. The officials, in short, know on which side their bread is buttered. Their continued employment is tied up with the successful performance of custody; and if society is not sure of the priority to be attached to the tasks assigned the prison, the overriding importance of custody is perfectly clear to the officials.... If custody is elevated to first rank in the list of tasks to be accomplished by the prison, the objective of maintaining internal order is a close second. And it must be admitted that under the best of circumstances the maintenance of order among a group of men such as those who are confined...would present formidable problems.

The problem of control in prisons springs from an inherent contradiction within the organization. An organization defined by the relationship between "keepers" and "captives" contains an underlying conflict that can potentially surface in open confrontation. Such an organization promotes, at times very powerfully, a "cold war" punctuated by an "us versus them" ethos shared, though on opposite sides, by both guards and prisoners (Johnson 1987). Open manifestation of this underlying organizational conflict, however, is usually contained, and at times largely overcome, through a precarious set of social controls. The problem of instituting and maintaining these social controls is expressed quite succinctly by Charles E. Silberman (1978: 531):

> Under ordinary circumstances, government depends on the consent of the governed; orders are issued and laws laid down on the assumption that they will be obeyed. The central dilemma faced by prison authorities is that they can neither expect cooperation from inmates nor govern without it.

The dilemma of control to which Silberman refers arises from the central contradiction between opposing forces within the prison organization which must be circumvented on a daily basis if the organization is to function in an orderly fashion.

Compliance from inmates is thus a formidable task that requires more than just the use of naked force. Prisons, like all organizations, operate through a variety of formal and informal structures of compliance. When these compliance structures are disrupted or break down, the inherent conflict within prisons between the keepers and the captives surfaces, and a crisis of control ensues. To understand the operation of prisons, it is necessary to understand the complexities of prison compliance structures.

Theory of organizational control and compliance

Perhaps the best conceptualization of compliance relations in the literature on complex organizations is Amitai Etzioni's (1970) "compliance theory." Each organization contains a predominant type of compliance structure. Such a structure entails a relationship between the type of power employed by authorities in an organization and a corresponding type of involvement on the part of subordinates in an organization. Three types of power can be employed within organizations: normative, remunerative, and coercive. Each of these tends to produce varying types of ideological commitment to, or involvement with, the organization by subordinates.

Normative power "rests on the allocation and manipulation of symbolic rewards" (Etzioni 1970: 104). Honors, titles, grades, expressions of appreciation, and even affection, can be used as power by authorities in an organization. These symbolic rewards elicit from subordinates a "moral involvement," designating "a positive orientation of high intensity" (Etzioni 1970: 107) toward authorities and the organization. The power of religious symbols and the devotion of parishioners in the Catholic Church is an example of such a compliance structure. In industry, the attempts to represent the company to workers as "a family" comprise efforts at using normative power. In prisons, such compliance structures have very limited applicability, though some rehabilitation programs contain important elements of normative power and on occasion instill a moral involvement on the part of some inmates who believe in the rehabilitative mission of the programs. Such a compliance structure assumes a sense of voluntary participation on the part of subordinates; thus it is extremely difficult to institute or maintain a normative compliance structure within prisons. This type of structure produces the strongest bonds of compliance between authorities and subordinates; therefore, it is most likely to be associated with organizations that are generally free of conflict.

Conflict under such a compliance structure arises only during a "crisis of belief," when the viability of symbols that had been manipulated as rewards breaks down. According to Irwin (1980) inmates' belief in rehabilitation, which had been relatively strong in California prisons in the late 1950s, eroded during the 1960s as Black Power advocates and other radicals challenged the ideology behind rehabilitation. The belief in these programs also weakened as it became clear to a growing number of inmates that actual job opportunities after leaving prisons as rehabilitated ex-offenders were extremely limited. In prisons, the efficacy of normative compliance, such as a belief on the part of inmates in the rehabilitative ideal, is contingent on actual (even if deferred) material benefits arising from compliance.

Thus compliance in the prison organization rests largely on the second type of power discussed by Etzioni. Remunerative power involves the manipulation of material rewards. Factory workers comply with their supervisors largely because of the remuneration, in the form of wages, they receive. Remunerative power creates in subordinates a "calculative involvement" of intermediate intensity. This compliance structure is precarious, depending on continual remuneration and advancement in the increment of remuneration. It produces very little loyalty on the part of the subordinate.

In prison organizations, material rewards can include the chance of better living conditions, possibility of early release on parole, a better prison job, or entry into a desirable program. The prisoner calculates the possible rewards to be gained through compliance with authorities and the possible privileges that can be lost for non-compliance.

Coercive control is the underlying source of power always available to prison authorities. It is constantly in the background in any prison setting, the visible signs being the bars, locks, walls, fences, guard towers, riot control gear, and guns. In times of order, coercion remains in the background. When the system of remunerative controls breaks down, coercion is relied upon to a greater extent. According to Etzioni, coercive power creates an alienative involvement, or an intensely negative orientation, toward authorities by subordinates.

Within prisons, the compliance structure offers a range of remunerative and coercive controls. Coercive and remunerative controls are not mutually exclusive categories. They lie on a continuum of control measures. The degree to which a control practice is remunerative or coercive depends on the relative position of the prisoner captured in the compliance structure. Thus, Erik Olin Wright (1973: 319) maintains,

> Some threatened punishments are simultaneously inducements: the threat of being denied a parole for resistance is also the inducement of being released for conformity. These escalated threats and inducements provide answers at every level of the system to the questions: What have I got to lose by resisting? What have I got to gain by conforming?

The extent to which an administration is losing control over a prisoner population can be measured by the degree to which prisoners answer "nothing" to these two questions. As a system of remunerative control breaks down and is replaced by a system that is predominantly more coercive, the answer to the two questions increasingly becomes, "I have nothing to lose and nothing to gain." Thus a purely coercive control structure is much less effective in producing compliance than one based on remunerative power and calculative involvement.

A wide range of remunerative and coercive measures increases the available rewards and punishments and places prisoners in more individualized gradients in their relationship to the structure of control. When the mass of prisoners calculate *individually* meaningful consequences arising from disorderly behavior, they are more likely to comply with authority. When the gradation of rewards and punishments narrows toward the more coercive end of the spectrum, forcing prisoners as a whole to lose ground relative to their former positions in the control structure, the probability that order will be maintained is lessened significantly.

A continuum of remunerative and coercive power exists at both the formal and informal levels within the organization. At the formal level, remunerative controls include reduction of time off sentence for good behavior, possibility of parole, and transfer to better housing, job, or program assignments. Coercive controls at the formal level include the loss of these rewards and the use of official disciplinary procedures and sanctions, such as solitary confinement and segregation.

Informal controls include what Gouldner (1954), in his study of industrial organizations, labels "indulgency patterns." These are informal means of remuneration that involve the overlooking by agents of authority of certain infractions by subordinates in exchange for compliance with larger organizational goals.

Sykes (1958) discusses the informal patterns of remunerative control that emerge between prison staff and inmates. Certain forms of disobedience by inmates are tolerated in exchange for visible appearances of compliance and order. For instance, contraband smuggling may be tolerated as long as inmates keep a cellblock clean and orderly. An indulgency pattern emerges in the prison in response to structural limitations of formal control mechanisms. As Sykes (1958: 52) explains, "the prisoner is already suffering from most of the punishments permitted by society, [thus] the threat of imposing those few remaining is all too likely to be a gesture of futility." Sykes (1958: 56-57) also recognizes that the guard's role as enforcer is undermined by the "claims of reciprocity":

> [A] guard cannot rely on the direct application of force to achieve compliance nor can he easily depend on threats of punishment.... The guard is under pressure to achieve a smoothly running tour of duty not with the stick but with the carrot, but here again his legitimate stock is limited.... [H]e finds that one of the most meaningful rewards he can offer is to ignore certain offenses.... Thus the guard...often discovers that his

best path of action is to make "deals" or "trades" with the captives in his power. In effect, the guard buys compliance or obedience in certain areas at the cost of tolerating disobedience elsewhere.

What the guard is buying is order, the primary purpose of the prison. The guard is creating for the prisoners a self-interest in order that corresponds to the prison administration's self-interest. The indulgency pattern, then, is a major informal mechanism, based on remunerative power, that obscures the underlying conflict between keepers and captives.

Informal controls can also be coercive. Beatings and other unauthorized acts of brutality against inmates are informal, coercive attempts at control. According to James W. Marquart (1986), informal patterns of physical coercion can become a major tool of inmate control. In his case study of a Texas prison, where he worked as a correctional officer in order to observe the prison setting, Marquart reports that "tune-ups," "ass whippings," and "back-stage" and "front-stage" beatings of inmates by guards were a major part of the prison's social control network.[7]

Compliance within prisons is complicated by the presence of an inmate social structure. Among inmates there are relations of status, power, and economic exchange. As with the relationship between staff and inmates, compliance relations among inmates also exist. Powerful inmates may be able to provide other inmates with desirable goods and services, obtained through both legal and illegal channels. These inmates have access to sources of rewards which give them power over other inmates. These remunerative sources of power provide these inmates with nonviolent means for manipulating other inmates' behavior. Often, these nonviolent sources of power are connected to formal and informal controls used by the staff over inmates. Inmate leaders may hold key jobs in the prison, which are rewards for their compliance and cooperation with prison officials. From these key jobs, inmate leaders are able to gain information, get other inmates into desirable jobs or program assignments, or gain access to illicit goods. Because of the formal and informal remunerative controls of the administration, inmates have access to sources of remuneration that in turn can be used for their control of other inmates. In this system of remunerative controls at both the staff-to-inmate and inmate-to-inmate levels, powerful inmates pull the inmate social structure toward cooperation with the administration's primary goal of order.

Shifts in control during "crackdowns" on corruption and periods of administrative succession

Order within the prison becomes more problematic when the accommodations, which are the basis for remunerative control between the administration and inmates, are disrupted and control shifts toward greater reliance on coercion. This shift can occur if the informal system of control based on remuneration (the indulgency pattern) leads to the discovery of a growing "corruption of authority" (Sykes 1958). It may also accompany a changeover in top prison administrators.

As a greater number of small informal concessions are made to inmates by individual staff members, a pattern of accommodation emerges in which staff begin to overlook not just small infractions, but major violations of prison rules. As informal remunerative controls get out of hand, their utility for creating order is undermined. Eventually, an obvious pattern of corruption emerges, and top officials' management of the prison is publicly called into question.

A crisis of control in the prison usually follows the discovery of such patterns of informal remuneration and corruption. A crackdown on the indulgency pattern often leads to noncooperation from inmates. If the administration responds to this crisis by resorting to coercion, the prison's compliance structure shifts from one that induces a "calculative involvement" on the part of inmates to one that creates an "alienated involvement," as Etzioni's compliance theory predicts.

A shift from remunerative to coercive controls is also likely to occur during a period of administrative succession, when new incumbents in top management positions change the direction of the organization. New administrators, in an attempt to gain greater control over their organizations, often formalize rules and refuse to recognize the existing informal patterns of accommodation between managers and their subordinates. Gouldner (1954) argues that administrative succession in industry is very disruptive for these reasons. Studies of prison organizations also indicate that when new administrators take over a prison and institute new policies, the result is often a period of organizational discord and disorder (Grusky 1968; Jacobs 1977; McCleery 1968; Stastny and Tyrnauer 1982; Wilsnack 1976).

The disruption becomes especially acute when the structure of control is suddenly altered by the administrative succession process. If the new administrator institutes policies that undermine accommodations which had provided formal and informal remunerative controls, the result is often a period of disorder. If accommodations are not reestablished, then coercive controls are relied upon in an attempt to restore order. During this shift toward coercive controls, a greater number of inmates perceive that they have nothing to lose by rebelling, and the inmate social structure moves toward confrontation with the administration.

Since the inmate social structure still includes a cohesive network of inmate relations (formed on the basis of the now disrupted remunerative controls), the rebellion at this stage will likely take the form of an organized inmate action, such as a work strike, that involves the leadership of the old inmate elite who had especially benefitted from the dismantled remunerative controls. If the collective action by inmates results in the reestablishment of accommodations, then order will return to the prison. This, Sykes (1958) maintains, is the normal cyclical pattern in a prison's history.

If, on the other hand, the collective action results in an escalation of coercive controls by the prison administration, aimed at undermining inmate solidarity, then a long period of disorder, which eventually fragments the inmate social structure, will ensue. The continued use of coercion by the administration further alienates inmates. As accommodations, which had induced inmate leaders' cooperation and given them sources of nonviolent power over other inmates, are dissolved, inmate leaders are no longer able to provide a stabilizing or cohesive influence over the inmate social structure. Relations among inmates themselves become more coercive as nonviolent sources of power dry up and are replaced with violence.

The shift from a compliance structure that is predominantly based on remunerative power to one that is predominantly based on coercive power often occurs with the discovery of corruption or with administrative succession. The shift usually produces a period of disorder. If the shift in the prison's compliance structure takes place concurrently with the external economic, political, and ideological changes discussed earlier, then the disruption of the organization leads to a prolonged crisis.

During the 1970s, the shifts in the larger society that undermined the dominance of corporate-liberal ideology, and specifically undermined the rehabilitative ideal, corresponded with and helped foster the movement in the prison from a system based on remunerative controls to a system that was dominated more and more by coercive controls. These corresponding external and internal changes produced an organizational structure within the prison that was more coercive and violent, and that led ultimately to a state of crisis and turmoil. The extreme example of these organizational changes is the Penitentiary of New Mexico (PNM) as it moved from a period of accommodation, based on remunerative controls, in the late 1960s and early 1970s, to a period of confrontation and fragmentation, produced by coercive controls, in the late 1970s. The social history presented in the next four chapters documents these organizational changes at PNM.

YEARS OF ACCOMMODATION, 1968–1974

In 1968, the Penitentiary of New Mexico (PNM) underwent an important transformation upon which the discussion in this chapter is primarily focused. The significance of this transformation can only be understood within the context of PNM's earlier history.

THE EARLY HISTORY OF THE PENITENTIARY OF NEW MEXICO

The Penitentiary of New Mexico, which was built in 1956 near Santa Fe, is the main prison for adult men in New Mexico.[1] Ground was broken for construction of PNM shortly after a series of riots in the early 1950s led to calls by prison officials, the press, and legislators for the closing of the old penitentiary.

The old Penitentiary of New Mexico, located about three miles south of the downtown plaza of Santa Fe, was constructed in 1885 as a Territorial Prison; it originally had 108 cells, each "furnished with 2 iron cots" (Department of Corrections 1976: 3). Additional wings were added in the early 1900s to raise the capacity of the old penitentiary to 300 inmates. Chronic overcrowding during the 1920s and 1930s led to construction of nearly double the cell space, which was quickly filled to overcapacity. By the late 1940s and early 1950s, the prison population at the old penitentiary stabilized near its capacity of 600 inmates. However, a series of riots, disturbances, and escape attempts rocked the old penitentiary in 1948, 1950, 1952, and 1953 (*New Mexican* 8/15/56). These disturbances led to a call for a new penitentiary (*New Mexican* 6/16/53).

Construction of the new Penitentiary of New Mexico, located on the rolling plains ten miles south of Santa Fe, was completed in April 1956. Amid much fanfare, following the warden's special invitation for parents to bring their children, thousands of citizens toured the new prison during a July 21, 1956, "open house," which had as its main attraction the chance to sit in the prison's new gas chamber (*New Mexican* 7/22/56). Inmates were moved from the old prison to the new PNM in August 1956.

The new penitentiary was touted as the latest advancement in architectural design, which afforded flexibility in classification for maximum, medium, and minimum security inmates. The "telephone pole" layout with separate, isolated housing units jutting off a main corridor stem was also useful, it was argued, for isolating disturbances (Morris 1983). The telephone pole architectural arrangement was originally designed by Alfred Hopkins and first used in the building of the U.S. Federal Penitentiary at Lewisburg, Pennsylvania in 1932 (American Correctional Association 1983). New Mexico was one of several states to employ the design in the 1950s. (See Appendix B for detailed description of PNM's physical layout.) Its unique feature is that inmates can be moved from one level of security and treatment classification to another within the same building. The layout of dormitories, cellhouses, and cellblocks had the potential basis for a "step system" in which inmates could advance toward greater freedom and responsibility through work and education programs. Though the new penitentiary's first warden, H.R. Swenson, stated in 1956 that the new penitentiary would use the "latest developments in the behavioral sciences" and "provide an atmosphere in which classification and treatment have an opportunity to achieve their goals" (Office of the Attorney General 1980b: 3), it was not until 1968 that the "treatment" potential of the new institution was first utilized. In fact, in 1958, shortly before he resigned as the second warden of the new PNM, Warden T.M. Woodruff told a legislative committee that "the major problem facing the penitentiary now is prisoner idleness. If all the jobs were counted up, there would be work for about 300 [of the prison's 1000] men" (*Albuquerque Journal* 3/30/80: 3).

PNM prior to the late 1960s was not a "treatment oriented" institution. In fact, it was similar to the authoritarian regime that, according to Jacobs (1977), prevailed at Stateville Penitentiary in Illinois before the 1960s. As Jacobs describes it, the authoritarian regime included independence of the warden from outside authority, so that his personal dominance over the administration of the prison was almost absolute. Outsiders had virtually no access to the prison. Professionals with loyalties to outside groups, such as academia or professional organizations, were completely distrusted by the administration. For both inmates and guards, rigid discipline was enforced. Harsh punishment, in the form of long periods of time in a "dark cell" for inmates, or dismissal from employment for guards, could be expected for rule violations. Daily life within the prison was highly regimented; prisoners walked single file and maintained silence. Treatment programs were nonexistent. With little due process or appeals of administrative decisions, rights for inmates (and for guards) was an alien concept.

Yet privileges were used as a way of keeping control and producing divisions and stratification among inmates. "[At Stateville, Warden] Ragen and his top staff made it a practice to offer many of the top jobs to inmate leaders and toughs" (Jacobs 1977: 44). And though discipline was strict,

> the organization could only function if innumerable exceptions were made. The captain's [inmate] clerks couldn't be "busted" and there were other "untouchables" throughout the prison whose inviolability was based upon stooling, indispensability, or personal relationships with the staff. This led to an arbitrary system of justice, whereby overlooking infractions was a reciprocity for certain inmate compliance, particularly the supplying of information. (Jacobs 1977: 42–43)

This reward system, based on highly personal and often arbitrary decisions of the warden and his staff, was a very effective mechanism of social control that produced both "greater disparity in the living conditions between the best-off and the worst-off inmates" (Jacobs 1977: 43) and loyalty to the authoritarian regime by an important segment of inmates who benefited from the system.

Many aspects of the authoritarian regime described by Jacobs also characterized PNM prior to the late 1960s. PNM's warden was virtually independent of outside authority. Until 1970, PNM was an independent agency reporting to the Governor through a Board of Penitentiary Commissioners. But in reality, the warden of PNM, with independent ties to the state legislative committees that provided funding for the penitentiary, did not answer to the Governor. An example, reported by a correctional officer (CO) who worked at PNM since its opening in 1956, illustrates the relationship before the late 1960s between the Warden and the Governor:

> These people from the news media came [to PNM's traffic control gate] and they had permission from the Governor [to interview two inmates]. The officer [at the traffic control gate] informed the Warden [Harold Cox, warden from 1959 to 1966,] that there was a couple of men from the media who wanted to talk to some inmates inside. The Warden comes out and he asks, "Are you people from the news media?" They say, "Yes. We'd like to talk to a couple of inmates. We have permission from the Governor to talk to a couple of inmates." The Warden said, "What do you want to know about them? Anything you want to know about anything in here you ask me. I'll tell you what's going on, what's what. But you're not coming in here." "Well the Governor gave us permission!" [To which the Warden responded,] "Well you go back and tell the Governor he runs the capitol and I run the penitentiary."

The newsmen did not get their interviews.

PNM in the middle 1960s was described by a former convict as containing a "repressive co-existence" between inmates and staff. Inmates did not question the orders of guards, did not "talk back," and generally stayed out of the guards' way. A veteran CO recalled his early years at PNM:

> Years ago you weren't allowed to talk to inmates and inmates were not allowed to talk to us. If an inmate wanted to talk to you he had to stand six feet away from you and cross his arms [as a signal he wanted to speak]. And then you'd say, "Okay. What do you need?"

The prison prior to 1968 contained minimal inmate programs. Like Stateville, PNM did not share in the movement toward rehabilitation that, during the 1950s and early 1960s, had influenced corrections systems in several northern and western industrialized states. A veteran corrections administrator, describing the prison in the early 1960s, stated that "programs were not of any importance at that time." An inmate high school, instituted in 1957 and administered through a local Santa Fe high school, was the only program that could be considered rehabilitative. Other activities, officially designated at this time as "vocational programs," were merely short-term, on-the-job training for the inmate jobs in the prison's shops, laundry, and kitchen.

Discipline was considered by former convicts to be "harsh, but consistent." Inmates were expected to walk single file in the corridors; their movement within the institution was tightly restricted. The "hole," solitary confinement in a dark cell, was the primary punishment for major rule violations and the primary formal mechanism for inmate control under the authoritarian regime. Former prisoner W.G. Stone (1982: 44–45) describes his ten-day stay in PNM's "hole" in 1962:

> The Hole is located in the basement of Cellblock 3, the lockup unit for troublemakers.... [These eleven] six-by-nine foot cells [have] no windows, no ventilation, no lights; just darkness.... Most of the time you're stripped and thrown in naked, as I was. All you're allowed is a thin blanket, a toothbrush, and a metal cup; a mattress is given to you at ten at night and taken away at six in the morning. They feed you one meal every three days, and six slices of white bread for the two days in between. There's a faucet in the cell, but there's water in it only when the guard comes and turns it on from the outside. He does that three times a day, morning, noon, and evening. You've got nothing to store the water in, so you've got to drink what you can.... The toilet is a hole in the floor that you squat over. It flushes from the outside. The guards think it's funny not to flush it for a few days in a row.... In the winter, it's freezing cold, so you don't have to worry about the odor. You have enough to do trying to keep warm with one thin blanket and no heat. The only time I

saw light was when [the guard] opened the door to give me the mattress or meals.

This prisoner's ten-day stay in the "hole" was relatively lenient. According to a veteran PNM staff member, "in those days [prior to 1968] if an inmate went to the 'hole' it was for fifteen days. When I first started there [in the early 1960s] inmates had as many as thirty days in the 'hole.' They'd bring them out at the end of the fifteenth day, give them like an afternoon off, and then back in they'd go." The "hole" remained in use until 1968, when it was closed down. It would not be used again, at least officially on any routine basis, until June 1976.

The "hole" prior to 1968 was generally used for major rule violations. "For a minor violation, an inmate was reprimanded or [given] a good 'ass-chewing' by someone, but he was never placed in segregation," said a caseworker, who was a correctional officer at PNM during the late 1950s and early 1960s when the authoritarian regime prevailed. A former inmate said of this era, "There was a lot of consistency. It was damn negative, but there is some stability in knowing where the hell you are. And under that kind of situation, people knew where they were. You got ten days in the 'hole' for this; you got your ass kicked out of your job for this; you went to isolation for 90 days or more for that. Everybody knew those things."

As in Stateville, inmate clerks were used in the hospital, records, and warden's and deputy warden's offices. These privileged positions gave inmates access to information and protection from disciplinary actions, as long as they cooperated with staff by letting them know of any potential problems that might disrupt the prison.

The potential for disruption increased during the early 1960s as inmate idleness and overcrowding grew. Following a series of economic recessions, PNM was chronically overcrowded by about 115 inmates from 1960 through 1963. On December 22, 1962, the population in the main penitentiary building reached 1,174 inmates, 152 over its capacity (at that time) of 1,022. In 1963, an average 1,140 inmates were housed daily in the penitentiary.[2] Yet during the early 1960s, there were no killings, violence, or disturbances. A veteran corrections official remembered this period:

> It just seemed that the population started to increase and increase and increase.... [In] 1962, I recall that we ended up one day for about an hour or two with a 13 hundred population count [which included 98 men at the Honor Farm and 22 women in the Annex Building]. Now this was something we never thought would happen.... [But] violence was a rarity. When it sprang up, we'd sit back and say "well why would it happen, particularly with those two inmates." And I can't recall specific cases, but I know from my experience and my recollection that they were just unheard of.

The authoritarian regime at PNM was apparently able to withstand this four year period of chronic overcrowding and idleness, since the prison remained orderly throughout the early 1960s. But this regime began to erode in the late 1960s and ended abruptly in 1968. The change occurred largely because of forces external to the prison.

SOCIAL MOVEMENTS OUTSIDE THE PRISON
DURING THE 1960s

Beyond the fences of PNM, social movements that affected major political institutions throughout the country were emerging. As discussed in Chapter 2, the roots of these movements can be traced to important demographic shifts following World War II that coincided with the infusion of large capital into U.S. agriculture, especially in the still "undeveloped" south and southwest. Old patterns of sharecropping (in the rural South) and communal use of grazing lands and forests (in northern New Mexico) were disrupted by this economic incursion. As machines increasingly replaced humans in agricultural work, and as the cost of competing in the agricultural business increased, people were driven from rural areas into towns and cities (Hodgson 1976). Many were able to take advantage of new opportunities in rising manufacturing and service industries in many U.S. cities. Many others, however, fell into urban poverty to become a source of cheap labor in many non-unionized industries (Braverman 1974).

It is no accident that the Civil Rights movement, which began in the mid-1950s through the leadership of Black religious groups and with the encouragement of antisegregation rulings of the U.S Supreme Court, coincided with this flood of migrants escaping rural poverty. With their traditional ties to the Black church, these new urban dwellers, especially in southern cities, looked to the church for both inspiration and help in dealing with the poverty and discrimination they faced in this new environment. The more established middle-class professionals among the urban Blacks provided the leadership against a long-standing pattern of discrimination, which became more intolerable with the arrival of this new and growing segment of the urban Black poor. Thus the ongoing struggle against segregation in southern cities was now linked directly to a movement against the growing poverty in urban areas. While the Civil Rights movement of the 1950s and 1960s fought first for political rights, economic rights emerged as the predominant issue in the late 1960s with Dr. Martin Luther King's plans for a Poor People's March (Hampton 1990).

The impact of the Civil Rights movement on the politics of the 1960s and early 1970s cannot be overstated (Davis 1986). It set both a moral tone and an example for other social movements of the era (Chafe 1986). The Civil Rights movement established through its struggles the idea of an expanding right to equal citizenship for all oppressed groups and, consequently, vilified those established groups who fought against this seemingly inevitable expansion of rights. The picture of Bull Connor's police dogs chasing nonviolent Black protestors in Birmingham, Alabama, would soon be transformed into pictures of Mayor Daley's police beating antiwar demonstrators in Chicago, Presidents Johnson and Nixon ordering bombings of civilian targets in Southeast Asia, police and national guardsmen killing students at Kent State and Jackson State, and state troopers storming the prison at Attica. These vivid images shaped the political ideology of the late 1960s and early 1970s. This ideology recast American liberalism and became the guiding force behind movements of Hispanics, students, women, and prisoners in the late 1960s.

The organizing efforts surrounding the Civil Rights movement also had an enormous impact on the federal government, directly spawning the ideas behind the War on Poverty programs of the early Johnson Administration. Some of the more radical approaches to combating poverty, including "community action" which involved participation of neighborhood leaders in poverty-stricken areas in directing and administering federal funds, came from veterans of the early Civil Rights movement and their allies in federal agencies (Lemann 1988; Piven and Cloward 1977). These early War on Poverty efforts attempted to harness (some would say co-opt) the enormous organizing energy, spawned in poverty-stricken areas by the Civil Rights movement, in order to create a new liberal coalition between the poor and the federal government. Established local political machines, which traditionally barred minorities from sharing in local patronage and power, would be circumvented by a new patronage system through the federal government that would create a new power base among the poor who could push for the expansion of their rights and economic opportunities.

This effort at collective political action for addressing poverty was short-lived. Local Democratic machines in such places as Chicago and Texas, sensing the political threat of an organized poor people's movement, successfully pressured the Johnson Administration and Congress to have federal antipoverty funds pass through local and state governments rather than directly to community action groups in poverty areas. This shift in control over the purse-strings was the first major weakening of the more radical aspects of the War on Poverty. Later, under the Nixon Administration, antipoverty efforts to an increasing extent focused on individuals rather than communities; organized antipoverty neighborhood groups were rapidly transformed into isolated, individual welfare clients. The War on Poverty was thus rendered, by the early 1970s, politically neutral, except as a "whipping boy" for conservative politicians, who later aided in its complete dismantling (Lemann 1989).

An important social and political movement by poverty-stricken Hispanics in northern New Mexico emerged in the mid-1960s. Directly inspired by the successes of Blacks in their civil rights struggles, a long-festering conflict over New Mexico land grants erupted into a militant popular movement in 1966. In the Treaty of Guadalupe Hidalgo, which ended the Mexican American War in 1848 and made New Mexico and California territories of the United States, the U.S. pledged to recognize the existing land grants given to Spanish families and their descendants in northern New Mexico by the governments of Spain and Mexico. Over the next century, these land grants, which included rich mineral, lumber, and agricultural resources, were taken from the descendants of the original Spanish families by Anglo business interests through various forms of fraud and deceit and legal mechanisms such as land confiscation for nonpayment of taxes (Barrera 1979). Taxing of land was unknown in the traditions of these Hispanic families, who often were not informed of the tax until the land was seized by local law enforcement agents (Blawis 1971). The land grants' "communal lands," which were not owned by anyone but had been set aside by local villages as common grazing land, were taken without compensation by the U.S Forest Service, which then charged fees for grazing permits. By the mid-twentieth century, Anglos owned four-fifths of the original land grant areas, and communal lands dropped from 2 million acres to 300,000 acres (Barrera 1979). This history of land seizure was "a major blow to the economic viability of the villages"; its disruption of a communal, subsistence economy is the primary source of the enormous poverty among many Hispanic families in northern New Mexico (Barrera 1979: 27).

In 1965, the U.S Forest Service reduced by 45 percent the number of grazing permits to local families while increasing the size of permits to large logging firms (Blawis 1971). For the local Hispanic population, which depended on the grazing lands for subsistence, the reduction in permits was an economic disaster. By 1967, more than 20,000 people left the small villages of sparsely populated northern New Mexico either to find work as migrant farm laborers or to join the growing segment of poor Hispanics in cities like Albuquerque and Santa Fe (Blawis 1971).

Over one million acres of the land grants were now in the hands of the U.S. Forest Service (and much more was controlled by large Anglo-owned interests). Local Hispanics, who believed that they were being deliberately squeezed out of the National Forests to make room for large Anglo-American cattle and sheep companies, logging firms, mining operations, land speculators, and developers, organized an alliance to fight for the land grants. Under the leadership of the charismatic Reies Lopez Tijerina, the *Alianza* grew by 1966 into a formidable, left-leaning political movement that fought not only for the land grants but also for Hispanic civil and economic rights. A parallel movement, *La Raza Unida*, also mobilized Hispanics in northern New Mexico. In 1968, Tijerina became a primary organizer of the Poor People's March with followers of Dr. King. *Alianza* and *La Raza Unida* also raised vocal opposition to the war in Vietnam, for which a disproportionately high number of Hispanics had been drafted.

Alianza's most dramatic moment was the June 5, 1967, armed raid on the County Court House in Tierra Amarilla, New Mexico. This attempt to place the local district attorney under citizen's arrest for violating the civil rights of *Alianza* members resulted in a confrontation with local and state police and kidnapping charges against Tijerina and other members of *Alianza*. The ensuing trials, which lasted through 1969, riveted the attention of New Mexico's citizens on the political struggle in northern New Mexico and on the poverty underlying it.

This climate of confrontation in northern New Mexico had an enormous impact on New Mexico state politics. During these years, the mobilization of Hispanics in New Mexico led to the election of state legislators who were able to form a liberal coalition, called the "Mama Lucy's" (after a northern New Mexico restaurant where they frequently met), that dominated the state legislature in the late 1960s and early 1970s.

Also, with the backing of large numbers of Hispanics from northern New Mexico, David Cargo, a liberal Republican, was elected Governor in 1966. Hispanics supported Cargo because local Democratic machines, often run by county sheriffs who had long been active in repressing the political activities of the poor in northern New Mexico, and the retiring Democratic Governor, Jack Campbell, were viewed as hostile to the movement taking shape in northern New Mexico. Cargo had made gestures of sympathy during his campaign for the plight of Hispanics living in poverty in northern New Mexico. Cargo was allied with the Nelson Rockefeller wing of the Republican Party, and shared many of the reformist ideas associated with these so-called "Eastern establishment" Republicans. Social programs for the poor and prison rehabilitation efforts that had been instituted in several northern and Pacific states during the late 1950s and early 1960s greatly influenced Cargo's views.

Governor Cargo, during the November 1967 trial of Tijerina, testified about the conditions that led to the militancy of northern New Mexico's Hispanic population. The following account appears in Blawis' (1971: 61–62) history of the land grant struggle:

The trial also saw the first of several appearances by witnesses including David Cargo, the Governor of New Mexico, who would describe to judges and juries the deprived situation of the inhabitants of northern New Mexico. Governor Cargo testified that "there is no dialogue between the people of northern New Mexico and the Forest Service." He detailed grievances of the Spanish Americans in the region, suffering, he said, from "bad roads, poor educational systems, trouble with disease and unemployment."

Another indication of Cargo's political orientation is presented by Blawis (1971: 109–110), who relays an account that appeared in the Santa Fe *New Mexican*:

On April 1, 1968, as Tijerina was preparing to assume New Mexico leadership of the Poor Peoples' March, Governor David Cargo met with a group of middle-class people in Los Alamos, urging them to "organize a few things" to fight poverty. Cargo said that he had made fifty-two trips to community meetings among the Spanish poor in the North, and was "struck by the hopelessness of the situation." One problem, he said, is "obtaining fresh water. In small villages it is normal for people to drink from drainage ditches or from contaminated streams." He mentioned the "extraordinarily high percentage of New Mexicans from rural, Spanish-American families who have died in Vietnam, because they're the ones drafted." [He said,] "Only one of four students in Taos and Rio Arriba counties and only one of six in Mora County complete high school, and 58 per cent of the people in these counties have a family income of less than $3000 a year." While some federal poverty programs have been beneficial, some have been "unadulterated baloney," he said. The people have "just lost all faith in government."

A political crisis, punctuated by growing radicalization of the poor and a sharp decline for a significant segment of the population in belief in the legitimacy of governmental institutions, directly affected the politics of New Mexico from 1966 to 1970. Cargo's strategy to address this crisis included attempts to bring the disenfranchised poor into a more responsive system that attempted in one stroke to alleviate the social and economic conditions fueling the movement and (perhaps of greater significance) to isolate or co-opt the more radical elements of the movement. Through his New Mexico Office of Economic Opportunity, the agency charged with "passing down" federal antipoverty funds, Governor Cargo instituted programs and aid for the northern New Mexico area, which one U.S. Congressman called "the Watts of rural America" (Blawis 1971: 94).

These economic and political crises had considerable impact on PNM in the late 1960s. The push of Hispanic families off traditional lands resulted in a flood of desperate people competing for low-paying jobs in the cities of Albuquerque, Santa Fe, and other New Mexico urban areas. These new urban dwellers soon scrambled into the unskilled and semiskilled jobs that were available. Many fell into an impoverished urban existence of sporadic work and chronic unemployment. Often family relations became strained, as the children of many of these new urban dwellers were drawn into the life of the streets, a life of drinking, heroin use, fighting, gambling, and crime. Children from areas like Albuquerque's South Broadway barrios began populating the state's juvenile reform schools and later graduated to the Penitentiary of New Mexico in Santa Fe.

Along the major east-west highway, U.S. 66, which runs through Albuquerque, other young, mostly Anglo, migrants from poor areas of Texas, Oklahoma, southern New Mexico, and California traveled through New Mexico on their way to or from such "meccas" of opportunity as Los Angeles. As they ran out of money and out of luck, some ended up at PNM for armed robberies, auto thefts, and murder. Blacks among these migrants who engaged in criminal activities were invariably sent to PNM, being overrepresented by nearly four times their proportion of the state population.[3]

Other migrants from the economic devastation of northern New Mexico were able to find jobs that allowed them to keep a precarious hold on lower-middle class respectability. The state government, the largest single employer in New Mexico, offered jobs for many of these migrants. Armed forces veterans who did not suffer disabling war injuries were often able to land jobs in law enforcement. Many correctional officers (COs) at PNM were raised in poor rural areas of northern counties and had served in the military. PNM offered a stable, though low-paying, alternative to the grinding poverty and uncertainties of the now disrupted, traditional agricultural work of their fathers and mothers.

Thus, in both the inmate population and the custodial force, the Penitentiary of New Mexico brought together the refugees of economic devastation who in urban areas were divided, respectively, into an impoverished lower class and a highly precarious, lower-middle class. These victims of economic "progress" now met as antagonists in the struggle between the keepers and the kept at the Penitentiary of New Mexico.

The Civil Rights movement created an ideological climate that not only affected the War on Poverty but also had an impact on corrections in the 1960s. The impact was felt most directly at the federal level and in more industrialized states where the urban poor were more restive. Radical movements had a direct effect on prisoners, especially Black prisoners, who were drawn from the urban areas most affected by these movements (Irwin 1980). The response from the federal level to the 1960s mobilization of the poor, including the accommodative strategies contained in the

War on Poverty, also influenced many young, college-educated corrections professionals who were emerging as major players in the shaping of corrections policies in the federal system and in several industrialized states (Jacobs 1977). These parallel movements from the bottom and the top of correctional organizations were reshaping prisons throughout the U.S. The general movements and struggles in the larger society that supported the granting of rights and power to disenfranchised groups affected the traditional authoritarian structures in prisons, including the Penitentiary of New Mexico.

THE END OF THE AUTHORITARIAN REGIME AND THE RISE OF A NEW TREATMENT-ORIENTED REGIME AT PNM

The authoritarian regime at PNM began to erode in 1966 with the death of Warden Harold Cox, who had held the wardenship since 1959. Felix Rodriguez was named acting warden until a permanent replacement could be found.

Rodriguez, whose imposing physical stature gave him a commanding presence, was a leader among a group of Hispanic corrections officers who, after serving in the Korean War, began working in New Mexico prisons in the early 1950s. Rodriguez began his prison career as a correctional officer (CO) in the old penitentiary on July 8, 1953, less than one month after the old penitentiary was shaken by the riot that led directly to its closing. Rodriguez's early career experiences in the immediate post-riot situation of 1953 had a lasting effect on his outlook about prisons. According to observers, he became sensitive very early in his career to the precariousness of the keepers' rule over the prison and to the uncertainties of prison order. Rodriguez worked his way quickly through the CO ranks to become an associate warden in 1958. Under the authoritarian regime in the early 1960s, Rodriguez was respected by both inmates and COs as being tough but fair. As a loyal deputy to Warden Cox, Rodriguez maintained the authoritarian practices that had existed in New Mexico prisons since statehood. As he rose in the prison administration, his associates from the group of Hispanic COs who had served together in the armed forces were placed in important posts within the prison hierarchy. This group of prison employees led by Rodriguez would continue to run the prison through 1975. A few of the middle-level administrators from this group would still hold important positions until after 1980.

As Rodriguez began his tenure as acting warden in early 1967, PNM was beginning to be moved by forces outside the prison. Inmates' perceptions and expectations were changing as a growing number of new prisoners who had served time in California and federal prisons entered PNM. As comparisons were made between these systems, with their many rehabilitation programs, and New Mexico's penal system, inmates began to voice their concerns to prison officials that New Mexico corrections be "brought up to date." Specifically, a group of mostly Anglo inmates began discussing with Rodriguez the need for new programs. While Rodriguez was receptive to their ideas, very little was done beyond the talking stage during 1967 toward initiating programs. However, this dialogue was the beginning of a new era in which inmate opinions would have some weight on decisions made at PNM. It also marked the beginning of a precipitous decline in the legitimacy of the old authoritarian regime.

Felix Rodriguez was the most important PNM administrator during the 1960s and early 1970s. Observers said that Rodriguez was very cautious and did not initiate changes on his own. He was no innovator. However, when confronted with a changing situation, Rodriguez was flexible and open to suggestion, especially if he perceived a change as a way of promoting a peaceful prison. Rodriguez was a very complicated man and a shrewd politician. Almost every conflicting group within the prison saw Rodriguez as the person to approach with problems, ideas, or complaints. He was a listening post for both staff members and inmates. This gave Rodriguez important information and a level of power unparalleled by any New Mexico prison administrator who came after him. He was one of the few administrators who could command allegiance from both COs and inmates, especially when relations between these factions worsened after 1968. Rodriguez's power and delicate balancing of opposing factions were always precarious, however, since they were dependent on compromises that could easily come unhinged by forces often beyond his control.

During his first few months in office in 1967, while Rodriguez was acting Warden, Governor Cargo conducted a thorough nationwide search to find a permanent replacement for Warden Cox. Cargo was looking for someone who shared his liberal vision of governance and could bring to PNM reforms which had been instituted in other states. For Cargo, prisoner rehabilitation went hand-in-hand with the war on poverty (and on the growing radicalism) he hoped to wage in northern New Mexico. Cargo would be the first activist Governor to bring significant changes to the Penitentiary of New Mexico.

In 1967, Governor Cargo named his agent for change at the penitentiary. J.E. Baker, a correctional administrator from the federal prison system, was appointed PNM's new warden in August 1967. Baker had a reputation as one of the most innovative correctional administrators in the U.S. He had been a strong force behind the wave of prison reforms in the federal system while associate warden for treatment at the U.S. Federal Penitentiary at Terre Haute, Indiana, from 1959 to 1964 and warden of the men's division at the Federal Correctional Institution at Terminal Island, California, from 1964 to 1967. During his wardenships at Terre Haute and Terminal Island, he had experimented with new rehabilitation programs and the implementation of inmate participation in the management of prisons. Baker's ideas about prison management were similar to those of Thomas Mott Osborne and Howard B. Gill, who in the early twentieth century had experimented with inmate participation in prison management (Stastny and Tyrnauer 1982). In 1964, Baker published an article in the *Journal of Criminal Law, Criminology and Police Science*, entitled "Inmate Self-Government" (Baker 1964), which laid out his philosophy of inmate management. Later, he expanded on these ideas in books entitled *The Right to Participate: Inmate Involvement in Prison Administration* (Baker 1974) and *Prisoner Participation in Prison Power* (Baker 1985), which survey the use of inmate participation in U.S. prisons.

Under Baker's wardenship at PNM, a new era of expanded opportunities and accommodations for inmates began. His approach to prison governance was parallel to many of the original ideas contained in the early War on Poverty programs of the Johnson Administration. These federal poverty programs initially promoted client participation and had the effect of circumventing local power elites (Lemann 1988, 1989).

In a similar fashion, Warden Baker attempted to circumvent the local elite in the custodial force, the middle-level administrators and correctional officers under Felix Rodriguez, by forging alliances with inmates to bring about changes in the prison. Most COs and middle-level administrators were opposed to any new programs or changes that would undermine the old authoritarian regime, which had given them unquestioned authority and power.

One of the most significant changes Warden Baker instituted was the closing of the "hole," the major control tool of the authoritarian era. He also reduced restrictions on inmate movement in the penitentiary and abolished the rule requiring that inmates walk single file in the corridors. These actions had an immense impact on the "repressive coexistence" that had prevailed between inmates and the custodial staff since the opening of PNM in 1956. As a veteran correctional officer said:

> Even some of the old tough inmates will tell you they had reservations about going to the "hole" because it does do something to you physically and psychologically. But once Baker got rid of the "hole,"...inmates would say, "Well, what the hell, I'll go to [disciplinary] segregation, I can do thirty days standing on my head in just regular segregation, three meals a day, I can kick back." To them it meant nothing anymore....

Baker brought in more relaxed rules and regulations for inmates.... There was a big, definite resentment by correctional officers. And there was an exodus of correctional personnel and a strong reaction against the Baker attitude of no back-up in enforcing regulations and policies.

These observations are supported by a former convict:

> So many different changes took place in the late 60s in terms of the make-up of that institution that changes began to take place in the officers.... Things were not in balance. The rules changed.... Baker stopped the "hole." And when that happened you could see the officers lighten up. They had no vehicle for discipline. Only ten percent maybe of their write-ups bore any fruit [resulted in punishment]. After guards write somebody up two or three times, the inmates begin to laugh [at them]. The guards lost control. They didn't have any authority. All of the authority was now vested in a new system.

Baker's new system attempted to forge direct ties with inmates through an array of new programs that had as a central feature inmate involvement in program development and administration. Using his connections with the federal government, Baker obtained funds for these programs from the Office of Economic Opportunity and other federal agencies. In 1968, a prison in which programs had had virtually no importance was suddenly transformed into a program-filled institution.

THE PROLIFERATION OF
REHABILITATION PROGRAMS

Programs that began in the late 1960s included several aimed at improving vocational and academic skills. The high school was transformed into a federally funded Adult Basic Education (ABE) program and placed directly under the auspices of PNM in 1968. During 1967 a group of inmates who had graduated from the high school approached acting Warden Rodriguez with the idea of bringing college classes in from the local College of Santa Fe. The idea was discussed informally with these inmates and with some of the Christian Brothers who administered the local college. A former inmate explained:

> The plans and the actual administration of the College Program was inmates. A stable team of inmates who came through the high school program had the initial concept as well as the continuing development of the college degree program. The impetus was placed upon it by inmates. By 1969 the program had gained enough respect both with the college administration and the inmates that it was possible to pursue programs outside the norm.

The plan for a college finally materialized after Warden Baker arrived and formally approached the College of Santa Fe in 1968. The College Program was started with an associate of arts degree with later expansion to a four-year bachelor's degree.

It soon became clear to inmates and to some of the Christian Brothers who were teaching classes that the College Program was not accessible to many inmates. Most inmates were ill-prepared to handle college level work, even though they had graduated from the prison's Adult Basic Education program.

In 1969 a college preparatory program, initially funded through the Office of Economic Opportunity as an "Upward Bound Program," and later funded with LEAA funds and called "Project Newgate," was instituted. Modeled on a program at the Oregon State Penitentiary, Project Newgate became the second college preparatory program in a U.S. prison. The program provided tutoring, remedial education, special educational classes in English and mathematics, ACT testing, psychological testing, and counseling services. It also provided funding to pay for college tuition and books, funding that continued for former inmates pursuing college degrees after they were paroled. One of the key aspects of Project Newgate was the requirement that all inmates desiring entrance into college undergo individual and group counseling. The Project Newgate staff, while working under the rules and regulations of PNM, were not penitentiary employees. They were employed by Eastern New Mexico University, which administered the funding for the project. Project Newgate served approximately 125 inmates at any one time, out of an average 660 total population, throughout the late 1960s and early 1970s. By 1972, 339 inmates were listed as participating in the College and Project Newgate programs (Department of Corrections 1972).

As an extension of the College Program, the School Release Program was instituted. Through this program, inmates attended classes on the College of Santa Fe campus during the day and returned to prison at night. Later, a number of inmates were placed on "24-hour release" at the college, where they lived in the college dorms, attended classes, and participated in work-study programs on campus along with the college's regular students. As many as twenty inmates per semester participated in school release during the early 1970s.

Women prisoners housed in the Annex Building also participated in these educational programs. In 1969, four women inmates attended a coeducational class in sociology held in the main penitentiary's Educational Unit. A 1973 lawsuit filed by inmate Shirley Barefield led to a federal court order compelling PNM to provide equal program opportunities for women. After that point, a greater number of women inmates were placed in the ABE, College, Project Newgate, and School Release programs. Women were escorted by COs from the Annex Building to the Education Unit in the main penitentiary to attend classes with male inmates.[4] The presence of women in the prison's college and Project Newgate classrooms made these programs even more appealing to male inmates. Several male inmates said their initial attraction to these programs was the chance to talk to women, something many of them had not done for years. Staff members and inmates reported that the presence of women put men on their best behavior. The privilege of being around women was something these inmates did not want to lose.

Federal funding, through the Department of Vocational Rehabilitation, was also used in October 1969 to start several programs aimed at giving inmates occupational skills. Training in auto body repair, carpentry, mechanics, plumbing, welding, and electronics was provided. In conjunction with these activities, a work release program was initiated in July 1969. A small prison industries program, initiated in 1967, included a furniture factory, sign shop, and printing shop which also provided some vocational training.

In September 1968, at the impetus of an Anglo inmate leader, a computer keypunching operation, overseen by a staff member but directly supervised by a convict, was opened. A former inmate explains:

> IBM came in and tested inmates on keypunch training in the institution. They had some inmates that tested very high, both in keypunch and management areas. It was decided a [computer] school would begin which would be taught by an inmate under the direction of a caseworker. So an inmate was selected and the school started with about six machines. It was intended just to teach the basics and then hopefully an inmate could go out and get a job. As it turned out, the inmates got interested, began to explore [possibilities] and took on contract work for the state.... [Eventually,] inmates did all of the keypunch work for the [State] Data Processing Center. The operation began with six inmates and grew to 111 inmates working around the clock [in shifts].

This program was the largest keypunch operation in New Mexico and had one of the lowest error rates of any keypunch shop in the U.S. (New Mexico Penitentiary 1969).

In addition to these educational and vocational programs, several programs aimed at improving inmates' social skills were also implemented in the late 1960s and early 1970s. Like the College Program and the computer keypunch shop, most of these programs were initiated by inmates. These programs involved direct contact between inmates and private citizen volunteers who entered PNM for an array of activities. These included the Chess Club, Toastmaster's Club, Gavel Club, JayCees, Dallas Cowboys'

Booster Club, Concerned Convicts for Children, Pre-Release Program, and Outside Friends Program. Caseworkers acted as official sponsors of the programs, but for the most part arrangements of activities were made directly between outside volunteers and inmates. "The convicts took the responsibility for doing most of it," said a former staff member. Activities included weekly meetings, banquets, escorted trips into town for inmates, and a variety of entertainment activities.

In November 1967, a Pre-Release Program was initiated by inmates associated with developing the College Program. The program provided community contact for inmates in the six months prior to their release. A number of students from the College of Santa Fe, as well as college instructors and other private citizens, volunteered to assist inmates in making contacts with employers and to teach them skills, such as writing a check or driving a car, needed for their day-to-day survival on the street. Most of all, the program allowed inmates to talk to "regular people" and especially to women who were part of the volunteer group. "All the meetings were supervised and everything," said an inmate, "but…they had females that you could go talk to for twice a week for a couple of months before you went to the streets. They kind of fit you back just a little bit you know."

Another organization that worked on a similar basis as the Pre-Release Program was the Outside Friends Program. The program was started in April 1973 by a Christian layman who had previous contacts with inmates in the institution. As a caseworker explained, the program matched a church member with an inmate "to have them develop friendship and rapport. And when the inmate was paroled, the church member would help him get a job, a place to stay, and reestablish him in the community. The program was working on a grand scale [in the early 1970s]. We had something like 200 people come in from the outside [every week]."

All of these programs "were initiated from inside by inmates," said a former inmate. "There was a lot of help from the Christian Brothers [at the College of Santa Fe] and staff members [from the prison's education programs] and some members of the prison administration itself. Notably, the strong man in the administration towards allowing these things to develop was Felix Rodriguez."

Baker and Rodriguez also used the prison's physical layout to implement their treatment regime. Some areas of the prison, such as Cellhouses 1 and 2, are more desirable places to live, since they provide a degree of privacy with larger individual cells that have doors rather than bars and individual cell windows on the outside wall of the cellhouse. In addition, Warden Baker gave inmates living in these cellhouses extra privileges, such as allowing them to decorate their cells, wear white, civilian-looking shirts, control the locking of their individual cell doors, and have a greater say in how their living unit was run. Inmates who had shown progress toward rehabilitation, by successfully participating in programs, maintaining orderly behavior, and following the rules, were rewarded with housing in these "honor units."

A NEW SYSTEM OF CONTROL EMERGES

The simultaneous elimination of the "hole" and implementation of programs affected inmates enormously. Despite correctional officers' fears that these changes would lead to disorder, they in fact created the basis for a much more sophisticated control system that maintained order in the prison. One of the secrets of effective prison rehabilitation programs, whether they actually reduce recidivism or not, is that they provide the basis for a network of control. As the 1870 Declaration of Principles issued by the American Prison Association proclaimed, "Since hope is a more potent agent than fear, it should be made an ever present force in the minds of prisoners" (quoted from Cloward 1960: 29). Or, as a PNM correctional officer explained, "I can control you a lot better by taking away something you really want, than by giving you a good ass-kicking."

As a system of rewards for good behavior, the proliferation of programs introduced a new compliance structure based largely on incentives or, using Etzioni's (1970) terminology, remunerative controls. Instead of going to the "hole" for punishment, an inmate could now be removed from participation in a program or from one of the honor units, or he could lose his chance to enter these. Such disciplinary actions became the major tools for inmate control in the new treatment regime's "step system," in which "a reward for being more responsible [is] more and more freedoms," explained a former corrections official, who added, "A logical freedom for them to exercise in the last stages before they get out is…self-government."

Warden Baker adhered strongly to the liberal ideology that promoted rehabilitation. (See his PNM annual report [New Mexico Penitentiary 1969] which lays out his "Forward Look" and "Challenge for Change" in corrections.) But it is not clear whether he completely appreciated the control functions of these programs. The side effect of control arising from these programs and the other innovations, however, was not lost on Felix Rodriguez, who came to understand during this period the benefit that programs had for maintaining order.

Inmates also understood the control functions of programs. Pressure from other inmates desiring program participation was an aspect of control provided through programs. An inmate said:

Rodriguez had security. He went out there and said, "O.K., you're going out there [on school release]...tell your buddy that you can't bring nothing in because you're going to be searched. And if you bring it in you're going to be responsible for causing the program to be ended, and you're not going to be real popular with the inmates." And those guys getting to go to college and sitting up there with them girls and going to church socials and stuff like that, no way they're going to lose that.[5]

Inmates reported that this was a period of excitement, hope, and expectations about changes in the prison. These rising expectations, at least initially, enhanced the legitimacy of the new treatment regime; and the programs provided a network of mutual support among inmates. A former inmate, who had been in PNM in the early 1960s, was paroled in 1967, and sentenced again to PNM in 1969, reports the changes he observed:

Former inmate: One of the first things I noticed was that there was mobility inside the penitentiary between units that hadn't been allowable before I left in 1967.... There was also an optimism present with Project Newgate and the College Program.... And right after I got [into Project Newgate] some Chicano friends of mine managed to get into the program. We would do a lot of studying together.
Interviewer: So there was a lot of support between inmates?
Former Inmate: Yes, there was.... And the programs themselves lent them more opportunity that wasn't there before. A clear example is that I had been nothing but a janitor until 1967.... But now I was respected because I was making a large-scale effort to do something about my condition. I had come up all the way from Springer Boys School [a juvenile institution]. I had gone through all the same route that they have gone through. And I made a complete turnaround. And I think this was somewhat encouraging to these other inmates.

This expression of belief in positive outcomes of these programs went beyond the mere calculation of material benefits; they also reflected elements of normative compliance with its "moral involvement" with the programs. This positive orientation toward programs provided control over a significant number of inmates who shared in this belief in the rehabilitative mission. Thus programs provided the prison organization with new networks of both remunerative and normative controls.

INMATE ADMINISTRATORS AND SOCIAL CONTROL

Even with the proliferation of programs and the loosening of restrictions on inmates, this was a period characterized by order. Escapes and violence were minimal. A primary reason for this low level of disorder was the presence of inmate administrators. A common feature of all the programs instituted by Baker was inmate involvement in both program development and administration. The group of inmates instrumental in initiating and administering the College Program and the Computer Keypunch Program had previously established reputations as "tough convicts," so many of them were already respected by the inmate population (Hart 1976b). Most were Anglo inmates who constituted an elite core within the inmate society. Most had been sentenced to PNM for murder; one had spent two years on "death row" before his sentence was changed to a life term after a retrial. A corrections official reported that inmates were utilized "in numerous places to assist the administration in getting the program across.... Inmates were placed in charge, in very high positions" in the IBM Keypunch Program, where "they were given free rein."

A former convict, who was associated with the prison's programs, gives a detailed account of the role of inmate administrators:

The [IBM Keypunch] Program was run absolutely and completely by one inmate and some inmate supervisors.... Now an interesting thing about this to understand is that there was no officer assigned to that shop. It was a dormitory area [in Dorm D-1] that had been cleaned out and the keypunch machines were installed. With the exception of the count and opening the door to let workers in and out [for the change of shifts], there was no officer in that place for two years or more. Now you talk about inmates having the ability to stabilize a situation in the prison. There was never a serious incident, never any incident, that occurred in that place. That's the only shop in the entire prison that could go like that with a two-year record of not even a fist fight. And the inmate that was in charge of that was a kind of a fuck-up [known as a troublesome inmate who had regularly confronted COs and was in the prison for murder] and naturally those are the people he knew the most; and when he saw a good thing he got a lot of those kinds of people around him.... But one inmate ran that entire program.... Many of the inmates involved in running the keypunch shop [later became] involved in administering the College Program.... What inmate administrators learned in the keypunch program was that if you keep a program together and police yourselves, the administration will allow you to go forward. So some of those inmates that had that experience moved to the college and carried that same attitude. And because of that attitude were able to keep, well you say "a lid on," what I say is to keep a college acting like a college should. In four or five years of my association with that place I can remember one or two fist fights and they were at the grill, not back in the Education Unit. That shows how the inmates respected the program.... Now the administration very quickly knew if there was something fishy going on. They weren't jumpy in those days so if an individual was getting out of line both sides knew it. And if they didn't get weeded out by those of us that were inside the program, they got weeded out on their own later. That was kind of understood and never really discussed with anybody.

A former staff member said these inmate administrators "were all very powerful in the inmate society." This staff member continued:

> They knew that social structure much much better than we did.... they could spot trouble. They could spot those that were there for other reasons than to help themselves.... All the men, I think, that participated in that [Education] Program appreciated what it did. They appreciated what they could get from it and they all valued it very highly. And if inmate staff spotted problems that could reflect on the Education Program either to the extent that it could get us in trouble with the Administration or with the Warden's Office, or disruptive behavior where somebody was trying to run games on Program professional staff, they let us know.

An inmate also discussed the lines of communication opened between inmates and staff through the inmate administrators:

> [In the early 1970s,] if you had a grievance, you'd walk right up to [gives names of inmate administrators].... They had the authority to tell the administration that the population is upset about eliminating a program and so they get together and have a big old conference and they get it worked out.

Another former convict also discussed the mediating role between inmates and staff that the inmate administrators played in the organization:

> These inmates [who administered programs] would act as mediators with other inmates. They were looked at by the general population as intelligent, as people who had been hardcore and had come through it, up through the system, had got their act together. The mere fact that they were working these key positions was a clear indication that they had made it. And that in itself was a status.... They would provide some on-spot counseling or clarification, or advice to inmates that were on their way to doing something that would have disrupted the program, particularly the College Program.

The use of inmate administrators was not without problems or contradictions. As a former convict said:

> Many of these convict administrators were mainly in it for themselves. My impression is that they were not so much interested in improving the quality of life in there and the programs themselves as they were in improving their own situation.

A caseworker also focused on what he saw as negative aspects of inmate administrators:

> *Interviewer:* Do you remember if the College Program and maybe a couple of other programs had inmates running them?
> *Caseworker:* Yeah, I remember that. I think a lot of the inmates that they had there shouldn't have been there.... They were running all kinds of games like you wouldn't believe. I think they should have inmate tutors and things like that, but when you start putting them up there in charge of management, you're asking for trouble.
> *Interviewer:* Cause they were doing favors for friends?
> *Caseworker:* Oh yeah, it was a very common thing, you know.
> *Interviewer:* Did that give those inmates a certain amount of power then in the population?
> *Caseworker:* It sure did, especially the kind of inmates that were running it.

Indeed, a very important aspect of these positions was the influence inmate administrators had on the selection of other inmates into programs. A former inmate administrator explains:

> Now Project Newgate very quickly gathered a lot of clout with the administration. Their recommendations were a fairly strong factor in who was chosen for school release [and parole]. One of the most important factors for who was chosen was who was funded and that's one of the things that gave Newgate clout. Now Project Newgate formed an internal committee which would meet and decide on who they would recommend to the [PNM] classification committee. That [Newgate] committee had the inmate college administrator on it, and that team of people would listen to an honest evaluation. And if that inmate did not believe someone was ready, the recommendation did not go; and if that inmate felt very strongly that an inmate should go and have an opportunity to show he could be successful, that committee would go along.... And Project Newgate's recommendations were followed somewhere in the neighborhood of 80 to 90 percent by the [PNM] administration.

These comments were supported by statements from other inmates, including another former convict who took part in administering programs:

> *Former Convict:* There was a selection committee at Project Newgate which I belonged to at one point.... [Other inmates] felt me out to see what I was capable of and what I wasn't capable of. I was consulted for various things. I even had requests for assistance in getting into the programs...
> *Interviewer:* Do you think that the fact that you and some other inmates had that kind of influence on selection built up your stature with other inmates?

Former Convict: Yeah, oh yeah!...
Interviewer: And in order to get into outside visiting programs like the Gavel Club, was it necessary for another inmate to sponsor you?
Former Convict: Yeah.
Interviewer: Or suggest that you get in?
Former Convict: Yeah.
Interviewer: And what would have been the benefits of something like the Gavel Club?
Former Convict: It gave you more visibility.... It gave the prison administration an indication that you were concerned about doing something about your condition, improving on it, and getting out and remaining out.
Interviewer: So these programs would help you with parole?
Former Convict: Oh yeah. It's like a resume, the more you build on it the better you look.
Interviewer: That would seem to imply that those inmates [who administered programs] had a considerable amount of power if they could help you get into a program that would help you get parole?
Former Convict: Yeah. Well see, eventually I even reached that particular position myself. I tried not to take it very seriously. I was very reluctant to support an inmate who I felt was very borderline. Although I did go out on a limb for one really borderline inmate. And he seemed to do really well. It was a touch-and-go thing, you know, it was just a daily task in trying to maintain him.

While the potential for abuse of this power wielded by inmate administrators was quite high and could lead to obvious problems within the organization, their influence over inmate placements in programs was a primary incentive for these inmate leaders' cooperation with the administration. Warden Baker's use of inmate administrators in some measure redirected the hierarchy of power within the inmate society. By relying on inmates who had already developed reputations as hardcore convicts, the administration handed these convicts an enormous source of nonviolent power. The influence they had on selection of inmates into programs meant that they indirectly could influence parole. (At that time, the Parole Board was not an independent agency. It was appointed by the PNM warden, who sat on the parole board as a voting member [*New Mexican* 2/11/70; Hart 1976a].) The trade-off was that these strong convict leaders now had a vested interest in maintaining their positions of power. And it was understood, although, as one of the former convicts quoted above said, "not discussed," that a major expectation of the administration was that these inmate administrators would help create an orderly prison. In the immediate vicinity of the programs, under their direct charge, they certainly kept order.

But their ability to "keep the lid on things" even extended beyond the programs into the larger inmate population. A veteran correctional officer, who had worked in the prison since 1956, explained this:

> *Interviewer:* Were a lot of convicts involved in helping administer those programs at one time?
> *Correctional Officer:* Yes, they were.
> *Interviewer:* Do you think those convicts maybe went back to their units and maybe helped keep the lid on things...?
> *Correctional Officer:* I know for a fact there were several that used to do that. Some even that were here in town [on school release] they had some rough sentences on them,...for murder, in fact. They used to work at school and some of them even conducted classes [in the ABE program]. And I know for a fact that they used to talk to the other cons both in the classroom and in their living units.
> *Interviewer:* So you think those convicts may have been bought into the whole system [to] help keep the place orderly?
> *Correctional Officer:* You have to, I think you have to have a man, an older con, tell you [other inmates] what to do, how to come around so as not to try and be acting tough like some of these young kids.

In addition to inmate administrators in programs, Warden Baker also instituted an inmate council to which prisoners from each living unit were elected by their fellow prisoners. "There was an inmate council, off and on again," reported a former convict:

> The inmate council in my estimation was never effective as a group...periodically a strong enough, smart enough inmate would get elected and that inmate could have an impact for a certain amount of time.... Now the council as a whole I would say long-term had no effect. But because the vehicle was there periodically there was a voice, so with that qualification, I would have to say the inmate council was a good thing.

Most observers agreed that the inmate council's primary beneficial function was that it provided an additional avenue for the warden to communicate with prisoners. It was another channel, along with inmate administrators in programs, through which the warden circumvented the old-line custody force.

A traditional holdover from the pre-1968 authoritarian regime was the use of inmate clerks in record-keeping and other administrative offices. These continued as positions of privilege and power for several inmates. In his 1975 investigative report on PNM, Attorney General Toney Anaya said,

> inmate clerks are used for various types of work within the correctional institution including the handling of accounting records, drug records

[for the hospital], personnel records and other confidential data such as psychological reports. All this work is being done by the inmate clerks without adequate supervision (Office of the Attorney General 1975: 23).

Inmate clerks in these sensitive positions had access to information, which is a potent source of power within the inmate social structure (Jacobs 1977; Sykes 1958). These inmates also had a vested interest in maintaining their positions and constituted, therefore, another stabilizing force within the prison society.

Thus an important aspect of the control system erected under Warden Baker, with the help of Deputy Warden Rodriguez, was a network of inmate power that gave strong inmate leaders a vested interest in maintaining order. This element of the control structure, along with the incentives built into programs and housing assignments, accounts in large part for the low level of violence and escapes during this period.

TREATMENT STAFF AS A NEW ELEMENT WITHIN THE PRISON ORGANIZATION

With the rise of programs, a new type of correctional employee was also entering the prison. The educational programs were administered by agencies outside PNM: the College Program by the College of Santa Fe; and Project Newgate by Eastern New Mexico University. This independence from PNM meant that outsiders to whom inmates could talk were in the institution on a daily basis. "It seemed to me like they were always going to bat for the inmates," said one inmate of these programs' employees. "These people who were running the place [Project Newgate], the outside people, they generally went to bat for the person who had an infraction of some kind." This was part of what gave the educational programs credibility with prisoners. They also gave inmates an avenue for expressing their anger:

> *Interviewer:* Back when you were there [in PNM in the late 1960s and early 1970s] and if you felt rage, were there staff people that you could have gone to and express that to who would have listened to you and maybe kind of defuse that for you?
> *Former Inmate:* Yeah. Mostly the people at [Project] Newgate. I wouldn't ever communicate my personal problems to anyone from the prison administration, the caseworkers and up, or even the guards themselves.
> *Interviewer:* So do you think the Project Newgate staff were a channel for the rage?
> *Former Inmate:* For a lot of us who were participating in that program, yes.

As programs progressed during the early 1970s, a core of new case-workers, oriented toward the goal of rehabilitation, were also entering the prison. They were a key element in the proliferation of the outside visiting programs. These caseworkers volunteered their time at no pay for the overtime, usually for one night a week, sometimes two nights, to supervise meetings between inmates and outsiders in the various programs.

With the arrival of these new employees, who were positively oriented toward programs, a new faction among the prison's staff was emerging that fully supported Warden Baker's attempts to remove the old authoritarian regime. These staff members, who had the closest contact with inmate leaders, represented an important new element in the prison organization. Not only did they represent a new direction in the goals of the prison, but they also became an important component in the network of control emerging in the prison. To the extent that program staff members allowed inmate leaders to function as administrators and advisors in program operations, program staff contributed to the maintenance of the nonviolent source of power these inmate leaders could use to influence the behavior of other prisoners. And to the extent that these program staff members intervened with the administration on behalf of inmates, the legitimacy of the prison organization as a whole was enhanced for inmates. A growing number of prisoners shared with these new staff members the belief in the rehabilitative ideal that was the expressed goal of the programs.

These inmates and these program staff members held to a goal that was in direct contradiction to the expectations of tight restrictions and inmate subordination held by most of the custodial force and members of the prison administration. Thus an important new faction within the prison organization composed of inmates and program staff members was spawned by Warden Baker's initiatives.

BACKLASH AND HOSTILITY FROM THE OLD-LINE CUSTODIAL FORCE

This new faction, however, met with very strong opposition from the custodial force, which largely adhered to the old authoritarian regime and felt completely undermined by the new direction the prison was taking. The proliferation of programs, inmate privileges, and a new type of employee created resentment from the old-line correctional officers.

Many of these COs had been raised in the rural poverty of northern New Mexico. They held very traditional, conservative values and were among the Hispanic poor who had been precariously moving into the lower middle class of cities like Santa Fe, working long hours at low-paying jobs, like those available at the prison. In their view, they had improved their situation through hard work. No one had developed any programs to help them! And they did not resort to crime as a result of their impoverished backgrounds. So, in the view of many of these COs, these programs were nothing more than an unnecessary coddling of people who had already proven their unworthiness of such consideration. The programs were seen as an element that fostered the disrespect inmates were now displaying toward the custodial staff. A veteran CO said:

> I've seen a lot of the disruption that those classroom programs caused. When I was in charge of Cellhouses 1 and 2, an inmate out of Cellhouse 1, which was the honor unit, come down laughin' like a loon. "What's the matter with you?" I asked. He says, "Oh, our instructor just told us that he could train an ape to do your job." And you get crap like this, you get college people coming in there to teach college courses to inmates, and the people that are teaching take a poor view of correctional officers.

For individuals who are struggling for middle-class respectability, as many of those in the custodial force were in the process of doing, the affront to their authority and respectability by established middle-class professionals, especially when communicated by inmates, caused a deep sense of class-based hostility. The social class differences—among the mostly Anglo, educated, young, middle-class professionals who staffed the programs; the less educated, mostly Hispanic lower-middle class COs; and the inmates from lower-class urban areas, who were now being given a lift up toward gaining middle-class educational credentials—were social forces underlying much of the resentment between the emerging factions within the prison organization. These class differences were directly reflected in the status differences within the institution itself, even in the differences in dress codes. Another CO expressed this status resentment:

> These [program] people come in. They're able to have beards and long hair. And they wear what they damn please—no ties, nothing like that. But yet, the correctional officer is told "you will wear a uniform. It will be pressed to a high degree. Your shoes will be shined to a very high shine. You will wear a tie. You will have your haircut." And then he sees these other people, all these other professionals coming in that have degrees, yet nobody says anything to them.... There's not only resentment but you're definitely going to have problems [getting cooperation between these program people and COs].

While education does not guarantee middle-class status, it is certainly an essential prerequisite. That inmates were gaining educational credentials was another source of resentment. One CO expressed the feelings of many correctional officers: "Right now if I wanted to go to school it would cost me a lot of money. And those guys [inmates] get it free." A long-running joke among correctional officers, which I heard repeatedly during 1975 when I worked inside the prison, was that if you wanted a college education, commit a crime and get sent to PNM. While these sentiments are an obvious exaggeration (inmates usually did contribute money toward their education and most inmates were denied admission into college because they could not pass entrance exams), they nonetheless express the enormous hostility that individual COs, who were getting no special help in their scramble for upward mobility, felt toward the programs, the program staff, and the inmates who participated in and administered these programs.

In addition to the programs, COs and middle-level prison administrators expressed direct hostility toward Warden Baker, who was perceived by these staff members as a dangerous radical who did not understand the realities of prison life. Warden Baker's closing of the "hole" and the loosening of restrictions on inmate movement were seen as undermining basic security. Baker was viewed by correctional officers as a warden who did not care about their safety. A middle-level administrator who worked under Warden Baker reports the following observations about correctional officers' fears for their safety:

> When Warden Baker came on board, he was the type of person who would because of his authority change things just for the sake of changing because he was the warden.... He would do such radical things as bring the entire [inmate] population of the prison, whatever the count was at the time, into the gymnasium, with the exception of those inmates in segregation, and bring all of his staff in there for a "chit chat" session with the inmates. You know, the staff are looking at each other and saying, "God. It just takes one guy to start something in here and they've got every staff member and the Warden right now, because we're outnumbered. It would take just one ass in that group and then we've had it." He did that twice. And that type of sudden performance by Baker worked a hardship on the staff because they became defensive never knowing what the heck he's gonna try the next time. He was throwing rules and regulations out so fast, changing the ones he had issued so fast, that the staff and inmates were both confused. Nobody knew what was happening.

Many COs expressed their resentment of Baker for the lax security and discipline he introduced. Baker was viewed as the source of inmates' lack of respect for COs' authority, which created, in their view, a dangerous situation. As a veteran CO expressed it,

Warden Baker...created a lot of problems. When I started working in May 1969,...the inmates had no respect for anyone in that institution. They'd kick grills, they'd holler obscenities to you, they'd push their way through, they'd do whatever they pleased and it was very hard to control. It's a wonder we didn't lose that institution at that time.

These observations about the lax security and the ample opportunities that inmates had to take hostages or even take over the institution during the late 1960s underscores the correctional officers' fear and resentment toward inmates. The fact is, however, that no incident occurred during the late 1960s. This had more to do with inmate motivation than security. The network of remunerative controls that Warden Baker had developed through programs held inmates back from creating disturbances. They calculated that there was too much to lose by rebelling and much to gain by maintaining order.

However, the lax situation contributed greatly to correctional officers' resentment and dissatisfaction. The turnover rate among COs was reported to be quite high during this period. "Probably a primary feeling of the officers was that they no longer had the power they did before," said a caseworker who worked in the prison at the time. "And consequently, they felt they no longer had control of the situation and decided to leave." But the majority of COs stayed, nurturing a growing resentment of the inmates and the programs that they perceived to be undermining their authority.

Though the COs' dire warnings about rising violence and escapes during this period proved to be wrong, they correctly perceived the loss of their authority. As a consequence, custodial staff morale was at an all-time low. "Mainly because Warden Baker had started the ball rolling. We lost total control of all the inmates. All the inmates, we lost total control of that. So they had no respect for us," lamented a veteran CO.

The consequence was that although there was no apparent increase in disorder as a result of Baker's actions, there was the beginning of an enormous rift between inmates and the custodial staff that would grow over the years and eventually lead to open and violent expressions of hostility. A former convict, who agreed that the period was marked by a low level of violence and disorder, said of this period, "Here's where 'who's in charge,' the uniformed guards or the convicts, begins to break down. And I don't think that changes overnight. I think that you had a calm before the storm."

RODRIGUEZ'S BALANCING ACT AS WARDEN

As deputy warden, Felix Rodriguez was trapped between the loyalty he felt toward his friends in the custodial force and his strong sense of obligation to be a loyal deputy to Warden Baker. Rodriguez was also aware that a growing number of young inmates, with whom he had been having dialogues, were not going to acquiesce any longer to the old authoritarian system. He realized that there was too much anticipation of change among inmates to allow a restoration of the old system. Many COs complained that Rodriguez became "pro-inmate" during this period because he helped implement the many changes that Warden Baker instituted. It is more likely, however, that Rodriguez was responding to a situation, over which he had little control, by trying to balance the opposing forces that were forming within the prison. This meant that he had to help accommodate the growing inmate power that was emerging from Warden Baker's innovations. As a result, Rodriguez alienated many COs who were adamantly opposed to any accommodations for inmates and who absolutely hated Warden Baker. This began for Rodriguez a balancing act he would be forced to continue even after he became the PNM warden in 1970.

Warden Baker's reign over PNM came to an end in February 1970, when a new department structure was being implemented. At Warden Baker's initiative, the legislature in 1969 created a new Department of Corrections which included a new position of Secretary of Corrections to oversee PNM, adult probation and parole services, and two juvenile institutions. For six months Baker unofficially held both the positions of PNM Warden and Secretary of Corrections. Though Governor Cargo attempted to appoint Baker as the permanent Secretary of Corrections, Baker ran into stiff opposition from legislative committees (*New Mexican* 2/18/70). Many disgruntled former prison employees talked to state legislators about Baker's allegedly heavy-handed management of corrections personnel and light disciplining of inmates (*New Mexican* 2/11/70). While the legislature was controlled by a liberal coalition, these legislators had a difficult time defending what many observers believed to be an attempt by Baker at "empire building." "Witnesses either praised Baker as the first really modern penologist to come to New Mexico, or condemned him as a tyrant and vindictive man" (*New Mexican* 2/18/70: A1). In addition, Democrats in the legislature used Baker's confirmation hearings to score points against Republican Governor Cargo (*New Mexican* 2/4/70) who, with his term as governor expiring, was planning to challenge an incumbent Democratic U.S. Senator in the fall 1970 elections. Amid this political maneuvering and public criticism, the legislature refused to confirm Baker as Secretary of Corrections. He then resigned as warden and left New Mexico (*New Mexican* 2/19/70).

Governor Cargo named Felix Rodriguez as the new permanent warden and appointed New Mexico psychiatrist Dr. John Salazar as the new Secretary of Corrections. These two correctional administrators quickly clashed over who was going to run PNM—the Warden or the Secretary of Corrections.

First, against Salazar's wishes, Rodriguez named as his new deputy warden, Horacio Herrera, who was part of the core group of prison administrators who had advanced up the organizational hierarchy behind their friend, Felix Rodriguez. According to a former corrections official, Dr. Salazar, a strong advocate of prison rehabilitation programs, wanted someone in the deputy warden's position who had a clinical background in inmate rehabilitation. But Rodriguez insisted on naming his own deputy. Within weeks a second confrontation emerged. Salazar instituted a first offenders program at the Los Lunas Honor Farm and wanted inmates transferred there for the program. Rodriguez, through Deputy Warden Herrera, refused to honor an inmate transfer specifically requested by Salazar. In this dispute over who had the power to transfer inmates, Salazar fired Herrera. Rodriguez and Herrera then went to Governor Cargo for his intervention. The Governor sided with these two PNM officials against Salazar. Governor Cargo asked Dr. Salazar to rescind the firing of Herrera and to cancel the transfer of the prisoner. After being Secretary of Corrections for only two months, Salazar resigned and released a six page resignation letter to the press. In this letter, Salazar said that he had attempted to centralize all department budgets and personnel, "but Rodriguez and Herrera, who run a Chicano conclave at PNM, resisted this.... In their attempt to show me that they were going to run the penitentiary rather than me, they went to the governor [about the dispute over transferring the inmate]" (*New Mexican* 4/30/70: A1). Salazar also told reporters that "Rodriguez and Herrera, when they went to Cargo, threatened to resign and told the Governor [who was now actively running for the U.S. Senate] a riot at the prison might result" (*New Mexican* 4/30/70: A1). Of this alleged threat, Warden Rodriguez said, "This I deny emphatically" (*New Mexican* 4/30/70: A1). The warden won this confrontation and thus maintained political control over PNM despite the new bureaucratic structure under which it nominally operated.

In Salazar's place, Howard Leach, a progressive but cautious corrections administrator, was named Secretary of Corrections by Governor Cargo. Leach had been executive secretary of the New Mexico Council on Crime and Delinquency and had done consulting work for Governor Winthrop Rockefeller of Arkansas when that state began implementing changes to its penal system in the late 1960s. Secretary Leach, who worked out of a small office in Santa Fe, deferred for the most part to Warden Rodriguez on decisions about PNM. Under Secretary Leach, Rodriguez would have undisputed control of the penitentiary.

In 1971, Governor Cargo, who lost the election for U.S. Senate, had to leave office under the state constitution's limitation on consecutive terms for governor. The Democrats regained control of the Governor's chair through a coalition that attempted to combine the political strength of New Mexico's ranchers with the growing influence of Hispanic voters. Bruce King, a rancher, was elected governor, and his running mate, Roberto Mondragon, a liberal Hispanic with strong support in poor areas of northern New Mexico, was elected lieutenant governor. Governor King was, for the most part, a "caretaker" governor who attempted little change. He retained Howard Leach as his Secretary of Corrections and Felix Rodriguez as Warden. He made no attempt to interfere with Rodriguez's administration of the prison, and, in fact, developed a close relationship with him.

It was during this period that charges began to be heard that an administrative clique, unaccountable to outside authority, was running the prison. That the prison was being run by administrators who really answered to no outside authorities was, of course, nothing new. What was new was the presence of outsiders in PNM who were maintaining daily contact with inmates through the prison's many programs. Since many of these inmates were engaged in a power struggle with the old-line custodial staff, from whom this administrative clique had emerged, it is not surprising that these inmates' sentiments were being communicated to outsiders. Partially as a result of the confrontation between this administrative clique and former Corrections Secretary Salazar, outside citizen groups, who had made contact with inmates through some of the new programs, began charging that a tight-knit group of prison administrators who were hostile to prisoner rehabilitation actually ran the prison (*Albuquerque Journal* 1/11/72).

Most of the members of this administrative clique were staff members who began working in the old penitentiary as correctional officers following the Korean War. They rose in rank behind their purported leader, Felix Rodriguez. After 1970, they held every major administrative position in the prison. Members of this group, however much they were old cronies, were not monolithic in their suspicion of programs. There was in fact a schism within this group between those who wanted to return to the tight-custody, authoritarian regime of the mid-1960s, and those who accepted not only the inevitability of the new programs but their positive benefits for control. Warden Rodriguez was notably in the latter camp. But he could not ignore the other faction.

Warden Rodriguez inherited a situation at the prison in which the traditional balance of power between the keepers and captives had been disrupted. On the one hand, inmates had gained an important voice in the prison organization. And program staff members were an important component in the information flow of the prison. Rodriguez depended on information from programs and inmate leaders as important avenues for taking the pulse of the institution. On the other hand, the uniformed custodial force and most of the middle-level corrections administrators, who had come up the ranks with him, wanted Rodriguez to tighten up the institution and retreat from the innovations that Baker had introduced.

Rodriguez attempted to bridge these contradictory forces within the prison. He developed a division of labor between himself and Deputy Warden Herrera. "Rodriguez imposed upon his deputy warden, Horacio Herrera, those kind of leadership things that had to do with the day-to-day involvement with the officers. I thought that was a pretty smart way to team it up," reported a former corrections administrator:

> I don't know Rodriguez to ever have done anything for or against a guard, either by act or by omission that hurt an employee, but yes his involvement was a lot more with the inmate, where Herrera was [in charge of] employee relations and security. And I thought it was a good trade-off. I don't see how one man could do all those things. It was clear that Rodriguez was absolutely in charge and I think he was a good delegator in the sense that Herrera had the role that he did.

Rodriguez was structuring his administration to accommodate the conflicting factions within the prison that had emerged with the late-1960s' innovations. He would deal with the new faction of inmates and employees involved with programs. His deputy warden would handle the clique of old-line correctional officers and administrators who resented the new freedoms and programs that former Warden Baker had introduced. This administrative structure, nonetheless, did not end the delicate and precarious balancing act that Rodriguez had to maintain to keep the prison running smoothly.

As a concession to the old-line custodial staff, Rodriguez attempted to reassert some of the authority of the uniformed personnel while keeping in place the rehabilitation programs begun by Baker. His goal was to slow inmate reforms. Few new programs were initiated and some were discontinued (including the Keypunch Program in November 1972). Also, an attempt was made to reestablish the COs' control over inmates. This reassertion of control, however, produced a reaction from inmates that made Rodriguez's balancing act even more precarious. As a correctional administrator who worked under Rodriguez reported:

> [After Rodriguez took over as warden] we started to implement procedures and policies, rules and regulations to attempt to control the inmates. They couldn't go some places now and they had to have clearance to go places. And they were resenting these [restrictions].... Once

you loosen up and then start to tighten up, the man who's doing the tightening is the S.O.B.

A caseworker also said, "Inmates were accustomed in the two years [under Baker] to that lax situation. It was difficult to come back and enforce the situation."

In addition to the reimposition of restrictions, inmates were also reacting to the slowdown in growth of new program opportunities. As a former convict explained:

There was an expectation among the inmate population that a realistic opening was taking place.... Inmates read more about correctional ideas than anybody else. And they see things going on in California, or Michigan...or wherever...and see the beginnings of it in here. But you have to keep in mind that the College Program, [Project Newgate, and other programs] touched [only a certain] percent of the population.... So once these programs were filled,...you have a lot of inmates there that are not being served. And that lends to the feeling of, "well, yeah, there's something for these guys but what about me?" And there's always a majority of the population that's in that situation...in spite of the fact that successful programming was finally taking place and even being successful, it was still successful with a small percentage of inmates.

Thus a significant proportion of inmates, who were expecting a continual rise in programs and other improvements, were becoming frustrated with the sudden slowing of innovations. Add to this the attempt by the administration to tighten up the institution by reimposing restrictions on inmates' movements, and it is not surprising that a confrontation soon developed.

THE 1971 INMATE STRIKE

An incident in October 1971 began as a work and food strike in which inmates refused to leave their housing units. But it soon developed into a small-scale riot that caused about $65,000 in property damage to six dormitories (Albuquerque Journal 10/7/71, 10/13/71; *New Mexican* 10/7/71, 10/8/71, 10/12/71).

The work stoppage was organized by inmates who were for the most part not participants in the programs. Most inmates (with some notable exceptions discussed below) refused to go to work on the morning of October 6, 1971. Inmates developed a list of demands which they gave to Warden Rodriguez. Rodriguez said he would interview inmates on an individual basis to see what grievances they had, but he would not respond to collective demands made by inmates. On the second day of the strike, "an

announcement [was made] over penitentiary loudspeakers that prison officials would not tolerate a boycott of meals and work routine beyond 11
a.m. [the next day]" (New Mexican 10/8/71: A1). Immediately, some of the
dormitory units exploded into rioting, which involved 10 to 15 percent of
all penitentiary inmates and lasted for about one and a half hours (New
Mexican 10/8/71). Notably, none of the rioting involved any assaults on
inmates by other inmates. Seven inmates suffered head injuries and broken
arms when correctional officers armed with clubs "were sent into dormitories with tear gas to evacuate the units" (New Mexican 10/8/71: A1).

Also of significance, not every unit participated in the rioting that
exploded after the Warden refused to negotiate collective demands and
the ultimatum for ending the strike was announced. Those units containing the inmate leaders involved in administering the college and keypunch
programs did not riot. A former convict gave this report:

> Interviewer: Was that 1971 incident somehow defused by some of the
> convicts?
> Former Convict: I won't go so far as to say that the entire situation was
> defused by inmates. I will tell you that the "fuck-up" block, Cellhouse 6—
> which to the guys that were in there once everything was locked down
> that was their whole world anyway—in that block an inmate came out
> and talked to everyone about what the hell are you doing involved in this
> [after an inmate broke out a window in the cellhouse]...And in that block
> 1 to 5 inmates defused the entire situation so that in that cellblock there
> was no damage, there was no riot. Now that's very real, and that took
> place with 68 inmates.... Now, for that group, and those were supposed
> to be, well many times the assignments get mixed, but you have to say 60
> percent of them was supposed to be the bad asses, but they were bad asses
> with pretty good minds and they hung together in a positive way.
> Interviewer: Now were these people some of the same people involved in
> these programs that you were talking about earlier?
> Former Convict: Yes they were. Now those...are the leaders of the college
> and the leaders of this other program [Keypunch], and these people
> helped stop this riot.
> Interviewer: Do you think that being involved in that programming that
> they really had something to lose because of this incident, that that just
> may have been the motive behind [stopping] it?
> Former Convict: I'm a graduate of all those programs and I can tell you
> very personally that that's exactly the reason.... The other thing was they
> wanted to break out windows and it was October.... But that was a very
> heavy incident and one of the few in my life, and I spent eighteen and a
> half years in prison, where I've ever seen a positive idea communicated
> from a few to a bunch that understood it and then the majority deciding
> not to fuck it up. There were dissidents in there but when they looked
> around and saw how small they were in number there was no riot.

This claim that the riot was defused by inmate leaders involved with programs was confirmed by other inmates and staff members, including a caseworker who was a correctional officer in 1971:

> *Interviewer:* I want to go back to an earlier event which was the 1971 incident. As I understand it, in that one there were cellblocks that just refused to participate.
> *Caseworker:* Right.
> *Interviewer:* And as I understand it, it also included [name of an inmate leader who administered the college and keypunch programs] and some of those people, who, I don't know if this is true or not, refused to participate and as I understand it, they kept Cellblock 6 from getting involved in that. Do you recall?
> *Caseworker:* Yeah. There were some units that didn't participate. Cellblock 6, though I think somebody broke a window or threw something and he was told to cool it. And they cooled it.

Other reports of inmates associated with programs refusing to participate in the riot were also given:

> *Former inmate:* It wasn't too long after I'd started [in] Project Newgate [in 1971] that that small riot occurred, where there was a lot of destruction of property.... But a lot of the inmates that were in Project Newgate didn't participate in it.... They just sort of hung around, I guess you could say. Didn't get into the main thrust of destroying things...or to do the riot itself.
> *Interviewer:* Do you think the fact that they didn't participate might have helped defuse that incident from becoming greater than what it was?
> *Former inmate:* It's very, very possible. You know, talking about myself personally, if I hadn't had that key position at Project Newgate and if I hadn't had the optimism as a result of participating in the program, I probably would have gotten pretty deep into that riot.... They had written out a whole plan for the strike itself including the key people and I had been selected as one of the key people for that strike. And I refused to participate. A work strike was called, a food strike was called, and as soon as morning work call was made, I just knocked on the door [of his dormitory] and I walked out and I went to work....There were like about two or three other inmates who went with me. The inmate that I had helped to get into the Toastmasters Club and Project Newgate went with me, and he had a reputation as a pretty violent person, because, you know, he's pretty fearless and inmates feared him.
> *Interviewer:* What about those Anglo inmates who were running the college, did they participate in that riot or did they pretty much stay out of it?
> *Former inmate:* No, they were mostly in the honor cellblock, Cellhouse 1, and my understanding is that they didn't participate in the riot.

The 1971 incident, which was the first disturbance at PNM since it opened in 1956 (*New Mexican* 10/10/71), demonstrated two things. First, it was not possible, without a confrontation, to reinstate the strict discipline and restrictions of the authoritarian regime that had been in place prior to 1968. Second, the network that former Warden Baker had created through the programs with inmate administrators did in fact provide a basis for control over a significant proportion of inmates. While program opportunities were not expanding, the existing structure of programs served important functions for control that certainly helped to dampen what could have been a potentially destructive riot. The importance had been driven home to Rodriguez of maintaining ties with programs and especially with the inmate administrators who had demonstrated during the 1971 incident the influence they held over a significant number of inmates. The 1971 incident also showed just how precarious the balance of forces in the prison had become.

THE EROSION OF CONTROL: APATHY, CORRUPTION, AND DRUG RACKETS

In the aftermath of the 1971 incident, charges of guard brutality against inmates were made (Albuquerque Journal 2/3/72). A high ranking member of the security staff, who was a long-time Rodriguez associate, was indicted for beating an inmate (*Albuquerque Journal* 3/30/72). The indicted staff member became a symbol for the old-line COs who still wanted a return to a more authoritarian structure. The custodial force, and many of the old-line administrators who had come up through the ranks with him, were becoming disenchanted with Rodriguez, who was increasingly seen as "pro-inmate." As a CO expressed it, "Rodriguez would go in there and talk to an officer for two or three minutes or just wave like that and talk to an inmate for an hour." This perception was enhanced when Rodriguez refused to intercede on behalf of the indicted staff member and agreed, as part of a bargain to drop charges, to have the employee banned from the prison and moved to a job in Central Office. "The staff felt he [the indicted employee] shouldn't have been taken to court because he was just doing his job. And then people felt that Mr. Rodriguez just left him hanging," said a veteran CO.

The indictment and subsequent removal of this employee, who had been the only captain under a system of relatively tight supervisory control of the custodial force, coincided with the creation of several captain's and lieutenant's positions. While this created some new promotion ladders for disgruntled correctional officers, the bulk of the promotions were filled with COs loyal to the administrative clique that had taken key positions as Rodriguez rose to power. A pattern of favoritism in promotions of correctional officers, which had been present for many years, now became even more apparent to line officers.

Many members of the custodial force viewed the Rodriguez administration as being as loose and undisciplined as the one headed by former Warden Baker. Many COs in fact tended to lump the two regimes together when asked to compare security and discipline under various wardens. These were invariably described by COs as "loose" in both the Rodriguez and Baker administrations. "Rodriguez was light," said a CO, echoing what most COs said in reference to the disciplining of inmates.

Correctional officers who complained about the favoritism and lack of support from supervisors and administrators, or who tried to take initiatives aimed at improving the working conditions for the correctional staff, were subject to ostracism, undesirable job assignments, being spied upon, gossiped about, and generally made to feel so miserable, that they would quit. As a high-ranking official who worked in the Central Office in the early 1970s said:

> Correctional officers were people who if they had any initiative and ability on their own, the system took it away from them because it was not a system that rewarded initiative and creative thinking. If you toed the line, minded your own business, obeyed the rules, made the post orders, you got along fine. Otherwise, you didn't last in the system.... Complaints would not have been welcome by the prison administration.

After the 1971 incident, with the unabated sense of dissatisfaction among COs, a growing apathy began to set in among the custodial force. "Of the officers that stayed...most of them operated with a total sense of apathy," said a former inmate. "There was never more than a very small core that I ever experienced that really gave a damn one way or the other. They did their eight hour shift and they split and if they thought something heavy was going to come down, ninety percent of them kept their mouth shut until they got out of the gate...in the late 60s and early 70s, that's when I think the greatest apathy set in."

The 1971 incident underscored the inability of the prison administration to reinstate tighter security procedures; the relative looseness that had begun under the Baker administration continued under Rodriguez. Since Rodriguez did not restore an authoritarian regime, as the custodial force had hoped he would, and since Rodriguez continued to be viewed as "pro-inmate" and nonsupportive of custody, the COs became demoralized and apathetic. "Inmates were going to run the place anyway," said a correctional officer, expressing this sense of demoralization.

By 1972, this apathy contributed to an organizational atmosphere from which emerged an informal pattern of deviance and corruption. Drug trafficking became a growing element of the prison organization. More inmates began entering the prison on drug charges, reflecting a rising use of drugs on the streets and the sudden availability of cheap "brown heroin," smuggled from Mexico, which flooded the southwestern U.S. from about 1972 to 1975. The inability of the PNM administration to place greater restrictions on the relatively free movement of inmates within the prison and the growing indifference among a demoralized custodial force facilitated this movement of drugs into the prison.

Inmates' unmet expectations for continuing program expansion can be understood as another source of growing illegitimate activities in prisons. Richard A. Cloward (1960: 28-30) argues

> that systems of incentives [like those of the prison's programs], although intended to secure conformity, constitute one of the major sources of deviant behavior in the prison...because the goals to which prisoners are enjoined to aspire are largely unavailable to them.... [Thus] the principal method of control now at the disposal of the custodian appears to be self-defeating—to have the unintended consequence of aggravating rather than resolving the problem of managing prisoners.... [D]eviance arises in the prison largely in response to discrepancies between aspirations for rehabilitation and expectations of achievement.... Disillusioned and frustrated, [prisoners] seek means of escaping degradation.... These prisoners pose a major problem for the custodian.... [But] pressures toward disruptive behavior are countered and channelized into adaptive patterns by providing access to higher status by *illegitimate means.* In other words,...the official system accommodates to the inmate system in ways that have the consequence of creating *illegitimate opportunity structures.* (Emphasis is Cloward's)

The experience of the Penitentiary of New Mexico in the early 1970s supports Cloward's observations. After Baker left, the expansion of programs ceased. Frustration on the part of those inmates who had been left out of the program expansion contributed to the disruption during the 1971 incident. These pressures toward disruption were then defused through an expansion of illegitimate activities. From the late 1960s to the mid-1970s, the flow of contraband drugs into the prison increased dramatically. Before the late 1960s, "drugs were practically unknown," according to a corrections administrator. "Drugs were not in discussion." But after 1968, and especially after 1972, there was "very definitely an upward curve" in the level of drugs in the institution, according to inmates, staff members, and officials. A former convict said:

Drugs have always been there, they'll always be in any prison.... The earlier years [mid-1960s] when I was there you knew certain individuals or certain groups that would score varying kinds of drugs, use them among themselves, sell them among themselves; and in order to replenish their drug supply, they'd go back out to the street for that small amount again. Very close-knit, very close-mouthed. That began to grow. More people got involved. First thing you know, everybody in the corridor knew who to go to [for drugs]. Now we are talking about the late 1960s, early 1970s. An upward curve definitely.

A former top corrections official agreed that "drugs were a problem, particularly during the later years [of his employment, which ended in 1975]." Most observers who were interviewed agreed that the highest level of drug trafficking occurred when Rodriguez was warden from 1970 to 1975 and that it increased most dramatically during this period. "I'd say from 1969 on was when heroin really started hitting Albuquerque and heroin would be coming in [the penitentiary]," reported a corrections official, who agreed that there was an upward curve of "street drugs" entering the prison in the early 1970s. The level of drugs "was highest under Rodriguez," said an inmate. "It [drug use] was quite heavy under Rodriguez," reported another inmate. Other inmates also reported the heavy availability of drugs: "There was all kinds of drugs. There was marijuana, there was heroin, there was pills." And a caseworker said, "There was considerably more dope floating around during the Felix Rodriguez administration.... Anything from heroin to pills and marijuana." These observations were backed up by scores of other interviews with staff members and inmates.

Drugs were also an important focus of a 1975 investigation of PNM, conducted by New Mexico Attorney General Toney Anaya, that found:

The free flow of contraband drugs into the Penitentiary is at an alarming level.... Although each Penitentiary official interviewed admitted that there was a contraband problem within the Penitentiary, it seems as though the procedures taken to counteract and solve that problem have been ineffectual and the problem has not received appropriate emphasis. It was admitted by prison officials that contraband is introduced into the Penitentiary by visitors, inmates and employees of the Penitentiary. No specific workable programs that have been undertaken to prevent or counteract such problems were mentioned (Office of the Attorney General 1975: 3 and 23).

The growing trafficking in drugs was not, as the 1975 Attorney General's investigation confirmed, accompanied by any serious attempts to stem the flow of drugs.

Interviewer: Do you think that the drug trafficking was tolerated?
Former convict: I think that the officer in the corridor for the most part could not have cared less. I feel that there were certain administrators who could not have cared less. Other administrators had they had good information I think would have made some attempt at a solution to the problem.... I do not recall a major drug bust in 12 years [from 1962 to 1974] in that prison. I do not even recall the attempt.

Testimony from another former inmate also points to the toleration of drug trafficking by the prison administration:

Interviewer: What were some of the ways that the drugs came in the institution?
Former inmate: Through the visitors...[inmates] working outside, you know, leaving the institution and returning back in the evenings or some time during the day. [Inmates] going out on furloughs. It was usually pretty apparent who brought it in too...because the heroin addicts would flock around the person or they would congregate in front of the man's living unit and they would holler his name out, you know, large numbers, and they were pretty well known as drug users. And they didn't care whether a guard was there watching them. That wasn't important to them at all.
Interviewer: So it seemed pretty loose in that way?
Former inmate: Oh yeah, extremely loose.
Interviewer: So do you think it should have been pretty obvious to the administration?
Former inmate: Oh yeah. Shit, you'd see ten inmates hanging out the window looking outside to see who came to visit who. And as soon as he walked past the Control Center after visiting with his relative or whoever, they would all follow up behind...you'd have to be stupid not to be able to know who was doing what.

The 1975 Attorney General's investigation also indicated that there were inadequate "precautions against tampering with examinations for detection of opiates in an inmate's body.... An inmate...has admitted altering the results of the Mor-Tek urine analysis and this admission was reportedly known by the administration.... The lack of procedural safeguards regarding all drugs at the Penitentiary is mirrored by the lack of safeguards for the integrity of the Mor-Tek urine examinations" (Office of the Attorney General 1975: 3, 13, 23).

As indicated in the 1975 Attorney General's investigation, some staff members not only overlooked drug trafficking but were actually involved in it. A former corrections official, in discussing the drug trafficking of the early 1970s, explained:

I think it was a combination of inmates and guards. See the way inmates worked guards is they would try to get a guard to make one mistake, to go along with one violation of the rules, and then they've got him because [the inmate would say] "you go along with me hereafter because if you don't I'll let it be known that you did so and so" and so on. [Thus, as a guard] you get stuck. You get more and more stuck the longer you work with them. This is the way these guys work and so pretty soon you get [guards] bringing things in.

The trafficking of drugs involved both street drugs, such as heroin, and drugs pilfered from the prison's pharmacy. The 1975 Attorney General's investigation reported very loose controls on pharmacy drugs:

> Inventory controls for hospital drugs are totally inadequate or non-existent.... There is no way under the existing practices to protect against large scale pilfering of drugs (Office of the Attorney General 1975: 3 and 22).[6]

The loose checks on pharmacy drugs and the lack of any serious efforts to crack down on street drugs entering the prison constituted an informal accommodation to inmates involved in these drug rackets.

TOLERATION OF DRUG TRAFFICKING AS AN INFORMAL ACCOMMODATION

This informal accommodation, in addition to the narcotizing effects of drugs, provided a second (the first being programs) major network of remunerative control over inmates. This network was informal because there was no official condoning of the drug trafficking. At the same time, however, as Attorney General Anaya alleged in his 1975 investigative report (Office of the Attorney General 1975), no effective steps were instituted to either safeguard against pilfering of drugs from the pharmacy or curb the flow of drugs coming into the institution through visits, through inmates leaving and entering the prison for furloughs, work or programs, and through some prison employees.

The growing tolerance of drug trafficking, with its effect of providing another avenue for inmate control, was not a product of any deliberate design on the part of administrators or staff. Rather, this pattern of nonchalance about drug trafficking was the result of a series of compromises made independently by many staff members. Over a period of a few years, small informal compromises, which involved overlooking certain infractions as trade-offs for the appearance of order in specific cellblocks or dorms by specific COs, eventually evolved into a general pattern of accommodating and ignoring what came to be some rather large-scale drug rackets.

Sykes'(1958) observations, discussed in Chapter 2, about the "corruption of authority" in prisons are particularly relevant to the situation at

PNM in the early 1970s. The administration did little to reverse this pattern of acquiescence to illegal rackets. But the unintended by-product of these compromises, at least in the short term, was order in the prison.

> *Interviewer:* So you think there was a lot more drugs when Rodriguez was warden here?
> *Inmate:* I think there was.
> *Interviewer:* Is that why there was the difference [in the level of violence, which was relatively low before 1975]?
> *Inmate:* I think that had something to do with it.... The drugs were here, you know.... But the tension wasn't that great.... As long as there were drugs, usually the people that were messing with drugs would go do it and stay to themselves. They weren't causing any trouble which surprised me.... I thought, "Man, they're gonna be 'O.D.ing' and killing each other and stuff," but that wasn't what was happening.
> *Interviewer:* Seemed pretty stable though? I mean there was just a pretty stable supply and people didn't really have that big a problem if they wanted it?
> *Inmate:* Right. And the junkies would stay to themselves. And the other people who were trying to straighten their lives up would stay to themselves. They weren't affected. And they weren't hassling each other or stealing from each other, which surprised me.

A former convict explains another component of the stabilizing effect of illegal prison rackets:

> *Interviewer:* Did these inmates [who controlled drug trafficking] in any way act to stabilize the institution? Would there be any connection between having a racket and wanting to keep things fairly cool...?
> *Former convict:* That's true, but you're not talking about controlling an institution. You're talking about whoever has the power in a small group controlling a group. And then with several groups of course it has the impact you're speaking of. But no one is ever thinking about control except for their own nest.
> *Interviewer:* Okay. But do you think it would have some sort of stabilizing effect, I mean, at least in those terms?
> *Former convict:* Absolutely. I was a gambler and in my area I saw to it everything was tight so the poker game didn't get busted up. And I had some help with that from a few other gamblers. The same thing would be for whoever had their thing. It assumes some strength which there always did exist in those groups.

Inmates involved in illegal rackets such as drug trafficking have a vested interest, as Cloward (1960: 33) suggests, in maintaining an orderly institution:

> [C]ertain prisoners, as they become upwardly mobile in these [illegitimate] structures, tend to become progressively conservative. This ideo-

logical conversion takes place because these individuals develop a vested interest in maintaining the higher positions they have gained. Seeking to entrench their relative advantage over other inmates, they are anxious to suppress any behavior that might disturb the present arrangements.

Disruptions would also risk the intricate connections that were necessary to keep a racket going. Thus the drug traffickers, just like the inmate administrators of programs, shared with the administration the objective of maintaining stability and order.

In 1975, I discussed drug trafficking with some former inmates, who had proven to be reliable sources for information, and a corrections department employee involved with intelligence and security activities. I was told, and this was later confirmed in interviews during the 1980 Attorney General's investigation of PNM, that inmates controlling the drug trafficking were largely Hispanics from Albuquerque who had been involved in drug use and sales on the outside and maintained connections with drug rackets in Albuquerque and Santa Fe after they were incarcerated. There was not just one group of drug traffickers, but several independent rackets which avoided, at least in the early 1970s, competition among themselves. There were several ways in which drug transactions took place, but usually inmates worked with confederates on the outside to finance the initial purchase of drugs and relay money to the outside. Once drugs entered the prison, they could be sold for about twice their street value. Inmates purchasing drugs might have money transferred by friends or relatives on the outside to other outside confederates involved in the transaction. Money could also be diverted from inmate accounts by having it sent out to relatives, both real and fake. Money was also smuggled directly into the institution through visitors. Money could be gained through gambling, loansharking, and extortion of young, "weak" inmates who had access to it from families with relatively higher incomes. Young Anglo inmates from more middle-class backgrounds, who entered the prison on drug related charges in greater numbers after 1972, were especially subject to extortion by some of the "heavies" associated with drug trafficking.

Inmates could also go into debt in order to purchase drugs. A chain of debts would be created in which repayment of a debt to one inmate was dependent upon the repayment of a debt from another inmate. These chains of indebtedness are not uncommon in prisons. Davidson (1974), in his study of San Quentin, observed a similar chain of indebtedness as a way of financing illegal prison rackets.

These intricate networks of drugs and money, and the chain of debts created by the drug trafficking, became an important feature of the PNM prison organization by 1974. These illegal networks provided a basis for informal controls within the organization. However, due to the growing corruption of authority that these networks entailed, this avenue of informal control also contained the seeds of a growing contradiction within the prison organization. This would lead to the destruction of the remunerative controls which had been largely responsible for the low levels of violence and escapes and the general atmosphere of stability and order.

SUMMARY: CONTROL DURING THE YEARS OF ACCOMMODATION

The relative order that prevailed from 1968 through 1974 was the result of some important formal and informal accommodations to inmate power. These accommodations provided structures of opportunity that held inmates in check.

A legitimate opportunity structure was instituted through the development of vocational and educational programs and a "step system" that allowed inmates to gain more privileges and freedom as they successfully progressed through programs. In addition, the network of inmate administrators and clerks provided an important nonviolent source of power for a number of inmate leaders. Help with obtaining access to program opportunities and the ability to gain information from the administration were the primary sources of power available through this network of accommodation. Both inmates in the programs and those in positions of power had a vested interest in maintaining an orderly prison.

Largely because of the gap between the expectations induced by the legitimate opportunity structure of programs and the limitations on the expansion of these opportunities, an informal, illegitimate opportunity structure in the form of drug trafficking began to emerge in 1972. Widespread apathy among COs also contributed to the rise of this illegitimate opportunity structure. Thus a second set of inmate leaders, who had a vested interest in maintaining their illegal rackets, helped to keep order in the prison. These inmates enforced order to facilitate the smooth operation of their rackets.

For those inmates who were shut out of both the legitimate and illegitimate opportunity structures, who became in Cloward's term "double failures," the choice of retreating into drug use, either with street drugs like heroin or those from the prison pharmacy, was readily available.

The system of remunerative controls, both the formal, legitimate incentives and the informal, illegitimate incentives, was effective in maintaining the appearance of order. The low levels of violence and escapes were due in large part to the presence of these controls.

Coercive controls, including lockdown in disciplinary segregation, were not used to any great extent. The maximum detention unit, or the "hole," was not officially used on any routine basis during this period after Warden Baker had closed it in 1968. Some inmates reported, however, that COs during the early 1970s did on occasion throw recalcitrant inmates, already locked in the regular segregation cells, into maximum-detention unit cells as an informal and unauthorized punishment. The regular disciplinary segregation unit (Cellblock 3), with a capacity for eighty-six inmates held an average of about fifty inmates from 1968 through mid-1975 (Office of the Attorney General 1980b: 18). The inmate population in Cellblock 3 was as low as thirteen in 1971. Cellblock 3 was used for both disciplinary and protective custody cases during the early 1970s. There was no designated unit for protective custody during this period. Prior to 1975, the percentage of inmates in disciplinary and protective custody lockdown was less than 5 percent (Office of the Attorney General 1980b: 18).

Thus inmates were controlled through a set of legitimate and illegitimate incentives. The prison was orderly and nonviolent, but it was full of contradictions that by 1975 began to put enormous strain on the organization and bring into play forces that would create dramatic and devastating change.

The contradictions involved with the corruption of authority could not go on unchecked. Drug trafficking would get out of hand and become part of a major public scandal.

The rift between COs and inmates that dated from the changes introduced by Warden Baker in 1968 was an ongoing contradiction within the organization which had been resolved through a pattern of apathy and resignation by much of the custodial force. Yet, the source of resentment against inmates, that inmates' power had been purchased at the expense of COs' power, was still present.

During 1975 and 1976, these contradictions would come to a head and force dramatic change upon the prison organization. These internal organizational contradictions coincided with the significant economic, political, and ideological shifts in the larger society discussed in Chapter 2. Together, these internal and external forces would cause the years of accommodation at PNM to give way to a period of open confrontation.

4

YEARS OF CONFRONTATION, 1975–1977

The Penitentiary of New Mexico (PNM) at the beginning of 1975 was to all outward appearances a calm and orderly institution. But beneath this surface appearance, internal contradictions that had been growing since 1971 strained the prison's organizational structure. Limitations on legitimate program opportunities, growing hostility between correctional officers (COs) and inmates, apathy among the custodial staff, and corruption of authority connected to drug trafficking threatened the balance of forces that Warden Rodriguez precariously maintained. In 1975, Rodriguez's delicate balancing act collapsed as the remunerative control structure, based on formal and informal trade-offs and incentives, unraveled.

FORCES OF CHANGE BEYOND THE PRISON'S FENCES

Events and trends outside the prison accelerated the movement of these internal contradictions toward organizational dissolution within the prison. The economic, political, and ideological shifts, considered in the theoretical discussion in Chapter 2, coincided with and exacerbated an emerging organizational crisis within PNM.

First, the recessions of 1974 and 1975 produced the largest rise in unemployment in the U.S. since the Great Depression. Rising unemployment disconnected increasing numbers of young people from the social controls provided by steady work and labor market participation; thus, greater numbers were joining the ranks of a socially marginal surplus population. Across the U.S., crime rates increased and incarceration rates began climbing dramatically (Box 1987). In New Mexico, the number of officially unemployed persons jumped 87 percent, from 23,500 in 1973 to 44,000 in 1975, representing a rise in unemployment from 5.7 to 10.4 percent of the labor force. Concurrently, the official number of "Index" crimes rose by 32 percent and the number of prisoners in all the state's adult prisons climbed by 59 percent, from 750 in June 1973 to 1,195 in November 1975. (The state's total population increased 6 percent during this period.)

Second, the political climate changed. Organized movements of the poor waned, partly because of the worsening economy that placed the unemployed and working class in more intense competition for jobs. This competition tended to fragment the poor politically and negated to a large degree the influence they had had in the late 1960s. In addition, the combination of repressive and co-optive measures by the federal government and many local agencies tamed the more radical elements of these movements. In New Mexico, the radical *Alianza* and *La Raza Unida* movements had disappeared by 1975. Tijerina had been convicted for his participation in the courthouse raid at Tierra Amarilla and was serving a prison sentence. Other former radical leaders had either been killed, locked up for various (in some cases possibly trumped-up) charges, or employed in federally funded antipoverty programs. As the movements died out, the social and political pressure that had been the impetus for the War on Poverty programs faded. Federal policies shifted during the Nixon Administration from community action to a greater emphasis on individual welfare grants. In the process, the poor became fragmented, isolated, demoralized, and disorganized. The political crisis emanating from the bottom of society in the late 1960s had been effectively contained by 1975.

Coinciding with this defeat of poor people's movements, the general political climate became more conservative. The old liberal coalition fractured as labor unions increasingly lost membership and political clout. And funding for social programs eroded with this decline in the once-solid liberal consensus.

The loss of federal funding and the shift toward conservative political power specifically affected New Mexico. In the late 1960s, the liberal-Hispanic coalition (the "Mama Lucy's") had its base in northern New Mexico and rose to power after the radical organizing in the state's northern counties. This coalition benefitted from the federal grants and antipoverty funds, which were used as an alternative patronage system to increase their political power and obtain jobs for their constituents in the northern counties. These antipoverty programs produced an opportunity structure for impoverished Hispanics of northern New Mexico, and provided the basis for the political dominance of the liberal-Hispanic coalition that controlled the state legislature throughout the early 1970s. The political mobilization in the north and the federal funding that was a response to this mobilization were the basis for this liberal-Hispanic coalition. By 1975, both the political mobilization and antipoverty programs had lost momentum. In the 1974 elections, the liberal-Hispanic coalition lost significant power in the state legislature. In the 1976 elections, this coalition completely lost control of the legislature to a group of southern New Mexico, Anglo conservatives.

This conservative political trend, which began to emerge strongly in 1975, coincided with a third important shift in the larger society. The ideology supporting rehabilitation as the goal of corrections came under a sustained and devastating attack from both the Left and Right (Cullen and Gilbert 1982). Academics also challenged the rehabilitative goals of corrections (Van den Haag 1975; Wilson 1975). Martinson's (1974) article on the rehabilitative effects of corrections programs purportedly demonstrated that "nothing works" in our attempts to rehabilitate offenders. In New Mexico, I witnessed powerful conservative legislators in 1976 hearings specifically use Martinson's article in their arguments against the continuation of funding for prison programs such as Project Newgate. Other studies which gave support to the rehabilitative effects of such programs, and specifically clarified Martinson's findings to show that "some things do work" (e.g., Palmer 1975), had been provided to these legislative committees by the Governor's Council on Criminal Justice Planning and the New Mexico Council on Crime and Delinquency. However, Martinson's study was the only basis for discussions at these hearings; the other studies, which deviated from the prevailing ideological trend, were ignored.

These shifts in ideology and political makeup of the New Mexico State Legislature coincided with the cutoff of federal funds. Many of the educational and other innovative programs at PNM, such as Project Newgate and the School Release Program, were funded with federal grants that the state was expected to match. After a three year start-up period covered by the federal grants, the state was supposed to provide complete funding for these programs. But with the political shift in the legislature and the ideological attack on rehabilitation, funding for most of these programs was not forthcoming as the federal grants ended in 1976. Throughout the U.S., many innovative correctional programs that had been federally funded were curtailed or eliminated as state and local governments did not continue the programs' funding. The major source for these federal funds, LEAA, was in its final years and had been increasingly moving away from direct funding of programs (Feeley and Sarat 1980).

As funding for programs at PNM was cut, other proposals for harsher treatment of offenders were being discussed by New Mexico legislators. By 1977, many of these proposals would be implemented. Of special significance were the discussions about eliminating parole and replacing it with a "flat-time," determinate sentencing structure that would generally increase the length of sentences. While determinate sentencing was supported by many liberals, who held to the "justice model" (Cullen and Gilbert 1982), it was largely the conservative arguments against "lenient" parole boards that constituted the major impetus behind these proposals. The conservatives clearly set the tone of the debate over fixed sentencing

(Greenberg and Humphries 1980). In New Mexico, these discussions led to enactment in 1977 of a determinate sentencing structure that eliminated parole.[1] Additionally, beginning in 1975, a new death penalty law was debated, with the conservative position in favor of it prevailing in 1978. Thus the rehabilitative ideal was abandoned by the legislature in favor of a hard-line, conservative approach to corrections.

These ideological shifts also affected local races in New Mexico for judgeships and prosecutors. In the 1976 elections, a number of liberal judges lost to hard-line opponents. District attorneys found their plea bargaining policies under attack by hard-line rivals who promised more jail time for offenders. Thus a new crop of conservative, get-tough prosecutors and judges replaced several liberals who had supported rehabilitation.

THE "ACTIVIST" GOVERNOR AND
THE FALL OF WARDEN RODRIGUEZ

As these more general shifts in the economy, politics, and ideology were emerging, the New Mexico Department of Corrections underwent a dramatic change. A new governor, Jerry Apodaca, took office in January 1975. Apodaca, like many Democrats around the country in 1974, following the Watergate scandal, ran on a "government reform" platform. A maverick liberal Democrat from southern New Mexico, Apodaca was an activist governor who sought to extend the control and influence of the Governor's Office throughout the executive branch. Under his leadership, the state moved from a "weak-executive" system administered by independent boards and commissions to a "strong-executive" system run directly through a governor's cabinet. Apodaca's plans for reform involved a massive reorganization of the executive branch, whereby commissions would lose their policymaking functions and become merely advisory. Each agency, including the Department of Corrections, would fall directly under the control of the Governor's Office.

Even before the reorganization was officially approved by the legislature in 1977, Governor Apodaca moved to take effective control of executive agencies. He attempted to appoint, as heads of departments, individuals who agreed to report directly to the Governor's Office. He could not, under the then current form of government, summarily dismiss agency heads, since these firings had to be approved by the commissions overseeing each agency. The current agency heads and their commission members were holdovers from the previous administration, headed by Apodaca's chief political rival within the Democratic Party, former Governor Bruce King. Many of these agency heads and commission members were set to resist Apodaca's reorganization plan. These agencies included the Department of Corrections, whose key administrators had managed the department during the King Administration with no interference or direction from the Governor's Office. "Having inherited us from the King Administration, we weren't [Apodaca's] people," said one of the King corrections appointees. The Corrections Commission, the Secretary of Corrections, and the Warden resisted Apodaca's moves against their independent status.

A dispute between Warden Rodriguez and Governor Apodaca quickly arose in the summer of 1975.[2] Initially, the dispute was over promotions at PNM. The Governor wanted one of his political supporters, who was the hospital administrator at PNM, promoted to a deputy warden's post. Warden Rodriguez refused to promote the administrator and informed Secretary of Corrections Howard Leach that the administrator was under investigation for improprieties. A report on the investigation, Leach informed the Governor, was being prepared by Rodriguez for the Secretary. The hospital administrator was accused of involvement in paying inmates' gambling debts and was in the process of being fired by Rodriguez. Governor Apodaca demanded a copy of the investigation's report, which Secretary Leach refused to hand over, since, he said, the investigation was "ongoing." "Howard Leach was not a politician," said a former state official. "He made the mistake of making himself appear to be taunting Jerry Apodaca with the contents [of the investigation's report]." In response, the Governor asked Attorney General Toney Anaya, who was also elected in 1974 on an anticorruption platform, to investigate the affair.

Anaya's investigation looked specifically at the case of the hospital administrator and at the prison's investigation of this employee. This 1975 investigation also focused on the general management of PNM. The Attorney General alleged that, to enable a prisoner to pay his gambling debts, the hospital administrator had brought him money from his (the prisoner's) family. This prison employee resigned after being cleared by the Attorney General of other serious charges against him. However, it was also alleged by Anaya that top prison administrators had obtained false testimony from inmates against the hospital administrator by promising them special treatment in return for their false accusations. Anaya went on to report the general mismanagement of the prison, including the placement of unqualified inmates in sensitive clerical positions and the lack of effective controls on drug trafficking, contraband smuggling, and pilfering of prison pharmacy drugs.

With the Attorney General's report and the documentation of serious allegations it provided, Governor Apodaca now had the ammunition he needed to remove his political enemies in the Department of Corrections. Under an onslaught of media publicity and pressure from the Governor's Office, Secretary of Corrections Leach was dismissed by the Corrections Commission in late August 1975. Though members of the Corrections Commission initially resisted Apodaca's request for Leach's dismissal, they refused to enter into a public confrontation with the Governor. "The Corrections Commission was weakened by having given in to the Governor and getting rid of Leach," said a state official. Leach's refusal to hand over the prison investigative report to the Governor, an alleged act of insubordination, was the basis for the removal.

Leach was replaced by Michael Hanrahan, one of the Governor's political supporters (*New Mexican* 8/28/75). Hanrahan had been a probation officer for ten years, director of the Albuquerque municipal court's probation office for five years, and, for the preceding two months, head of Apodaca's newly created, full-time parole board, which was made independent of PNM in early 1975.

Hanrahan inherited a central office located in an old two-story house near downtown Santa Fe that housed "three or four professionals to operate the department," said a corrections administrator. At that time, "the penitentiary was running itself," said the administrator. Removing PNM's independence was the object of Apodaca's next moves and a specific instance of his overall objective of bringing all executive agencies under the direct purview of the Governor. A successful move against his political enemies in the Department of Corrections would send a clear message to every state agency and commission that Apodaca's reorganization was for real.

Through Hanrahan, Apodaca now had the power to remove the top administrators from PNM. Armed with Anaya's report, the Governor asked in September 1975 that Hanrahan fire both Warden Rodriguez and Deputy Warden Herrera. Hanrahan removed Deputy Warden Herrera, eventually allowing him to resign after a prolonged public battle and threats of a lawsuit. However, he acceded to demands by Corrections Commission members, who still had policymaking authority over corrections and had to approve Hanrahan's decision, that Rodriguez be assigned to another position in the department.

Governor Apodaca, who had publicly stated that he would not interfere with the decisions of his new corrections secretary, reluctantly agreed to allow Rodriguez to take a post in the Department of Corrections Central Office, but only on condition that Rodriguez be barred from entering or having any contact with PNM. Rodriguez was named to a newly created position, Director of Adult Programs, that had no supervisory authority over any prison in the state, including PNM (Department of Corrections 1976). "From 1975 to [January] 1979 the penitentiary was pretty much autonomous, reporting directly to the [Secretary] of Corrections instead of going through the Director of Adult [Programs]," reported a corrections official. "[Rodriguez] had no input into any of the policy changes or anything else during that time." Another corrections official said, "What they did was kick him upstairs and put him out to pasture." And a third corrections official reported that Rodriguez "didn't have any meaningful leadership role. He was cut out with respect to the penitentiary." Rodriguez's new position was undefined and, at least initially, involved few responsibilities. "His authority quite frankly was limited at the request of the Governor," said a high-ranking corrections official. "I went to the Governor and said, 'Governor, what do you want to do with Felix Rodriguez? I'd like to use whatever experience he has.' The Governor said, 'That's fine. I just don't want him in the penitentiary.' What I did with Mr. Rodriguez, I said, 'Felix, you stay away from the penitentiary, just stay away from it.'" Rodriguez's official responsibility was the planning of new adult institutions. He was to have nothing to do with PNM as long as Apodaca remained governor. Thus, Governor Apodaca won his battle with the top administrators at the Department of Corrections. The Rodriguez era at PNM came to an abrupt end in September 1975, and Rodriguez himself now waited from his do-nothing position in the corrections Central Office for the political tides to change.

RISING AND FRUSTRATED EXPECTATIONS
AMONG INMATES DURING THE PROCESS OF
ADMINISTRATIVE SUCCESSION

Inmates at PNM anticipated very positive changes with the removal of these top administrators. The new Secretary of Corrections, Mike Hanrahan, made many gestures indicating new initiatives and expanded inmate programming. The most significant move was Hanrahan's appointment in September 1975 of Lloyd McClendon as his administrative assistant (Hart 1976b; *Santa Fe Reporter* 6/10/76).

McClendon was a former convict at PNM who began his sentence for murder in 1964 on death row. His sentence was changed to life imprisonment after a retrial in 1966 of his original conviction. Under the parole provisions in effect at the time, prisoners serving life sentences were eligible for parole after ten years of their sentence. McClendon, whose prison name had been Lloyd Miller, developed a reputation as a mean, tough, and fearless convict (Hart 1976b). McClendon also had outstanding leadership and organizational skills. He was respected by other inmates as a spokesman, and slowly gained the respect of many staff members including Felix Rodriguez, who allowed him to advance in the prison's educational programs. He was the primary organizer of the highly successful Keypunch Program and later was one of the key inmate administrators of the College Program. He earned an associate of arts degree and eventually gained a position in the prison's School Release Program, through which he earned a bachelor's degree in accounting and business education. In 1974, he was paroled from PNM and hired as the grants manager for the Governor's Council on Criminal Justice Planning. He and some former staff members from Project Newgate, who now worked for the Governor's Council, formed the nucleus of a group of state employees who continued to push for rehabilitation programs at PNM. In this position, he was instrumental in obtaining federal funds for innovative programs, including the continuation of the penitentiary's education programs. During the summer of 1975, he became an unofficial advisor for the new parole board, created by Governor Apodaca and headed initially by Mike Hanrahan. During the fall of 1975, McClendon taught inside the penitentiary a psychology course which he specifically designed for inmates. He also was a consultant for Attorney General Anaya's investigation of PNM in the summer and fall of 1975. As previously noted, shortly after Hanrahan was appointed Secretary of Corrections, he named McClendon as his administrative assistant. Given his unique background and the respect he had attained among inmates as "a tough con who made it," McClendon's appointment to this high position signaled to inmates that enhancement of programs was in the offing.

Despite these optimistic signals, the overall policy direction for New Mexico corrections was actually unclear and undefined. Hanrahan "remained deliberately vague on his goals in his new job" (*New Mexican* 9/14/75: A2). A Santa Fe grand jury, after examining PNM in January 1976, wrote the following about the Department of Corrections' lack of policy direction:

> As a result of the change in administration, it needs to be determined or at least clarified by the Department of Corrections whether the concept or policy of the Department for this penitentiary is one of "rehabilitation," "humane confinement," or some third definition, combining both. Whatever the concept or policy, as soon as it is determined, it should be communicated to the inmates, for there is a strong feeling among many of them that the policy has shifted from "rehabilitation" to "humane confinement" to their great disadvantage. (Office of the Attorney General 1980b: B-13)

This lack of policy direction had immediate consequences for PNM and ultimately meant that inmates' expectations about program expansion would not be met. Governor Apodaca, after naming Hanrahan to the Secretary of Corrections post and giving his blessing to Hanrahan's appointment of Lloyd McClendon as administrative assistant (actions that signaled approval of expanded rehabilitation), moved in a contradictory direction in finding a replacement for Warden Rodriguez.

In late September 1975, Governor Apodaca's staff began a frantic search for a new warden. The name of a recently retired federal warden, Ralph Lee Aaron, was given to Apodaca's staff. After a hastily arranged meeting between Aaron, Hanrahan, and Apodaca's chief aide, Nick Franklin, at the Dallas-Fort Worth International Airport, Aaron was selected to replace Rodriguez as PNM warden. The choice of Aaron was not a deliberately contradictory move, but represented administrative decisions made in ignorance of prison organizational dynamics, and betrayed a lack of any clearly articulated goals or direction on the part of the Governor and his new Secretary of Corrections. None of the decision-makers involved in Aaron's appointment had any experience working in prisons. Secretary of Corrections Hanrahan had been a probation officer before being named as head of the new adult parole board, a position he held for only two months before being named to the Secretary's post. Other people knowledgeable about prisons, including former prisoner Lloyd McClendon and representatives from the New Mexico Council on Crime and Delinquency, were not consulted in the choice of Aaron. Aaron's background and beliefs about corrections were not carefully checked. But with the lack of direction and goals for correctional programming, it is doubtful that a detailed understanding of Aaron's background and beliefs would have made much difference. Apodaca was eager to appoint a new warden because he was coming under attack from the Corrections Commission, the New Mexico Council on Crime and Delinquency, and the local Santa Fe District Attorney for creating a leadership crisis by forcing corrections officials out of office (*Albuquerque Journal* 8/28/75, 9/22/75; *New Mexican* 10/3/75). A former federal warden was available whose name had been given to the Governor by the Federal Bureau of Prisons. How could Apodaca possibly go wrong with an experienced federal warden? So a decision was made to hire Aaron, who took over as PNM warden on September 26, 1975.

Aaron's 32-year experience in the Federal Bureau of Prisons had been primarily at the bureau's maximum security penitentiaries, including his last appointment as warden of the U.S. Federal Penitentiary at Marion, Illinois. As a Federal Bureau of Prisons spokesman said, "Marion is our 'Big House,' it replaced Alcatraz" (*New Mexican* 9/25/75: A1). Aaron was thus a veteran of the type of penitentiary in which the emphasis was not on corrections, but on tight control, regimentation, and security. Marion was also a "Big House" in Irwin's (1980) meaning as a leftover from an earlier era when prisons were solely operated as authoritarian regimes and rehabilitation was a foreign concept. With this experience, the new warden held strong beliefs about how a penitentiary should be managed. A penitentiary should be run like a "tight ship" under the strict command and control of the warden. Rehabilitation programs, especially those involving contact between inmates and citizens, had no place in a penitentiary.

The Penitentiary of New Mexico by 1975 was anything but a tight ship. Upon his arrival in Santa Fe, Warden Aaron was aghast at the loose control of the prison. His hand-picked deputy warden, Clyde Malley, a retired 28-year veteran of the federal prison system who had been associate warden at the U.S. Penitentiary at Leavenworth, Kansas, arrived in New Mexico a few weeks after Aaron. Malley described PNM as "a national disgrace." "The inmates," he said, "were running the place" (*New Mexican* 6/16/76). What Aaron and Malley observed was lax security and loose discipline at the prison. There was little control over the movement of prisoners within the institution. The custodial force was demoralized and apathetic. Post orders, the most basic instructions for COs' performance of duties, were not to be found. No one could locate the riot plan or the escape plan, which gave instructions for responses to such events. The food service was found to be "deplorable," with often partially cooked food and unsanitary conditions (*Albuquerque Journal* 9/27/75: B10, 12/13/75: A12; *New Mexican* 12/14/75). And the prison was crowded well beyond its then 822-inmate capacity, reaching 1,018 inmates on November 15, 1975 (*Albuquerque Journal* 11/16/75).

Aaron and Malley also found the prison to be, from their perception, dangerously open. Outsiders, including the press, entered the prison grounds without permission. The outside friends and other citizen-contact programs brought hundreds of civilians into the penitentiary each week. The work- and school-release programs had scores of inmates leaving and entering the prison on a daily basis. From Warden Aaron's point of view, following the institutional designations in the federal prison system, these types of programs might be appropriate for a "correctional institution," but not for a "penitentiary" that contained inmates serving long sentences. With the rampant drug trafficking, Aaron saw this more open programming as a serious threat to security (*Albuquerque Journal* 2/10/76).

In addition, the idea of inmates having any voice in administrative decisions or in programs was completely foreign to Aaron's and Malley's experience. The Warden runs the prison, not the inmates. This also applied to former inmates. Warden Aaron was extremely upset that former prisoner Lloyd McClendon was on the Department of Corrections staff. "What concerns me is the use of ex-offenders in the system with the authority to give me guidance. With Lloyd McClendon in the office, he is calling me, giving me directions, asking information for inmate files and is in charge of inmate grievances," said Aaron in a newspaper interview (*Albuquerque Journal* 5/29/76: A1). He informed both McClendon and Secretary Hanrahan that McClendon would have nothing to do with PNM as long as Aaron was warden. McClendon was not allowed into the penitentiary to teach his college class or for any other reason. From Warden Aaron's viewpoint, a former inmate could never be trusted. In addition, he felt that dissension and demoralization among the custodial staff would only increase with a former inmate involved at a high level with the administration of the prison.

In short, Warden Aaron and Deputy Warden Malley were poised to move the prison organization in a direction diametrically opposite to the plans and expectations that had been evolving among inmates and treatment-oriented personnel. As a corrections official said, speaking of Warden Aaron, "He'd come from Marion, which is the so-called 'toughest federal penitentiary,' and that is what he wanted here." Governor Apodaca and Secretary Hanrahan had placed in the warden's position an administrator who was fundamentally at odds with the goals of expanded programming and rehabilitation.

ADMINISTRATIVE SUCCESSION
AND THE DISRUPTION OF
REMUNERATIVE CONTROLS

Given his background in maximum-security federal prisons and his marching orders from the Governor to clean up the mess at PNM, it is not surprising that Warden Aaron began instituting drastic changes that were aimed at tightening up the prison. Deputy Warden Malley was the primary administrator in charge of carrying out the new direction set by Warden Aaron. He was assisted by another new administrator, Deputy Warden Robert Montoya, who had also been hired by Aaron from out of state.[3]

Aaron wanted to wrest control of PNM away from inmates and curtail the flow of drugs into the institution. First, inmate administrators were removed from their positions in programs. Civilian staff would handle the operation of programs without the input of inmates. Second, many programs were discontinued. The school-release and work-release programs were stopped in early 1976. Furloughs from the prison were drastically curtailed. Programs involving outsiders entering the prison were also cut back, many being eliminated entirely. A Santa Fe grand jury, which routinely toured and reported on PNM, wrote in its January 1976 report:

It appeared that the emphasis under the former Secretary of Corrections [Leach] and the former warden [Rodriguez] was one of "rehabilitation." It now appears that the emphasis under the new warden [Aaron] is to be one of increased controls and discipline but decreased "rehabilitative programs." (Office of the Attorney General 1980b: B-14)

As a corrections official described it, programs at PNM "just seemed to come to a screeching halt." One of the caseworkers who sponsored the "Outside Friends" program discussed how his program was eliminated:

When Aaron came in it seemed like right off he wanted to know what was going on. So I was taken into the [Warden's] office and advised him what the program was about. He pulled me in there not really interested in whether it was doing any good or not but [wanted to know] what the hell is it doing there?...His comments [about the "outside friends" volunteers] were "a bunch of [inmate] sympathizers." That was his reaction—"a bunch of sympathizers, what are we going to do to get rid of them?" And so he began an effort to get rid of them.... He pulled the caseworkers together and said, "You guys don't have to come out here to supervise that [program]." He didn't give it to them as an option, he made them understand that he was very disgruntled with the program. He'd rather not see them out here supervising, so that left me. And so I have to sponsor the program, do everything else that everybody else had been doing before.... He got his classification chief to put pressure on me to let it go. After awhile they realized I was not going to give up the program.... [Then] they boycotted the program at the classification committee, and so the numbers dwindled. They just sucked us dry. They put restrictions on us that discouraged [volunteers] from coming in, [made them] fill out ridiculous questionnaires...fingerprinting the people that had already been there three or four years. And so they got what they wanted and it really sank away. They reduced us to almost nothing.

While Aaron was clearly opposed to the programs on ideological grounds, he had a ready justification for curtailing these programs because of the high level of drug trafficking. "Almost anything that showed any positive future for inmates had to go," said a corrections official. "Like anything else that goes in corrections, it goes in the name of security; it goes in the name of tightening things up." Aaron and Malley made it clear that they did not tolerate drug trafficking. For the first time in years, systematic searches of the institution were made. Visitors were screened and searched upon entering the prison. Inmates who were leaving and entering the prison for work-release or school-release programs were searched. And every member of the prison staff was now subject to being searched. A few COs were actually caught bringing in contraband and were given the choice of resignation or prosecution. Other employees were thus put on notice that the smuggling would no longer be tolerated. While the crackdown by no means eliminated drugs from the institution, it did disrupt tremendously the established networks of drug trafficking. The level of drugs in the institution after this crackdown appeared to have dropped and remained low throughout the remainder of the decade. By the late 1970s, the sniffing of inhalants (paint, thinner, and glue smuggled from prison shops) had replaced heroin as the major drug of choice.

Along with the crackdown on drug trafficking came an attempt to generally improve security. A pass system was instituted to control inmate movement within the institution. Inmates could no longer move freely within the prison, as they had been able to do since 1968. Concertina wire (rolled strands of wire with razor sharp barbs jutting out in all directions) was placed between and on top of the double perimeter fence. Post orders were developed, and formal CO training was instituted.

Deputy Warden Malley was the primary official in charge of the security enhancement. Almost all of the post orders (which were still in operation by 1980) had Malley's signature of authorization. Malley established rules and regulations to formally govern all aspects of prison life. "There was in-depth work done on policy statements for this institution," said a CO. "Everybody including the inmates knew where they stood. If you breached a policy you were in trouble." And a caseworker stated, "With the Malley era the policy statements had grown. We had a four-inch [thick] notebook of policies that kept building.... What we used to have in a couple of lines now it's four or five pages." Such a formal structure of regulation had never before existed at PNM.

With the tightening up of security and new restrictions on inmate movement, Aaron and Malley were now implementing policies that Rodriguez and Herrera were unable to institute in 1971, when their attempt to tighten up the institution resulted in an inmate disturbance that forced these administrators to back off.

Aaron and Malley also removed many of the key administrators who had run the prison under former Warden Rodriguez. The superintendent of correctional security (SCS), who had served under Warden Rodriguez, was replaced in early 1976 and, along with some of the other leading members of Rodriguez's former administration, was transferred to the Los Lunas Honor Farm. Aaron and Malley both felt that Rodriguez's former top administrators were resisting the changes in security they were attempting to institute. They both felt that the poor security was a result of demoralization and apathy among COs. This was brought home to Warden Aaron after an escape of six inmates on October 19, 1975, which was not discovered by the staff until almost a day after it occurred (*New Mexican* 10/20/75; 10/22/75). One of the new prison officials brought in after

Rodriguez was removed responded with the following when asked to describe security when he arrived at PNM in 1975:

> Well in the first place they had a very, very incompetent staff.... For every one that took pride in what he does, there's three or four that don't.... The captains [were] very indifferent...they didn't follow directives from the Warden's office. I read a number of these reports [after the 1980 riot] that talked about these grills being left open...that's very true, I saw with my own eyes, on a couple of occasions one involved the captain [who] walked right through both of those gates, one evening after a training meeting [in 1975]...both of those grills were left open, which is a cardinal sin in running a prison. But that shows how lacking in knowledge of a penitentiary to stand there and permit both of those gates be left open.

Thus security was viewed by these new officials as extremely loose in 1975. The enhancement of security was the primary objective behind Warden Aaron's initiatives.

The effect of Warden Aaron's actions, however, was the elimination within a matter of months of all the key elements of the remunerative system of control that had provided order throughout the early 1970s. The formal trade-offs and accommodations instituted through the programs were erased. "When the wardens changed and all school release and work release and furloughs were shut down, the institution made one of its first steps toward being unmanageable. [These programs] were carrots for good behavior," said a corrections official.

Inmates involved directly in programs, and those who desired to attain program status, now had less incentives. The inmate administrators, who had gained power through the programs, lost their influence over program decisions, and lost the basis for the power they had held over other inmates. These formal trade-offs between the administration and the inmates, which made up an important aspect of the remunerative control system, were in a very short period eliminated. The informal trade-offs connected with the tolerance of drug trafficking also were eliminated with the crackdown on drugs. Thus the basis upon which inmates had been controlled and order maintained in the early 1970s was completely disrupted.

Would it have been possible to keep intact positive elements of the remunerative control system while removing the negative elements associated with drug trafficking and corruption? The answer is yes, but only under conditions of a coordinated, systematically thought-out policy of control. It would have been possible in the view of many inmates and correctional staff members, with whom I discussed this, to have cracked down on drugs while simultaneously expanding program opportunities. In this way, legitimate incentives could replace illegitimate ones. The turmoil associated with the crackdown on drugs, while inevitable, could be reduced. However, no one with decision-making authority, from the Governor's Office, the New Mexico State Legislature, or the Department of Corrections, had a clearly articulated policy of control. The officials who best understood PNM, and who understood the importance of incentive controls, were former prisoner Lloyd McClendon and former warden Felix Rodriguez. Rodriguez was in exile at Central Office, and his advice about PNM was neither sought nor given. After sparring with Warden Aaron in late 1975, McClendon's access to PNM and his influence on Secretary Hanrahan waned. Both Rodriguez and McClendon had been effectively stripped of their decision-making authority and thus had little power. The only officials with decision-making authority who had a clear idea of what to do were Warden Aaron and Deputy Warden Malley, who acted in a policy vacuum. No one else in authority could offer an alternative to the direction being set by Aaron's and Malley's decisions.

Also, the only way to expand positive elements of the remunerative control system would be to gain a legislative commitment for increased funding of inmate programs. Given the conservative trend that was rapidly emerging in the mid-1970s, such a commitment from the legislature would have been extremely difficult to elicit even if the Governor and Secretary of Corrections could have articulated a coherent policy of control and set a clear direction for the department. Governor Apodaca, however, had been giving only an ambivalent, luke-warm public endorsement of inmate rehabilitation programs (*New Mexican* 9/14/75). Without a clear policy direction, a legislative commitment for expanding rehabilitation programs was impossible. Thus under the conditions of policy disarray and the conservative trend in the legislature, it was not likely any other direction would be taken once Warden Aaron was placed in charge of the prison. The remunerative system of control, in both its positive and negative aspects, could not survive.

OUTSIDE OPPOSITION TO AARON AND THE GROWING POLICY VACUUM AT THE TOP LEVELS OF THE CORRECTIONS DEPARTMENT

Warden Aaron's actions, however, were not without opposition. They created an enormous amount of political fallout for a warden who, in the federal system, had been insulated from both political and community reactions. Outside groups who had been involved in many of the programs that the Warden was curtailing expressed their dissatisfaction. Some of the Christian laymen involved in the "Outside Friends" program, who had supported Apodaca in his campaign for governor, complained bitterly to the Governor and Secretary Hanrahan about the restrictions imposed by Warden Aaron. "Aaron got some opposition from Senator Domenici's office, from the Governor's office, and several prominent community leaders just objected [to Aaron's actions] very vehemently," reported a former corrections official. Dr. Charles Becknell, a very liberal-minded education expert who had headed the University of New Mexico's Black Studies Program and was appointed in 1975 by Governor Apodaca as director of the Governor's Council on Criminal Justice Planning, also complained to Apodaca about Aaron's restrictions and his alleged arbitrary removal of inmates from programs that the Governor's Council funded. The press was upset at the Warden's restrictions on their access to PNM. (Press contact had been open to an unprecedented degree during the period of the 1975 prison investigations conducted by Attorney General Anaya.) Finally, members of the Secretary of Corrections' staff and the Corrections Commission were angry with Warden Aaron, who saw their oversight of PNM as an intrusion into his autonomy. "Mr. Aaron felt first of all there should not be a Corrections Commission.... He felt he should not have to report to anybody but the Governor, not even to the Secretary [of Corrections]," reported a former corrections official. A series of highly publicized disputes between Aaron and the Central Office led to Aaron's resignation in May 1976.

After Warden Aaron resigned, Secretary of Corrections Hanrahan chose Aaron's deputy warden, Clyde Malley, as the new warden. Hanrahan's open dispute with Aaron hurt him politically. Aaron left the state with a barrage of public criticism aimed at Hanrahan, whom Aaron characterized as "unqualified" (*Albuquerque Journal* 5/29/76: A1). Largely because of this political damage, and his lack of prison experience, Hanrahan deferred entirely to Malley on decisions concerning PNM. "Malley told the Secretary of Corrections what to do and how to do it," said a corrections official. Hanrahan did not question decisions made by Malley. "The Secretary was not making decisions [about PNM]," said another corrections official. "The Warden was making them and the Secretary was buying it lock, stock, and barrel. Anything Malley wanted he'd approve." Members of Hanrahan's Central Office staff were becoming disenchanted. "Mike Hanrahan had not much to operate with because he very quickly ran into these two people [Aaron and Malley] who set up a situation where he could *not* get information out of his prison," reported a former Central Office staff member. "Very quickly, the Central Office and the penitentiary became two islands. Central office was only loosely catered to." Thus, PNM was still administered with little oversight from above. "Aaron and Malley were essentially not answerable to anybody, Governor or anybody else," said a state official. "And I guess they had some sense of encouragement from the judiciary and the press that toughness [in penal policies], in the climate of rising crime, was a good thing."

Lloyd McClendon, the former prisoner who Hanrahan had hired as his administrative assistant in a flourish of gestures about program expansion, became discouraged with the direction PNM was actually taking and with the lack of a coherent policy in the department. In November 1976, McClendon left New Mexico and subsequently became a corrections official in Ohio.

The policy vacuum at the top levels of corrections continued throughout 1976, allowing Warden Malley to proceed with the hard-line policies initiated by his predecessor. This new policy direction was strongly supported by the custodial staff who were now reasserting their power within the organization. However, these policy changes were leading to a confrontation between the PNM administration and inmate leaders, who began organizing a collective inmate response to the new administration.

CONFRONTATION BETWEEN INMATES AND THE NEW ADMINISTRATION AS THE CUSTODIAL FORCE REASSERTS ITS POWER

Malley was keenly aware of the poor morale among the custodial force. He was sensitive to the concerns of COs, and especially to their desire to take back control. "When Malley came in [he] was of the attitude and concern...that the institution had gone to hell and the inmates were running it," said a veteran CO. "Malley came in with a train of thought that we're gonna wrestle control away from the inmates and *we* are gonna be running it. And he did clamp down." Almost every CO described Malley as supportive, respectful of their position, and someone who would back them up. "Officers' pride went up a lot," said a CO. "Malley did that for the staff, gave them more pride and added security." Malley's primary concern was the improvement of officer morale. The loss of power that COs had experienced during the Baker and Rodriguez administrations had created a deep-seated animosity among most of the custody force toward inmates and treatment-oriented personnel. The concessions that inmates had gained from former Warden Baker, and which had been reluctantly retained by Rodriguez in his attempt to balance the forces of conflict within PNM, had within a period of six months been dismantled by Aaron and Malley. Most of the custodial force applauded the curtailment of programs, the removal of convict administrators, and the loss of other special privileges for inmates. The COs felt that they were now getting the upper hand over the inmates. Malley named Robert Montoya, who had been hired by former warden Aaron at Secretary Hanrahan's request, as his top deputy warden who would carry out a further clamp-down on inmates.

The curtailment of programs and special privileges, however, soon led to an open confrontation between the prison administration and inmates. A former PNM inmate (Stone 1982: 92-93) describes this period:

> During the spring of 1976, the residents at [the] Santa Fe [penitentiary] spent their free time scheming on ways to get the administration to change their tune. They knew the only effective means of doing that was to catch the public's attention; this meant staging some kind of uprising to protest conditions, which were intolerable from every point of view. Besides Malley's oppressive regime, the institution was infested with rats and cockroaches, the toilets didn't work, and the food was, as usual, bad. Back and forth through the vents went talk about what kind of action to take. It was decided that the entire population would stage a sit-down strike while the warden had a chance to look over their list of grievances and demands.

On June 14, 1976, two weeks after Warden Aaron left, and immediately upon Malley's official takeover as warden, inmates began a massive sit-down strike. The timing of the strike at the point of transition between wardens was a clear challenge to Malley's authority and was aimed at changing the direction of prison policies that had been set by Aaron and Malley. Prison officials at the time reported that 600 of the 912 inmates residing in PNM that day refused to leave their cells and dormitories for work assignments and meals (*Albuquerque Journal* 6/16/76). Other estimates by inmates and staff members with whom I talked place the number of strikers at closer to 800, with every dorm and cellblock participating in the strike. "The inmates seemed very organized," said a caseworker. Many of the organizers of the strike had been former inmate administrators of the educational programs and of the outside visiting programs. The strike was modeled after the 1971 inmate strike, except that this time inmates involved in programs participated. The level of participation in the strike demonstrated the high degree of inmate solidarity during this period.

On Monday morning, June 14, 1976, after inmates refused to leave their housing units, lists of demands and grievances were slipped to COs at the entrances of several housing units. The exact wording of these complaints is not known, since none of these lists survived the incident. But the general nature of the grievances and demands, described to me later by former inmates, focused on the return of the recently eliminated programs, inmate participation in program administration, improved food, recreation, medical and counseling services, fewer restrictions on visiting, and the opening of regular lines of communication between the press and inmates. The inmates were in large part demanding a return of accommodations lost after Aaron and Malley took control.

Sykes (1958) argues that prison disturbances come in cycles. Accommodations to inmates, he argues, create prison order. When these accommodations are disrupted, as they often are after a discovery of "corruption of authority" which leads to a tightening up of prison security, prison disturbances occur and a period of disorder ensues. According to Sykes, order is restored as prison administrators reinstitute accommodations by giving in to inmate demands. Sykes' scenario fits fairly closely with the events before and after the 1971 incident in which inmates used a work and food strike to force Warden Rodriguez to retreat in his attempt to tighten up the institution. Again, in the 1976 strike, Sykes' prediction that administrators' attempts to tighten up an institution would lead to a disruptive response by inmates is also supported. However, Sykes' prediction that such inmate disruptions would lead to a reinstitution of accommodations, and to a new period of order, is not supported by the events that transpired after the 1976 strike.

The week of June 14, 1976, can be pinpointed as an important watershed in the history of PNM. For it was during this week that a new structure of inmate control was inaugurated. As one inmate said, the prison administration during this week "just let the hammer down."

Instead of listening to individual inmates' grievances, as Rodriguez had done following the 1971 strike, Warden Malley and Deputy Warden Montoya began a process of identifying and segregating the strike leaders. "They called everybody out of their unit one at a time and threatened them with lockup.... They were trying to individual everybody out and hold interviews and lock up the instigators,...the strong people," reported an inmate. A staff committee interviewed inmates in the gymnasium and captain's office one at a time to ascertain if the inmate wanted to continue in the strike or go to work. Inmates were also being asked to identify the instigators of the strike and were threatened with lockup if they did not cooperate (Stone 1982). Strikers and other inmates who refused to cooperate were placed in disciplinary segregation, Cellblock 3. It soon became clear that most inmates were refusing to give up the strike as Cellblock 3 was quickly becoming overcrowded. The overflow was being moved into Cellblock 4.

The last group of inmates scheduled to be interviewed were in the south wing dormitories. Inmates in the dormitories refused to come out for individual interviews. COs then locked the dormitories and systematically went from one dorm to the next using tear gas to subdue the striking inmates. "The inmates just started breaking everything inside some of those dormitories, not all of them," reported a CO. "We had three or four units [Dorms B-1, B-2, E-1, and E-2] that were involved in that, but we had to go in one unit and the rest, they gave up."

The official report to the press from penitentiary officials that day described "an incident [in a dorm] in which 40 inmates attacked 15 other [inmates]" who wanted to leave the strike (*Albuquerque Journal* 6/17/76: A1). But correctional officers and inmates did not report to the Attorney General's investigators in 1980 any such incident. "There wasn't that many incidents between inmates and inmates, in fact I don't think there was any," reported a CO who helped to subdue inmates during the strike. The only incident reported by COs involved an inmate who was allegedly beaten by other inmates in the bathroom of Dorm B-1 before it was tear-gassed. But inmates said that this particular inmate was beaten by prison officials after the dorm was subdued. The inmate himself subsequently filed a lawsuit against Deputy Warden Montoya and another staff member, alleging that they had beaten him (*Santa Fe Reporter* 9/3/81). The allegation against Montoya and the other staff member was never proven.

There are also conflicting reports about the way in which inmates in these dormitories were subdued. Most inmates agreed with the following account:

> *Inmate:* They brought us out of the dormitories. They had shot tear gas in on us and…were waiting for us when we came out the door…. They were on both sides of the hall and we were having to shed our clothes from the door of the unit until we got into the hallway. And then when we got into the hallway it was just a whipping all the way down…from when we came out the door to lock up…. You could dodge a few, but you couldn't dodge them all.
> *Interviewer:* What did they hit you with?
> *Inmate:* Axe handles.

Most inmates and some staff members described the scene as a "gauntlet" (Office of the Attorney General 1980b: 20). Whether the hitting of inmates was authorized by top prison officials is not clear. An inmate said, "Not all of them would hit you but a few of them [did]." But this inmate, along with other inmates interviewed by the Attorney General's office in 1980, identified high-ranking captains and prison supervisory personnel, along with other key personnel, as some of the prison officers who were hitting inmates. Warden Malley, however, denied to the Attorney General's investigators that such a gauntlet occurred (Office of the Attorney General 1980b: 20). A CO, who confirmed that prison officers were armed with axe handles and that inmates were made to "walk single file to [Cell-blocks] 3 and 4," said, "There was no beating unless you [the inmate] are going to fight. If you want[ed] to fight, then your ass [was] mud." But another penitentiary staff member said, "There was a lot of 'getting-even' swings with those axe handles.... The officers finally were in a position [for instance] to smack that inmate that told him to get screwed three weeks ago.... That's what the hits were about." Whether there was an organized, officially sanctioned gauntlet could not be confirmed. That members of the prison staff hit inmates during the breaking of the strike is almost certain. The strike was suppressed with coercion and violence. As one CO told me during an interview, "We were finally showing them [the inmates] who was in charge." The years of pent-up resentment against inmates, who were disrespectful of COs, had gained power at their expense, and dared to embarrass the first warden in years who had shown correctional officers any respect, now came out with a vengeance.

For the prison's top administrators, the strike demonstrated a high level of organization and cohesiveness with obviously strong leadership among inmates. From the perspective of these administrators, this inmate leadership, which clearly threatened their rule of PNM, had to be broken up.

After being subdued in their dormitories and "escorted" down the main corridor, these 300 striking inmates joined another 200 strikers who were already locked up. "They were locked up in Cellblock 3 and Cellblock 4," said a CO. "I remember we had 2 or 3 in a cell." In the 11 maximum detention units (the "hole") in the basement of Cellblock 3, which had not been officially used since 1968, inmates who had physically resisted COs' attempts to subdue the strikers were jammed as many as 6 to a cell.

> *Inmate:* I got put in the hole in 1976 for a sit-down strike that they had here. They put me in the hole where they would just feed me one bread or one bologna five o'clock in the morning and again at five o'clock at night. With no mattress...six of us inside of a cell and we'd have to sleep on each other.
> *Interviewer:* With no mattresses or anything?
> *Inmate:* No mattress. All you could use for a pillow would be one of the [other] person's leg or his arm or something. Squashed in there like a sardine can....
> *Interviewer:* How long did you stay in?
> *Inmate:* I stayed there ten days in the hole.
> *Interviewer:* How many people were inside [the cell] during this period?
> *Inmate:* The first three days it was two of us, then for seven days after that there was five to six of us in there.... Then from the hole they released me to the upper class Cellblock 3, which is segregation. They kept me there another four months or so.

This inmate's case was not unusual. A caseworker reported that in response to the strike inmates were very likely to be locked up in Cellblock 3 for seven months "under the guise of pending further investigation."

The investigations were conducted to identify the strike leaders. As other inmates were released from segregation over the weeks following the strike, many of the strike leaders "were retained in segregation for months and some for years" (Office of the Attorney General 1980b: 26).

In a further attempt to break the inmate leadership and organization, many inmate leaders "were transferred to other states" (Office of the Attorney General 1980b: 26). "When Malley came in he got that interstate compact to transfer prisoners," said a correctional supervisor. "We had extensive meetings. We talked to all the [corrections] personnel about [inmate] leaders. And we got all the leaders out of state." A corrections official reported that "the inmates had developed strong cliques. We attempted to break those up." A CO said, "Well, I saw Malley do that here. He got a string of about twenty or thirty troublemakers, and he used to call it 'the banshee strikes at night,' and all of a sudden the next morning you'd wake up and there would be three guys gone. They were gone to the federal [system]." The inmate leaders who had provided cohesion and organization in the inmate society had now been effectively removed through transfer or segregation in Cellblock 3.

THE RISE OF A COERCIVE CONTROL STRUCTURE

The response to the June 1976 strike ushered in an era in which coercive controls replaced the remunerative control structure that had been in effect since 1968. The inherent conflict between the keepers and captives, which had been obscured by the remunerative-control structure, was surfacing with the shift in controls. The division between the staff and inmates, overcome to some extent by the formal and informal trade-offs, now became wider. According to a caseworker:

> We used to have a monthly meeting [of staff and top PNM administrators] at the gymnasium, a kind of "state of the penitentiary address.".... [Deputy Warden] Montoya would talk about the different policies that [were] being implemented.... Then [Warden Malley] would take over the podium and he was a tremendous public speaker...a real challenge...he would speak in terms that everybody would understand...the essence of what he was saying was this: "They [the inmates] are the enemy and we are the vanguard. We have to protect ourselves and the public from this enemy." It was the "us and them" syndrome.... He would quote things that were happening in other penitentiaries across the country...gory details of killings and maimings...riots and stabbings...[reports on inmate] sympathizer groups...and inmate unions.... It definitely worked.... This is what began to rally not only the [middle-level] clique [of correctional supervisors], but it began to rally a lot of

people where everybody [among the staff] began to snitch off everybody else: "I saw this guy out there and he was shaking hands with an inmate in the hallway," those kind of things.... And it gave [the captains] license to intensify [the coercive control of inmates].

The coercive controls were most evident in the increased use of disciplinary segregation. "Malley was a better disciplinarian," said a CO. "[He] opened up the 'holes' again [which had been officially in disuse since 1968]. [The 'holes'] might be inhumane; they might be unconstitutional. But they do accomplish the job. With Malley the cons right away knew there was going to be a...stricter situation." A caseworker said, "That [policy] of don't use segregation lasted until Malley came in and reinstituted the maximum detention unit [,the 'hole']." The opening of the maximum detention units greatly affected COs, who had pinpointed the 1968 closing of the "hole" as the time when they "lost control" to inmates. "When they opened the 'hole' back up," said another CO, "naturally morale went back up because the officer felt that [inmates] had really been creating problems for us. This way they can be properly disciplined by placing them down there."

The official reopening of the "hole" in 1976 meant that it was used on a routine basis for the first time since 1968.[4] While in the "hole" an inmate wore only "boxer shorts." He was fed two bologna sandwiches a day. "At eleven o'clock at night they'd come and give us a blanket. That was it. We'd have to sleep on the cement on one blanket. And at seven o'clock in the morning they'd take it away from us," reported an inmate who in 1978 was placed with two other inmates in a maximum detention unit cell.

Segregation was organized into a "step system" for punishment. An inmate explains:

> When Malley got here, they put segregation in steps. Step one being the "hole" [in the basement of Cellblock 3], step two is the south side [upper tiers] of Cellblock 3, step three is the north side [upper tiers]. When you first come in, if you're on investigation, you go straight to step two. If you get charged you go to the "hole." You stay a week in the "hole," and then step two. Step two you can't have any personal property and you don't get any dessert on your tray...and no canteen. Nothing. You've got what they give you and that's it. And then when you go to step three, they give you personal property, you can make canteen once every two weeks.

Thus the continuum of rewards and punishments at the formal level was moved significantly toward the more coercive end of the spectrum. The removal of administrative positions for inmates and the sudden curtailment in inmate release and outside visiting programs removed the primary rewards from the formal step system that had prevailed in the early 1970s. In their place, the maximum detention unit (the "hole") was reopened, and a generally greater reliance on disciplinary segregation ensued.

At times between late 1976 and 1978, "more than 200 inmates in [the disciplinary unit] Cellblock 3 (with a capacity of 86)" were placed 2 and 3 to a cell (Office of the Attorney General 1980b: 27). At some points during the 1976 to 1978 period, "we had 25 percent of the institution in [disciplinary] lockdown," reported a corrections official. Even after the period of crackdown following the June 1976 inmate strike subsided, the disciplinary cellblock remained chronically overcrowded. There were on average about three times as many inmates locked in the disciplinary unit after 1976 as there had been prior to 1976. "Cellblock 3 was so overpopulated," reported a CO. "We would get a guy on a major report [who] we were going to lock up; but then there wasn't any room in segregation." Inmates reported that quite often there were three inmates to a cell. "They put me in the hole for eight days and there was three of us in the hole," said an inmate. A caseworker in charge of segregation units said:

> It was 1977. I remember watching these guys [in the upper tiers of the segregation unit] crawling up the wall. Three of them together where they have to organize such things as sitting and standing. And [they would] come up with schedules, "you sit and I stand." And a guy sleeps in the top bunk and another one in the bottom and another one there in the aisle in the little 9 by 6 [foot] cell.

The shift toward coercion at the formal level of control paralleled a similar shift at the informal level of control. The crackdown on drugs removed a major informal mechanism of control: toleration of drug trafficking. "They did tighten up a lot on the dope," reported a caseworker. "They cut off the supply." Correctional staff members and some inmates credited Warden Malley with significantly disrupting the flow of drugs into the institution. Replacing this informal control of tolerating drug trafficking was informal coercion. A squad of COs specially trained to handle inmate disturbances and recalcitrant inmates was formed in 1976 following the June strike. The squad was called the "S.W.A.T. team" by staff and the "goon squad" by inmates. The squad was used mostly for moving resisting inmates to the "hole." The squad wore protective jumpsuits and helmets and were armed with shields and batons. Most COs said that excessive force was not used by the squad, but only enough force to subdue inmates who were fighting the COs' efforts to move them. But some COs did report that if an inmate "got into it" with the COs, then there was retaliatory beating of the inmate as he was thrown into the "hole." Also, if inmates in segregation threw "water or piss or food at you," said a CO, "well according to the rules there was nothing you could do, but it was done, you know, guys were taken out of there and whipped." Several inmates reported that these beatings occurred frequently.

During the evening of June 25, 1977, inmates rioted in Cellblock 3, "leaving much of the maximum security cell block in ruins. Warden C. J. Malley said the riot leaders were the same inmates who led the last major [disturbance] in June 1976 .... Malley said a squad of guards specially trained to handle outbreaks was called in to restore order" (*Albuquerque Journal* 6/26/77: A1).

A correctional officer supervisor reported the following incident that occurred in the early morning hours of June 26, 1977, following this disturbance in Cellblock 3.

> *Correctional Officer Supervisor:* We were called in about three that morning. The inmates in the top tier in the north side of Cellblock 3 had torn the place apart.... So myself and [another officer], they sent me and him to oversee [a civil disturbance "S.W.A.T" team].... So we went in there.... We pulled all the inmates from the north top tier out. And the officers that weren't assigned to my civil disturbance team, those that were *not* assigned to it, they were hitting the inmates...
> *Interviewer:* You mean they were using excessive force?
> *Correctional Officer Supervisor:* Yeah. They hit them, and I know they beat the shit out of one downstairs. I knew what was going on....
> *Interviewer:* Did you report this to anyone?
> *Correctional Officer Supervisor:* Yeah, I sure did.
> *Interviewer:* Who did you report it to?
> *Correctional Officer Supervisor:* To [gives name of PNM official]. [Name of an official] was there. In fact, [name of another official] was there, too. They sort of looked the other way.
> *Interviewer:* They were in [Cellblock] 3 at the time this was going on?
> *Correctional Officer Supervisor:* Yeah.

Beatings of inmates were not anything new at the Penitentiary of New Mexico. (Morris [1983] gives several examples.) Following the 1971 inmate strike, it will be remembered, COs beat inmates, and a correctional supervisor was indicted and removed from the prison for allegedly beating an inmate at that time. But after 1976, with the creation of this special squad, beatings of inmates, whether for retaliation or in the course of subduing a fighting inmate, became more routine. As the testimony from the above quoted correctional officer supervisor alleges, these actions were overlooked and tolerated by some PNM officials.

The step system in segregation, in which inmates were removed from step two in the upstairs of Cellblock 3 to the step one "hole" in the basement, often required the physical removal of an inmate who fought all the way to the "hole." As segregation and the "hole" became more widely used, inmates resisted the punishment by fighting with the guards. The actions of these squads constituted an informal coercive control that had not, at least to this degree, been present in previous years.

Another indication of the shift toward greater coercion in the control structure was the nature of offenses for which inmates could be locked in segregation. With the greater restrictions on inmate movement, there were suddenly more acts for which a prisoner could be punished. And prison officials were generally sending inmates to segregation for relatively minor offenses.

> *Interviewer:* What's the littlest thing that it takes to get into segregation?
> *Inmate:* Not walking single file.
> *Interviewer:* What was the littlest thing when Rodriguez was warden in 1975?
> *Inmate:* Fighting.

A veteran PNM staff member concurred:

> When [former wardens, from 1957 to 1975,] Rodriguez, Baker, Cox, and Woodruff were there, for a minor violation an inmate was reprimanded or [given] a good ass-chewing by someone, but he never was [placed] in segregation.... But in the Malley era a lot of inmates were being sent to segregation for minor rule infractions where they could have simply gotten off with a reprimand.... A greater number of inmates were sent to segregation for minor violations.

A long-term inmate said:

> I don't think I had ever seen segregation being used so much like the way it was since 1977. It was for anything. I don't care what it was. Even if they *thought* you were doing something, they'd drop you off [at segregation]. And people would be there for unlimited periods of time, for nothing.

And a correctional officer said, "From little reports over nothing they make them out to be big ones."

Indeed, the distinction between major and minor offenses was becoming blurred, as inmates reported:

> *Inmate 1:* I had a situation where I was locked up for being in the hallway at 12:30 p.m. without a pass, which is my lunch time.... I spent 89 days in [Cellblock] 3 for being in the hallway without a pass at lunch time.... [Then] there was a fight in the kitchen with knives. One guy spent seven days and the other spent eight days. I spent 89 days for being in the hallway without a pass at 12:30 p.m.... The rules are ad hoc.... The rules are petty. And there's no schedule for disciplinary procedures, [no time limits for various offenses].[5]

Inmate 2: If I even get pulled over by a captain for my hair or my mustache, I cop an attitude and tell him off,...and the man don't like my attitude, he locks me up. That's gonna be the same penalty as if I went and stabbed somebody, I'm still gonna lose my parole board either way for six months. There's no distinction for the crime.

The Disciplinary Committee was not following the due process procedures laid out in PNM's policies. As an inmate said, "They are supposed to take you to a hearing in 72 hours. [But] you stay in segregation from 13 to 21 days just waiting to go to the kangaroo court [officially the Disciplinary Committee]." The Attorney General, after his 1980 investigation, concurred: "There are many instances when the 72-hour period goes by without a hearing" (Office of the Attorney General 1980a: K-1).

During the investigation of a minor violation, inmates were often placed in segregation while the charge against them was pending. An inmate said:

[Before 1976] when Rodriguez was warden...you wouldn't get locked up. You'd get a report; sometimes they'd just send it in the mail. And then you're told when you're suppose to come down for a hearing in front of the [Disciplinary Committee]. [After 1976], you get a report and you're locked up. You go from lockup to the [Disciplinary] committee.... People would be put in there for indefinite periods for investigative purposes.

And then, after being officially charged and given punishment in segregation by the Disciplinary Committee, "[a]n inmate placed in segregation must later request a release and then the Segregation Committee reviews the request. The same person chairs both the Segregation Committee and the Disciplinary Committee" (Office of the Attorney General 1980a: K-1).

Much of the effort of the Disciplinary and Segregation committees was aimed at breaking up inmate groups and reducing the power of inmate leaders. A correctional supervisor said, "We were unjustifiably locking up people because of hearsay. And a lot of the major leaders inside the institution were being locked up for no reason at all.... Anybody that wanted somebody locked up at that time was." In fact, any attempts by inmates to organize or present grievances were met with segregation. An inmate said:

We had about 600 people sign a petition for long hair and beards. This was back in 1977. They locked up about 60 people from the joint over that request...found a bunch of people guilty for "instigating"...left them in [Cellblock] 3 for eight, nine, ten months.... They just didn't like us trying to organize anything.

Thus segregation became the major tool of inmate control. Inmate groups were broken up and inmate leaders segregated in a coercive attempt to wrest control of the prison away from inmates. In the process, punishment was often arbitrary, and established disciplinary procedures were routinely violated. The distinction between minor and major offenses was becoming unclear, as more inmates were being locked in segregation.

A correctional administrator who witnessed these changes in the use of segregation said, "When the officer locks up people on any minor thing, then it becomes one punishment for everything that is being done. [As a result,] your security is going to fall down."

INCREASING SIGNS OF DISORDER

And indeed, security did seem to fall down. Even with the pass system, stricter controls on inmate movement, increased use of punishment in segregation for rule violations, and the placement of concertina wire on the perimeter fence, inmates escaped from the prison in record numbers. During the period in which the crackdown on drugs and the enhancement of security was being initiated, from October 1975 to June 1976, there were eight escapes from the institution and several inmate fights that involved inmates being cut and stabbed. "One serious stabbing and several cuttings," recalled a corrections official. "But none of an extremely serious nature like cutting any of the main arteries." Nevertheless, given the virtual absence of violence in the preceding seven years, the increased incidence of violence in early 1976 was alarming.

This sudden upturn in early 1976 in the level of disorder might partially be explained by the crackdown on the drug trafficking. "I remember one of the things inmates talked about was the fact that the drugs had been cut off by the federal wardens [Aaron and Malley] quite a bit. It created a lot of tension," reported a caseworker. An inmate concurred, "Aaron came in, security tightened up, people started escaping, people started stabbing each other.... Sure, they got rid of the drugs, but the violence got worse, the tension [increased]."

As drug connections became strained, the stability in the drug market was disrupted. This led to an intense competition between inmate drug dealers and, more importantly, to a disruption in the chain of debts among drug-using inmates. As inmates pressured each other for payment of debts so that their own debts could be paid, incidents of violence increased. While I was still working at PNM in late 1975, inmates on the school-release program talked about the increased harassment, threats, and pressure from other inmates to bring drugs in through the program after the crackdown began in early October 1975. Inmates recounted to me that much of the violence and escapes were related to the increasing pressure and competition surrounding the now-strained drug operations. Then in mid-1976, violence and disorder escalated even more. "Malley came in. That's when it really changed," said an inmate. "He's the one that started all the security. That's when all the escapes were happening.... So right away the security came down and everywhere we went we were told not to do this or do that. It just created a lot of tension.... They keep you more and more down. They just put more and more rules on us." And another inmate said, "There was more escapes during Malley's administration than there has ever been. When, yea, there was security. But that's exactly what the problem was. It was security but directed at the wrong angle." During Malley's wardenship, from June 1976 to March 1978, there were thirteen successful escapes from the institution. Adding to this the eight escapes that occurred during Aaron's wardenship, the rate of escapes was higher from October 1975 to March 1978 than at any time in PNM's previous history. In addition, incidents of violence, discussed in greater detail in Chapter 5, increased, as the first inmate killing of the 1970s occurred in August 1976 (*New Mexican* 8/17/76).

INMATES' NONVIOLENT RESISTANCE
THROUGH A CLASS-ACTION LAWSUIT

The increase in coercive controls soon led inmates to another strategy in their struggle against the prison administration. Throughout the U.S., prisoners were filing lawsuits to relieve poor prison conditions (Crouch and Marquart 1989). The federal courts since the late 1960s had intervened in the administration of state prisons, reversing the traditional "hands-off" approach. Judges appointed during the 1960s held to a more liberal position that contrasted sharply with the conservative trends in state legislatures after 1975. It was generally to these federal judges, the last holdovers in the federal government of the 1960s' liberal coalition, that inmates addressed their class-action suits.

After the prison administration's crackdown on inmates following the June 1976 strike, conditions at PNM became increasingly intolerable. In addition to the usual poor food, poor medical care, and generally unsanitary conditions that had existed for several years, the prison by 1977 and 1978 was very overcrowded. The prison population was 1,150 in June 1977 and reached a high of 1,272 inmates during 1978. The overcrowding in the segregation unit made conditions there especially bad. Double and triple celling of inmates in segregation had become routine practice by 1977 and 1978. Disciplinary procedures lacked due process and were arbitrary. Inmates were often locked up longer in segregation for investigation or for minor infractions than they were for major violations. The restrictions and curtailment of programs led to a high rate of inmate idleness. Approximately 60 percent of inmates had meaningful activity (in jobs or programs) for no more than three hours a day; another 30 percent were involved in no activities (Governor's Council on Criminal Justice Planning 1978b). These conditions, along with restrictions on mail and visiting privileges, became the basis "for the most sweeping reform ever proposed for any single prison in American history" (Morris 1983: 49). The reforms were set forth in an inmate-initiated lawsuit against the State of New Mexico.

The lawsuit placed the inmates' struggle against the PNM administration within the federal courts. According to Roger Morris (1983), who conducted extensive interviews with the major plaintiffs in the case, the lawsuit arose out of a specific incident. In 1976, an inmate who was seeking medical help for heroin withdrawal at the prison hospital was thrown into the "hole" in Cellblock 3, where he was allegedly beaten by guards, including being kicked "repeatedly in the scrotum" (Morris 1983: 47). After being released from segregation a month later, the inmate's health deteriorated. Dwight Duran, another prisoner who was a boyhood friend of this inmate, attempted to nurse him back to health, but his condition worsened. Duran and other inmates pleaded for almost a year with authorities to hospitalize their friend. "Simply for making the request they, too, were threatened with the hole" (Morris 1983: 48). Later, when the inmate was examined at a Santa Fe hospital, he was found to have "an advanced malignant tumor on his testicles" (Morris 1983: 48). The inmate was transferred to a locked ward in the state mental hospital, where he died two weeks later.

As a result of this incident, Dwight Duran, along with inmates Lonnie Duran and Sharon Towers (housed in the Women's Annex across the street from the main penitentiary building), wrote a hand-printed brief that they filed in federal court in late 1977 on behalf of themselves "and all those similarly situated." The brief charged the state with operating a prison under conditions that constituted cruel and unusual punishment. The suit was joined by the American Civil Liberties Union (ACLU) in 1978 as one of their major cases challenging prison conditions in the United States.

The lawsuit, known as *Duran v. Apodaca*, represented the last organized non-violent attempt by inmates to bring about reforms at PNM. Prisoners were now confronting the Department of Corrections with the threat of judicial intervention. The federal courts were being brought into the struggle between keepers and captives at the Penitentiary of New Mexico.

Initially, the ACLU suit, according to inmates, "boosted morale." Inmates reported, "Everybody was looking forward to changes"; and "We thought everything was going to change." The expectation of change engendered by the ACLU suit was also bolstered by inmates who had been coming from other prisons from around the United States. "Nowadays every joint on the West Coast and every joint on the East Coast don't care if you grow your hair and your beard," said an inmate. "They'll give you a pair of Levis, let you have some identity. You are not a robot anymore.... People want their identity in here." These sentiments were echoed by a CO:

> All these people coming from these different prisons bring ideas to our prison system. [They say] over there we can wear beards, we can wear civilian clothes, we can do this and that. We can have motorcycle races on weekends in the yard. Walla Walla [prison in Washington State] had all those things. These people come down here and they tell [our inmates about these privileges]. Naturally...they are going to want the same and equal opportunities as these [other prison systems have]. That poses a big problem. These other institutions are giving away a lot more things than New Mexico is.

The lawsuit, in combination with an awareness by inmates of greater privileges in other prisons, led PNM inmates to expect that conditions would soon change. For the next three years, however, from 1977 to 1980, the lawsuit would drag on in negotiations, with no final resolution until the summer of 1980.

CONFRONTATIONS AMONG
TOP CORRECTIONS OFFICIALS

Ironically, specific reforms called for in the ACLU suit against PNM paralleled correctional planning efforts initiated by the Governor's Council on Criminal Justice Planning. Both the ACLU suit and efforts by the Governor's Council were aimed at improving conditions and enhancing rehabilitation and due process at PNM. The fact that PNM had been moving in an opposite direction from these efforts reflects the confused policies and contradictory appointments made by the Apodaca Administration. Governor Apodaca oversaw the appointment of hard-line wardens Aaron and Malley to the state penitentiary while he simultaneously selected Dr. Charles Becknell, an outspoken liberal, as director of the Governor's Council on Criminal Justice Planning. These appointments eventually led to an open confrontation between these top criminal justice officials.

When Becknell took over as director in the spring of 1975, the Governor's Council was little more than a conduit for passing federal law enforcement funds along to local and state criminal justice agencies. Under Becknell's leadership, the agency emerged as New Mexico's leading policy coordinator for criminal justice and corrections matters. More importantly, it became the spearhead for Apodaca's drive to reorganize corrections as part of his state reorganization plan.

Within the Governor's Council, Becknell assembled a staff of planners that included former treatment-oriented personnel from Project Newgate and PNM's other educational programs. The grants manager for the Governor's Council in 1975 was former inmate Lloyd McClendon, who had been one of the key inmate administrators in the late 1960s and early 1970s responsible for organizing PNM's innovative rehabilitation programs. McClendon was highly influential in corrections planning at the Governor's Council and helped Becknell choose his planning staff. These former associates of PNM's treatment programs, and the other like-minded staff members whom they recruited in 1976 and 1977, formed the nucleus of a planning staff that was ideologically committed to rehabilitation and inmates' rights. Dr. Becknell, whose liberal inclinations paralleled the goals of these key staff members, relied heavily on these planners for setting his agenda for corrections.

One of the first significant initiatives of the Governor's Council under Becknell's leadership was the development of Criminal Justice Standards and Goals for New Mexico that were based on National Standards and Goals initiated by the federal government. In 1973, the National Commission on Criminal Justice Standards and Goals was established to provide priorities for criminal justice planning and for the allocation of LEAA funds. The National Standards and Goals Project was an effort to provide a framework for rational planning so coordinated efforts within criminal justice agencies could be mobilized. LEAA in the mid-1970s made it very clear that states adopting the Standards and Goals would be in a better position to receive federal funds.

The National Standards and Goals presented a far-reaching blueprint for improvement in criminal justice practices and prison conditions. Criminal justice planning agencies in other states largely ignored LEAA's National Standards and Goals initiative (Feeley and Sarat 1980). New Mexico's criminal justice planning agency was one of the few that took the Standards and Goals project seriously. In the early 1970s, federal funds were often the only source of revenue for prison programs in New Mexico. Corrections planners and treatment-program personnel could not afford to risk one of their few funding sources. Thus in late 1975, the New Mexico Standards and Goals Project was established within the Governor's Council on Criminal Justice Planning. Lloyd McClendon, while he was still grants manager at the Governor's Council, was a primary force behind initiating the project. Florence Slade, a former Project Newgate counselor at PNM and by 1975 a corrections planner at the Governor's Council, was also influential in starting the project. Its initial director, Jack

Weber, soon became the chief aide to Lt. Gov. Robert Ferguson, who was chairman of the New Mexico Standards and Goals Committee. In July 1976, John Ramming, a lawyer who also had been an inmate at PNM during the early 1970s, was named director of the Standards and Goals Project. And, in 1976, I was hired as the Standards and Goals corrections planner. The New Mexico Standards and Goals Project was thus staffed and heavily influenced by people who had worked or been incarcerated in PNM during the years of accommodation in the early 1970s, when programs constituted a major element of the remunerative system of control. They represented the treatment-oriented staff members and inmates who had formed an important alliance in the prison during the early 1970s.

The Standards and Goals report was developed with input from the New Mexico Council on Crime and Delinquency and a select group of criminal justice practitioners and private citizens from around the state. It reflected a liberal approach to corrections that was in direct opposition to the policies being implemented at PNM by wardens Aaron and Malley.

The 1976 New Mexico Standards and Goals called for several reforms that were similar to those proposed two years later in the ACLU suit. First, a major emphasis was on the development of community-based alternatives to confinement within the Department of Corrections. A cornerstone of the goal was the initiation of a classification mechanism within the department that allowed prisoners to be assigned directly to community-based facilities after sentencing. Under the then-current sentencing laws, all New Mexico prisoners were sentenced directly to PNM and were under control of penitentiary officials. The approach called for in the Standards and Goals would have offenders sentenced to a central classification facility, where they could be placed either at PNM or in less restrictive surroundings, including community-based programs. This standard attempted to address the problem of overcrowding by diverting nonviolent offenders from PNM, thus avoiding the construction of new maximum security facilities. The standard also moved effective control of the correctional system away from the PNM warden to a centralized treatment-oriented staff.

Second, rehabilitation was seen as the primary goal of corrections. "Each correctional agency should immediately develop and implement policies, procedures, and practices to fulfill the right of offenders to rehabilitation programs" (Governor's Council on Criminal Justice Planning 1976: 304). Educational and vocational program expansions were detailed in the Standards and Goals report.

Third, standards for due process in disciplinary procedures were outlined in detail. Minor violations had to be clearly specified and differentiated from major violations. Minor violations could result only in reprimands and loss of commissary, entertainment, or recreation privileges "for not more than 24 hours." Punishment for major violations included loss of good-time, loss of program and housing assignment, or transfer to segregation. The least restrictive alternative was called for, consistent with staff and inmate safety. Rules for conducting disciplinary hearings for major violations were promulgated, including time limits for hearings, rights to cross-examination and representation, and the requirement that "substantial evidence of guilt" be found before imposing a sanction. Related to the due process rights was a standard calling for a code of offenders' rights that stated, "Except where the nature of confinement necessarily requires modification, offenders should be entitled to the same rights as citizens" (Governor's Council on Criminal Justice Planning 1976: 392).

Fourth, Standards and Goals focused on prison conditions. Minimum standards were set for medical care, recreation, clean and healthful surroundings, and protection against physical abuse. In addition, the social environment of major correctional institutions was to be less coercive. "The institution should adopt policies and practices that will enhance the individual identity of the inmate and reduce regimentation in the institutional setting" (Governor's Council on Criminal Justice Planning 1976: 360).

Fifth, the Standards and Goals called for greater inmate participation in the decision-making process. Specifically, "Inmate committees should be developed to assist the administration in an advisory capacity.... Participatory management should be adopted.... An ombudsman independent of institutional administration should receive and process inmate and staff complaints.... Inmate newspapers and magazines should be supported under supervision...of the administration.... Inmates should be provided opportunity to have input to news media" (Governor's Council on Criminal Justice Planning 1976: 358). Along with these standards were the outlines for formal grievance procedures and guarantees for free expression and association, restrictions of which had to be justified by compelling reasons of safety and security.

And finally, the Standards and Goals set forth an outline for a reorganization of New Mexico corrections. Since the Standards and Goals had no legal authority, governmental structures had to be developed which would give them such authority. Legislation was requested to unify all correctional programs under one agency (not specified in the standard) that would oversee correctional research, information gathering, and planning. The thrust of this final group of standards was to implement Apodaca's reorganization plan. It was well understood by most of the planners that the Governor's Council would become the "oversight agency" called for in the standard.

Coinciding with the 1976 Standards and Goals Project was a second major initiative of the Governor's Council. Funded by LEAA, a comprehensive Corrections Master Plan for New Mexico was developed with a consulting group, Approach Associates, from Berkeley, California. The consultants studied the corrections system of New Mexico and concluded that the majority of the inmates at PNM were less sophisticated, less violent, and less hardened than inmates in other states (Governor's Council on Criminal Justice Planning 1978b). The Master Plan called for a coordinated corrections system, increased programming for rehabilitation, greater emphasis on community-based corrections, and a comprehensive classification system. The Master Plan recommendations paralleled those of the Standards and Goals, and, again, echoed many of the reforms that would in 1978 be called for in the ACLU lawsuit. The Master Plan, like the Standards and Goals, laid out a direction for PNM that was contrary to the policies set by wardens Aaron and Malley.

> *Interviewer:* Was there any conflict between the policies that were coming out of the Master Plan of Dr. Becknell and Warden Malley's [policies]?
> *Corrections Official:* Well absolutely.... Dr. Becknell supported the Master Plan...the conditions that we laid out in the Master Plan were the conditions over which Malley was warden. Those are the same conditions that were the basis for the ACLU...suit. So we were here at the same time seeing the same things, identifying the same problems, coming to a lot of the same solutions [as were called for in the ACLU suit]. So insofar as Dr. Becknell supported the Master Plan, its recommendations were in direct conflict with Warden Malley. His philosophy as well as his daily operation of the institution was in direct conflict with everything the Master Plan was about. I mean from inmate rights, to correspondence, to grievance, to overcrowding, to access to programs...the whole gamut.

The cornerstone of the Master Plan was development of an Intensive Classification Center (ICC). The ICC would give the central corrections agency control over inmate movement, which by law had been controlled by PNM. The ICC would be empowered to place new inmates in less restrictive environments of medium- and minimum-security facilities and even in proposed community-based programs that would be run by the Department of Corrections. The ICC could monitor and regulate the inmate population at PNM. According to the plan, the ICC, in conjunction with research and planning components in corrections, would forecast inmate population growth and plan new facilities around inmate characteristics and program needs. The Master Plan called for a new medium-security facility and several minimum-security facilities to relieve overcrowding at PNM, which would remain, under the Master Plan, the only maximum-security institution in the state. The ICC would coordinate classification and transfers for all of the facilities.

The ICC as a classification and planning tool fit in well with Apoda-ca's reorganization plan, which sought to centralize state agencies' activities. The Governor's Council took the lead in pressing the legislature for the reorganization of criminal justice agencies. The reorganization, if passed, could potentially provide the basis for an actual implementation of many of the Standards and Goals and Master Plan recommendations through executive decree, and would allow the Governor to press the legislature for further funding of their other key elements. During the legislative session of 1977, Apodaca's reorganization plan was considered. It was not presented to the legislature as a liberal reform designed to change the direction of PNM. In fact, it is doubtful that Governor Apodaca understood it as such. Rather, it was presented as a more efficient, effective, and rational means of governing state agencies. But the planners within the Governor's Council were quite certain that reorganization would be the catalyst for instituting the liberal reforms that had been called for in the Standards and Goals and the Master Plan. It was seen as an opportunity to change the direction of corrections programs and move PNM away from the hard-line policies that had emerged since 1975.

The legislature passed Apodaca's reorganization plan in March 1977, but it did not go into effect officially until April 1978. The inherent conflicts that arise in any transition from one form of governance to another were exacerbated by this one year lag in implementation. For a full year, the officials charged with running corrections were unsure of the eventual authority structure within the department. The Corrections Commission, whose policymaking authority would end in April 1978 under reorganization, still held their power during the implementation phase. The Governor's Council on Criminal Justice Planning, which had no administrative connection to the corrections department prior to reorganization, would emerge under reorganization as the lead agency in the newly reorganized department. But until April 1978, the Governor's Council had no legislatively mandated authority over corrections. Caught within this transition was the Central Office of the Corrections Department, which was destined under reorganization to become one of four divisions within a new Department of Criminal Justice.

In February 1977, Mike Hanrahan resigned as Secretary of Corrections. During the legislative session in which reorganization was passed, Charles Becknell was named acting Secretary of Corrections, while he also retained his post as director of the Governor's Council. This joint appointment meant that administrators from the Corrections Department could raise no public objections to the reorganization plan, which was fully supported by both Governor Apodaca and Charles Becknell, while it was being considered by the state legislature. Shortly after the 1977 legislative session passed the reorganization bill, Becknell relinquished his role as acting Secretary of Corrections and returned to the Governor's Council, where he led the implementation of the reorganization. The new Secretary of Corrections, Ed Mahr, a former newspaper reporter and chief administrator of the district court in Albuquerque, entered his job knowing that his position would soon be subsumed within a newly reorganized departmental structure.

While the reorganization would not take effect legally for a year, Governor Apodaca ordered his department heads to proceed with operations as if the reorganization was already in effect. This caused immediate conflicts, especially between the Corrections Commission and Charles Becknell. "The Corrections Commission very clearly resisted the reorganization," said a state official. "They did not like Becknell because he would not report to them. And they did not like being left out of day to day decisions.... They were totally opposed to the recommendations of the Master Plan,...[they] felt that they were not consulted enough during the Master Plan [development]. It was a question of their being policymaking or advisory."

The conflict between Becknell and the Corrections Commission came to a head in January 1978 just prior to that year's legislative session when funding for the ICC would be considered. The ICC, which was the cornerstone of the Master Plan, was opposed by the Corrections Commission. The Chairman of the Corrections Commission, Bud Richards, had close personal ties with the powerful, conservative chairman of the Senate Finance Committee, State Senator Aubrey Dunn. Under pressure from Governor Apodaca, the Corrections Commission had approved $8 million for construction of the ICC. The bill that was eventually drafted for legislative approval called for $13.4 million. Commission Chairman Richards contacted Senator Dunn to tell him that the Corrections Commission had not approved this allocation of funds. Senator Dunn let the Governor and Becknell know that he would not pass the appropriation without approval of the Corrections Commission, even though they were going to lose their policymaking authority in three months. According to a state official, "Charles Becknell called Bud Richards and said, 'Bud, you're killing our ICC.' And [Commission Chairman Richards] said, 'You're damn right, Charles, I'm killing it.'... So the ICC was killed." This incident underscores the conflict-filled atmosphere under which the corrections administration was operating during 1977 and 1978.

There was also conflict between administrators involved in the reorganization over how to proceed with the ACLU lawsuit. Secretary of Corrections Ed Mahr and Governor's Council Director Becknell differed strongly on the concessions that should be made in resolving the lawsuit. A corrections administrator said:

I saw representatives of Becknell's office ready to give inmates *everything,* everything they asked for [in the ACLU suit].... They were fighting for inmate rights.... [Secretary Mahr exclaimed in a meeting with Becknell's representatives,] "Who's going to run the penitentiary after this is all over? Lonnie Duran [an inmate plaintiff in the suit] can run it. I'll make him warden!" We had some terrific battles over that.... But then [Becknell's people] persisted, [so] we went to mediation [instead of fighting the suit in court]."

Becknell and the staff members under him at the Governor's Council were clearly gaining the upper hand in setting policy for state corrections. Despite the loss of the ICC, Becknell's people were getting their way in the state's response to the ACLU lawsuit. The state agreed to court supervised negotiations with the plaintiffs and to a series of negotiated consent decrees mandating changes at PNM. In addition, the structure of the new Criminal Justice Department placed Becknell and his staff from the Governor's Council in the lead policymaking positions.

In April 1978, the Governor's Council and the Corrections Central Office moved from their old separate quarters into a three-story building in downtown Santa Fe to form the nucleus of the new Criminal Justice Department. Under Governor Apodaca, it was very clear who was running this new department. Charles Becknell was named Secretary of Criminal Justice in overall command. Under Becknell were four division directors, including Ed Mahr who had been Secretary of Corrections under the old structure and now was Director of the Corrections Division. Administratively attached to the Corrections Division was the Corrections Commission, which no longer had policymaking authority, but still heard inmates' appeals and grievances and could offer advice on policies—advice which could now be largely ignored. Beneath Mahr was the Bureau of Adult Institutions, which was headed by Felix Rodriguez, who now had nominal authority over PNM since it fell under this bureau in the new organizational chart. (Despite being the head of this bureau, Rodriguez was still under Governor Apodaca's ban against entering or having any contact with PNM, a ban that Corrections Director Ed Mahr continued to enforce.) This new organizational setup meant that within the space of eight years, PNM had moved from a relatively independent agency to a sub-bureau agency four steps removed in the chain of command from the Governor's Office.

The new Criminal Justice Department included not only the Corrections Division, but the State Police Division, Public Defenders Office, and Adult and Juvenile Parole Boards. To coordinate these diverse agencies, the reorganization created two new divisions, the Administrative Services Division and the Technical Support Division. The latter two divisions were staffed largely by planners and administrators from the old Governor's Council on Criminal Justice Planning.

Charles Becknell and the Administrative Services Division were housed on the top floor of the new department's three-story building. The Corrections Division and its director, Ed Mahr, were housed on the bottom floor, which was half underground and a virtual basement. This arrangement reflected the power structure of the new Criminal Justice Department. A former corrections official who worked in the corrections Central Office said:

> [the Correction Department's old] Central Office was decimated by the Criminal Justice Department. There was an administrative assistant to the Secretary of Criminal Justice who was telling [Director of Corrections Ed Mahr] what to do.... The Administrative Services Division was created and all the administrative functions...[like] personnel and budgets...were moved to the third floor.... They got this power over everybody [in corrections]. They ran roughshod over us.

Becknell and the Administrative Services Division moved quickly in early 1978 to assert control. "The Central Office staff not only of Corrections but also of the State Police really resisted reorganization," reported a state official. It was largely because of this resistance that Becknell attempted to consolidate administrative functions under his direct control. Because Becknell enjoyed Governor Apodaca's strong support, these agencies were compelled, at least initially, to follow his lead.

Despite Apodaca's support of Becknell and his initiatives for consolidating the new department, the reorganization was bringing to a head the contradictions in Governor Apodaca's earlier administrative appointments to corrections. The lack of clear policy direction in 1975 and 1976 had led to the simultaneous appointments of Becknell, a liberal, as director of criminal justice planning and Malley, a hard-liner, as warden of PNM. These two strong-willed administrators who had opposing philosophies and goals clashed in early 1978, a few weeks before the reorganization officially went into effect.

Becknell, who was in a constant battle with the Corrections Commission over the reorganization and implementation of the Master Plan, had forbidden Warden Malley to communicate directly with the Commission. All communication to the Commission was to proceed through Ed Mahr and Becknell. Under former Secretary Hanrahan, "Malley was in charge and that's the way he wanted it," reported a state official. "He saw the penitentiary as a separate institution where he could do his own thing." Now the warden was coming under the supervision of state officials who had very clear ideas about how corrections should operate. And these ideas were directly opposite those of Warden Malley.

From Malley's perspective, his new superiors had no expertise in corrections and did not understand the nature of maximum security institutions or the hardcore convicts that populated them. The Corrections Commission had generally been supportive of Malley's operation of PNM and could easily elicit from Malley opinions that were contrary to the policies Becknell was trying to institute. Becknell and Mahr were especially incensed at Malley when he allegedly expressed his opinion at a Corrections Commission hearing about a proposed minimum-security facility at Roswell. "He went before the Commission and told the Commission [that] Roswell will do no good [in alleviating overcrowding at PNM]," reported a former corrections official. At that very moment, across the street in the state capitol, Ed Mahr was seeking to persuade reluctant state legislators to fund the facility because, he told the legislators, it would significantly reduce the crowding at PNM.

Direct contact between Malley and the Corrections Commission, which was a normal procedure before the reorganization was passed, became the reason for firing Malley. Becknell and Mahr claimed that Malley was misleading the Commission about their policy implementation. But at the core of the dispute was both a philosophical difference between Becknell and Malley and a political struggle between Becknell and the Corrections Commission. On March 10, 1978, Becknell and Mahr went to Governor Apodaca and told him that they were going to dismiss Malley. The Governor asked them if they had the support of the Corrections Commission and they replied that they had not yet informed them. The Corrections Commission was that day having a meeting across the street from the Governor's Office. According to an official who was present, the Governor said to Becknell and Mahr, "Well, you go over there and you tell them I support you and if anyone of [the commissioners] don't support you, you call me and I'll fire their ass." Warden Malley was thus officially terminated that day from his job by Ed Mahr during the Corrections Commission hearing.

In March 1978, three weeks before the reorganization was officially to take effect, Becknell was clearly in the driver's seat and enjoyed the strong backing of Governor Apodaca. At that point, it appeared that dramatic liberal reforms at PNM could proceed with little opposition from within the Corrections Division. The confrontation between Becknell and Malley had been decided in Becknell's favor. As he officially took over the new Criminal Justice Department in April 1978, Becknell had a clear mandate from the Governor.

The Malley era at PNM was over. The confrontation between two opposing views of corrections during Apodaca's administration ended with Malley's firing. Upon leaving New Mexico, in a parting shot at those who dismissed him, Malley warned that PNM "is going to burst at the seams until the inmates burn it down to get attention" (*Albuquerque Journal* 3/24/78: A1).

SUMMARY: YEARS OF CONFRONTATION

Governor Apodaca oversaw from 1975 to early 1978 a correctional apparatus that was in confrontation at several levels: between former Warden Rodriguez and the Governor; between new PNM administrators and inmates; and between liberal and hard-line factions. During most of this period, New Mexico corrections lacked a coherent policy direction. Many of the officials in conflict with each other had been appointed by Apodaca in the context of this policy disarray.

Key changes in the control structure over inmates set a confrontational tone at PNM. The rapid removal of accommodations connected to remunerative controls produced organized inmate opposition in the form of strikes and lawsuits. In response, the prison administration attempted to isolate inmate leaders and reduce their influence through a coercive crackdown.

Near the end of his term as governor, Apodaca appeared to be resolving the conflicts (that he had helped to nurture) by squarely backing a particular faction of administrators and their more liberal goals and plans for corrections. However, these spring 1978 developments, which promised more progressive correctional policies and a resolution to much of the conflict plaguing PNM, soon evaporated as Apodaca's newly reorganized Criminal Justice Department became an ineffectual bureaucracy. As discussed in the next chapter, Apodaca's reorganization quickly became a bureaucratic quagmire in which implementation of any policies, including the Standards and Goals, Master Plan, and resolution of the ACLU lawsuit, became bogged down. As Apodaca was forced by state constitutional requirements to step down as governor, his reorganization of New Mexico corrections could not be carried through to a consistent conclusion. New Mexico corrections and PNM then slid into a period of disorganization and fragmentation.

5

YEARS OF
FRAGMENTATION,
1978–1980

By April 1978, a promising movement toward a liberalization of corrections policies appeared to be set. Charles Becknell, the liberal administrator armed with his Standards and Goals and Corrections Master Plan,
officially took over the top position in corrections with the full backing of
Governor Apodaca. The hard-line warden at the Penitentiary of New Mexico (PNM) had been removed and could now be replaced with someone
loyal to the department's top administration. And the U.S. District Court
gave a positive reception to the inmates' legal suit by mandating a negotiated settlement between inmate plaintiffs and the State of New Mexico.

A liberalization of policies, however, did not take place. In 1978 and
1979, an administrative paralysis set in within the new Criminal Justice
Department. Agencies at the lower levels of the organization drifted
toward disarray while the top levels were immersed in political infighting.

ADMINISTRATIVE CONFUSION IN
THE CORRECTIONS HIERARCHY

As Governor Apodaca's reorganization finally took effect in April 1978, he
would be forced to leave office in less than a year because of the New Mexico Constitution's ban on consecutive terms. A new governor would be
installed in January 1979. Whether this new governor would follow
through with Apodaca's initiatives was up to the vagaries of shifting political winds. The Republicans were coming increasingly under the influence
of the emerging New Right. Their election to the governorship would
drastically move corrections policy in a hard-line, conservative direction.
Republican influence in the New Mexico State Legislature, while not dominant, was a major factor in the coalition of legislative conservatives who
had successfully passed a new death penalty statute and a determinate sentencing structure. These measures passed despite the lobbying efforts of
Becknell's staff and their allies with the New Mexico Council on Crime
and Delinquency.

One of the major ironies for the newly reorganized Criminal Justice

Department was that these hard-line penal statutes passed as a result of compromises, between Governor Apodaca and legislative conservatives, aimed at keeping his reorganization plan intact. Governor Apodaca signed these bills into law. His commitment had, after all, been to his vision of a strong executive structure, rather than to a liberal corrections policy. Once again, Apodaca's reorganization moved in contradictory directions dictated by a growing political and ideological conservatism. In order to save his reorganization, he was forced to give in on key elements of the liberal agenda, an agenda that was rapidly being whittled away not only in New Mexico, but nationwide.

Governor Apodaca was very similar to President Jimmy Carter in his ideological orientation. Both ascended to office on government reform programs and both fixed their governmental agendas upon technical rather than programmatic changes. Government reorganizations, along with "sunset" and "sunshine" legislation, were seen as ways of fine-tuning government to make it more effective. Liberalism during this period, especially as practiced by political leaders like Carter and Apodaca, lacked the broad programmatic agenda of the Kennedy-Johnson era that was aimed at partial transformation of societal structures, not just refining governmental structures. Basically, this was liberalism sans the guiding philosophy or vision of liberal ideology. This liberal philosophy had included a belief in our ability to reform not only society but also to reform individuals who had broken the law. The discrediting of rehabilitation as a goal of corrections represented one of the most significant setbacks for the liberal agenda, for it struck at the heart of the underlying vision. That liberals during the late 1970s assisted in the discrediting of rehabilitation meant that they aided in the decline of their basic ideological beliefs. Francis T. Cullen and Karen E. Gilbert (1982: xxviii-xxix) make this point very clearly:

> by discrediting rehabilitation and endorsing the punitive principle of just deserts (or retributive justice) as the preferred goal of criminal sanctioning, liberals have provided a new and potent legitimacy for the philosophy of punishment. In so doing, they have inadvertently and dangerously created optimal conditions for a conservative campaign to establish "law and order." For once they have agreed that inflicting pain—and not treatment—is the only justifiable purpose of sanctioning offenders, liberals no longer are able to debate *if* punishing is a wise or humane policy but only how much punishment should be meted out.... the rehabilitative ideal has long provided liberals with a coherent framework which could be invoked to unmask repressive policies as both scientifically unfounded and non-humanistic in spirit.

Any ideological movement that begins to lose its vision will soon lose its political force. In the late 1970s, the Apodacas of American politics represented a form of liberalism that had lost its soul. This lack of vision accounts for the fact that basic positions on the death penalty and determinate sentencing could so easily be traded for the technical governmental reforms represented by Apodaca's reorganization. During the 1977 and 1978 legislative sessions almost every legislative measure drawn from the New Mexico Standards and Goals for adult corrections was either defeated, allowed to die in committee, or traded away for the passage of Apodaca's reorganization legislation. At the time, it seemed ironic that at one stroke the Governor and the legislature instituted a reorganization of corrections that put one of the most liberal, reform-minded administrators (Charles Becknell) over corrections while enacting a stringent fixed-sentencing law that would ultimately undermine any reforms that Becknell might initiate. When I asked one of Apodaca's chief aides in charge of steering criminal justice bills through the legislature why the Governor had not vetoed these measures (a veto which very likely could have been sustained), I was told, "Everything had to go for the 'reorg' bill." The price of the reorganization was the collapse of the liberal corrections policies proposed in the Standards and Goals. While reorganization had been one of the goals for corrections enunciated in the Standards and Goals, it became the *only* goal for adult corrections that survived the legislative process. Under these circumstances, reorganization became a means for governing corrections with no articulated or coherent objective guiding the governing process. It was the ultimate victory of process over substance. And it became the seed of a governmental paralysis that would fragment New Mexico corrections for years to come.

The fragmentation of corrections was not inevitable in April 1978. The reorganization could be effective as long as an administrator at the top of the agency had a vision and direction and, more importantly, that this administrator enjoyed the clear backing of the Governor. In April 1978, this was the case. Despite the legislative setbacks for liberal policies, the reins of the correctional apparatus were in the hands of an administrator, Charles Becknell, who very strongly endorsed liberal reforms. The implementation of reforms could proceed, albeit with difficulty, as long as Charles Becknell had the backing of the Governor's Office. The selection of Apodaca's successor, then, was crucial to Becknell's progress toward these reforms; clearly a Democrat was essential as the next governor, but not just any Democrat. The new governor had to proceed with the reorganization and give Becknell a free hand to implement administratively as many of the liberal reforms as were called for in the Standards and Goals. Of the two contenders in the Democratic primary, only Lt. Gov. Robert Ferguson held such a promise. He had been the chairman of the Standards and Goals Committee and was a strong supporter of Apodaca's reorganization. His opponent was former Governor Bruce King, an Apodaca political enemy who was gaining support among the many disgruntled agency heads who had lost out in Apodaca's reorganization. He was making it quite clear that he meant to alter the reorganization, a message that was warmly received by administrators in the State Police and in the former Corrections Department who had been absorbed under the new Criminal Justice Department. Playing to state agencies by candidates for the governorship is a very important tactic since state government is the number one employer in New Mexico and state employees are very active in organizing local politics. In April and May of 1978, state employees from the Criminal Justice Department spent their off-duty hours working in one of the Democratic candidates' campaigns for the June primary election. The former director of the Standards and Goals Project, Jack Weber, became Ferguson's campaign manager. Becknell and several members of his staff also worked in the Ferguson campaign. Members of the State Police and the old Corrections Department establishment supported Bruce King's attempt to return to the governorship. The future of the reorganization would be settled at the ballot box.

In the event, Bruce King prevailed in the June 1978 primary. From June until January of the next year, Apodaca became the ultimate lame duck, waiting for a successor who planned to alter his governmental centerpiece, reorganization.

King went on to defeat the Republican candidate by a very close margin. In the closing days of the fall campaign, Bruce King prevailed upon Charles Becknell to deliver the state's small but crucial Black vote by promising Becknell that he would be re-appointed as the Secretary of Criminal Justice. "Becknell's family is very politically strong in the southeastern part of the state," reported a state official. "Becknell made a commitment to King after Bob Ferguson lost the primary...and he did deliver the votes that he said he would deliver with the Black community." King won one of the closest races for governor in the state's history. The Black vote, which turned out heavily and went solidly for King, provided the margin of victory. Thus Becknell would be retained in the new administration as head of the Criminal Justice Department.

However, King's support of Becknell was lukewarm at best. "Becknell's relationship was not as clearly defined with the King administration as with Apodaca's," said a state official. While King, as promised, put Becknell's name forward to the State Senate as his Secretary of Criminal Justice, he offered no words of support as Becknell underwent the harshest grilling of any cabinet member by state senators that people observing these events could remember (*New Mexican* 2/6/79). "Dr. Becknell's confirmation hearings under Governor King...became quite racist and there was a lot of doubt that the State Senate would confirm him as Secretary," said a state official. "King was just letting the Senate do his dirty work.... [T]hose confirmation hearings thoroughly emasculated Dr. Becknell's ability to run the department; psychologically it was a real drain on him.... [After those hearings] nobody knew who was calling the shots [in the Criminal Justice Department]." After these grueling Senate hearings, Becknell was confirmed as the Secretary of Criminal Justice (*New Mexican* 2/7/79). But he would oversee a department that Governor King and the legislature were rapidly dismantling.

The State Police were removed from the new Criminal Justice Department, since one of Governor King's strongest campaign supporters had been the Chief of the State Police who, before Apodaca's reorganization, had always reported directly to the Governor. During the 1979 legislative session the State Police became an independent agency once again. One of the four divisions of the Criminal Justice Department was thus removed, leaving the Technical Support, Administrative Services, and Corrections Divisions. The Technical Support Division, which included the correctional officer training component, was "zero budgeted" by the legislature, effectively eliminating this division. Its functions had to be taken over by the Administrative Services Division with no increase in its funding. "In fact, the only way we could start training was with an LEAA grant," reported a department administrator.

The clear intent of the legislature and Governor King was to undo former Governor Apodaca's reorganization of corrections. The Corrections Division and the Administrative Services Division were combined into a new Department of Corrections. Becknell's position, Secretary of Criminal Justice, was redesignated Secretary of Corrections; and Deputy Secretaries (instead of Division Directors) now oversaw each of the department's remaining divisions. "If you look at the organization chart for 1979," reported a Corrections Department administrator, "you can see...deputy secretaries dangling out there with nobody under them.... It was top-heavy." With the removal of the State Police, many of the coordinating functions of the Administrative Services Division were no longer needed. "In [the] Corrections [Division] we had ten people including secretaries and I think Administrative Services had something like fifty-four positions," reported a corrections official. "I don't think it was anybody's fault other than the fact that the State Police got pulled out so that left all these positions in there that had been handling state police matters.... it wasn't thoroughly defined as to what the function [of the Administrative Services Division] was."

Yet Becknell and his staff still attempted to run the department through the Administrative Services Division. During 1979 "there was an even greater feeling of 'us versus them' between the Corrections Division and the Administrative Services Division," said a corrections official. The Administrative Services Division continued to develop plans for implementation of Standards and Goals. "It was very ineffective planning because it had no executive or legislative backing," said a planner who worked for the Administrative Services Division during 1979. "We did a very poor job of disseminating to those legislators and the Governor the problems we were having." In fact, during 1979 the Administrative Services Division became increasingly isolated from the decision-making process as it lost power under Governor King. Becknell, who had been weakened by the confirmation hearings, and the planners in this division became cloistered from the day-to-day running of the department and focused their energies on planning programs that had little chance of being implemented.

Another decision by Governor King that undermined Becknell's power occurred soon after the Senate confirmed Becknell as Secretary. In a controversial move (*Santa Fe Reporter* 4/12/79), Governor King appointed Felix Rodriguez (the former PNM warden who had been removed from that position by Governor Apodaca in 1975) to the Deputy Secretary's post that directly oversaw the department's Corrections Division. Secretary Becknell had no input into this decision. "This was the Governor's appointment," said a corrections official. The former head of the Corrections Division, Ed Mahr, had resigned on April 13, 1979, because, said a state official, "the [former] Secretary of Corrections [Mahr] was no longer running corrections." On the one hand, his power had been initially moved through Apodaca's reorganization to Becknell's office, and on the other hand, with the inauguration of Governor King, Felix Rodriguez, Mahr's subordinate, was given greater influence than Mahr in the day-to-day running of corrections. Before Mahr resigned, Governor King met frequently with his old friend Felix Rodriguez. "There was no relationship between Felix Rodriguez and [former] Governor Apodaca, [but] a very strong relationship between Felix and Governor King," said a corrections official, who added, "I don't think Becknell and Governor King had a good relationship at all." Though Becknell was his nominal superior, Felix Rodriguez, unlike Becknell, had the ear and trust of the new Governor.

Another complicating factor undermining Becknell's control of the department was Governor King's apparent promise to the Corrections Commission that he was going to restore their policymaking power. A state official said that when King took office in 1979, "the [corrections] commission felt that they were going to become policymaking." In fact, the chairman of the Corrections Commission announced at a commission hearing in 1979 that Governor King had through executive order given the

Commission back its policymaking power. "I attended that meeting," reported a corrections staff member. "I think that was a political move on the Governor's part to pacify those Commission members.... Governor King was paying political dues." Governor King could not, of course, through executive order reverse the reorganization legislation that had made the Corrections Commission merely an advisory body. And this move was not made by the legislature during 1979. But the apparent message from Governor King clearly made the Commission members think they were effectively, once again, in charge of formulating corrections policies. "In conversations with the Governor [King], he has given the Commission more and more things he wants looked into [in which we] have the final word," reported a member of the Corrections Commission.

Thus, in 1979, Governor King gave signals to at least three different factions within the department that they were in charge: Becknell through his official appointment and confirmation as Secretary; Rodriguez through his appointment as Deputy Secretary overseeing the Corrections Division and his close personal relationship with the Governor; and the Corrections Commission through close contacts and promises from King that they would be restored to their policymaking status. Even though these three entities within the department were often moving in contradictory directions and were in constant conflict, Governor King assured each of them, at least privately, that they had his full support. In contrast to Apodaca's activist style, King was the ultimate "caretaker" executive. But, unlike the situation during his first term in the early 1970s, King was now in a position that demanded strong executive direction. Instead, after the partial dismantling of the reorganization, Governor King left it to the various factions within the Corrections Department to sort out policies as best they could.

By the summer of 1979 a situation had evolved in which top administrators of the department were moving in several different, often conflicting directions. Secretary Becknell and the Administrative Services Division continued with their attempts at long-range planning and organizing such activities as training of correctional officers. Their plans, while laying out good blueprints for correctional practice, gave no immediate answers to the actual day-to-day problems facing administrators on the line. Their efforts at instituting a training program were hampered first by the lack of state funding and later by the lack of cooperation from supervisors at PNM who would not give new correctional employees time off from their shifts for training (Office of the Attorney General 1980b).

Meanwhile, Deputy Secretary Rodriguez, who more than anyone else in the department was now in charge of responding to day-to-day crises, did not have clear legislative authority to set policies within the department. His problem was in many respects opposite to that of the Administrative Services Division. Where they could plan, they did not have the effective power to implement. Where Rodriguez was in a position to implement, he could not plan an effective strategy for action. The immediate reality of day-to-day crises within his division was obviating any attempts through long-range strategies to overcome the underlying sources of the constant emergencies that Rodriguez was facing. "We're too busy managing our day-to-day brush fires," said a department official. "If you have brush fires in front of you, you just never get around to these other good things that should happen in the system...sort of like wearing blinders and worrying about the day-to-day problems and [not seeing that] if we implement some of these things in the [Master] Plan, we wouldn't have these brush fires everyday." Rodriguez settled into a reactive style of "crisis management," necessitated partly by the nature of the situation but also by his lack of administrative skills. The official whose 1975 investigation was largely responsible for Rodriguez's removal from PNM, former Attorney General Toney Anaya, said, "Basically, I think Felix is a good man, but a poor administrator." Indeed his track record as warden of PNM, as documented in Anaya's report, demonstrated, in the words of the former Attorney General, that "there was some atrocious administration going on there (at the Penitentiary [in 1975])" (*Santa Fe Reporter* 4/12/79: 3). And the situation by 1979 had become much worse and even more contradictory than it had been in 1975 when, as warden, Rodriguez's delicate administrative balancing act had collapsed.

During 1979, Rodriguez became the chief corrections administrator in charge of negotiating, with the ACLU and inmates Dwight Duran and Lonnie Duran, a settlement of the lawsuit against PNM. He also oversaw the many changes occurring at PNM, including renovations of the physical plant, supervision of a new and inexperienced warden, growing violence among inmates, and one of the highest turnover rates among correctional officers in the nation. He visited the prison for the first time in nearly four years during the spring of 1979. What he witnessed was an institution in turmoil, not the relatively calm prison he was forced to leave in 1975. He was now in charge of administering this turmoil with no clear policy guidelines and no experience in dealing with a prison that was rapidly coming unglued. The key players among the middle-level administrators and among the inmate leadership had changed, leaving Rodriguez with few of the old networks he had relied upon for information and control prior to his ouster in 1975. Yet there was really no one else among New Mexico's corrections officials who had any experience dealing with the complexities of prisons.

The split and isolation within the department between the Corrections Division and the Administrative Services Division, and the "loose

cannon" that the Corrections Commission had become in opposing virtually every initiative from Becknell's office, meant that corrections policymaking was completely stalemated. In addition, the state corrections
department was becoming increasingly disorganized as a result of repeated
administrative successions. One warden and one secretary of corrections
had administered the prison from 1970 to 1975, but there were four wardens and four secretaries from late 1975 through 1979. This rapid series of
administrative successions resulting from the changeover in governors was
having by 1979 a devastating effect on correctional policies and on the
operations at PNM.

The administrative confusion produced at the top levels of government by Apodaca's reorganization and King's subsequent partial "de-
organization" allowed PNM to drift toward disaster. Ironically, the reorganization, which was designed to make agencies like PNM more
accountable to higher authorities, led to a situation in which the middle-
level administrators at PNM ran the institution in their own fashion, with
little or no supervision or policy guidance from above.

THE MIDDLE-LEVEL "CLIQUE" AT PNM

After Warden Malley was fired in March 1978, management of PNM fell
to a group of middle-level supervisors. Under Malley's wardenship, fairly
tight controls had been placed by the warden's office over these middle-
level supervisors. A correctional officer discussing Malley's control of the
prison's operations said, "He gave all of us [tight supervision]. Even the
inmates knew that if we [the COs] didn't walk the line we'd hear from
him." By most accounts, Malley had been a "hands-on" administrator
who controlled the activities of his subordinates. He was also supportive
of his line personnel. "If an officer had a gripe or couldn't get help from
the supervisor," said a CO, "he'd talk to Mr. Malley [who]...talked to the
supervisor to find out why he didn't help him out or what happened."
Another correctional officer agreed that under Malley, "you had better
cooperation from supervisors. They would help you.... Malley used to
make sure the supervisor would help with any problems." Malley had created a structure of accountability over the line supervisors to ensure consistency in prison operations and support for the front-line correctional
officers. His development of post orders and specifications of duties were
an attempt to professionalize the custodial staff and their immediate
supervisors. From the accounts of correctional officers, this structure had
some success in restraining the captains and lieutenants, many of whom
had a tendency to run their shifts as little fiefdoms. "There was a feeling of

line staff that they were getting more support from the Malley administration," reported a caseworker. According to correctional officers, when Malley was fired, "there was a lot of open comments [such as] 'now Malley's gone, we're going to go down the drain.'" The structures of control over the custodial staff that Malley had constructed "fell apart after he left"; and the relationship between supervisors and COs "deteriorated very quickly," according to correctional officers. The vacuum left by Malley's departure was filled by this group of middle-level administrators who ran the prison with no accountability to their superiors, including the two successive wardens who followed Malley in 1978 and 1979.

The primary consideration for Malley's replacement seemed to be loyalty to the corrections Central Office rather than penitentiary experience. After serving as acting warden for two months, Levi Romero reluctantly agreed to be named as permanent warden of PNM on May 25, 1978. Romero had worked under Corrections Division Director Ed Mahr in Central Office as the division's finance specialist overseeing the budgets of PNM and the other division bureaus. He had become a very loyal and close friend of Director Mahr. After the conflicts with former Warden Malley, loyalty to the Central Office and Director was a primary consideration. Romero, however, had never worked in a prison. Most people in corrections considered Romero's appointment to be a temporary move until a more experienced warden could be hired. "Romero was supposed to be a caretaker," said a corrections official. He remained as warden for almost a year, resigning his position a week after Ed Mahr announced that he was stepping down as head of the Corrections Division.

When Felix Rodriguez was appointed the new Deputy Secretary overseeing the Corrections Division in April 1979, he also chose a warden who had limited penitentiary experience but who was a loyal follower. Jerry Griffin, appointed PNM warden in April 1979, had been an administrative aide to Rodriguez for several months during the early 1970s when Rodriguez had been warden. He soon became an area supervisor for the Adult Probation and Parole Office in Santa Fe. In March 1978, he was named superintendent of the new minimum-security Roswell Correctional Center.

This facility, one of the satellite institutions called for in the Master Plan to relieve overcrowding at PNM and enhance community-based programming, was considered a successful venture under Griffin's leadership. By early 1979, the new facility, which housed about 130 inmates transferred from PNM, had been partially responsible for reducing the PNM inmate population from 1272 inmates on March 3, 1978 to 957 inmates on October 15, 1979. The Roswell Correctional Center experienced no incidents and, after an initially cool reception from the Roswell citizenry, was sending inmates into the community on work and school release. Griffin's successful supervision of the opening and first year of operation of the Roswell Correctional Center had endeared him to Central Office. Roswell was one of the few successes that the department could point to in the late 1970s.

As warden, Griffin had only tenuous control of PNM. By 1979, the middle-level clique of administrators was entrenched, and Griffin did not make a move to assert his authority over them until January 1980. Thus from March 1978, when Warden Malley was removed, until January 1980, when Warden Griffin attempted to rein them in, a group of middle-level administrators ran the prison with no supervision or control over their activities.

The middle-level administrators included the deputy warden, Robert Montoya, who had been brought to PNM in November 1975 by former Corrections Secretary Hanrahan and former Warden Aaron. Reporting to Deputy Warden Montoya were the most sensitive posts within the institution, including the Chief Classification Officer, the Intelligence Officer, the Associate Warden for Inmate Management (who chaired both the disciplinary and segregation committees), the heads of all educational and industry programs, and the Superintendent of Correctional Security (SCS). Beneath the SCS were the shift captains and lieutenants who directly supervised the COs and inmates on a daily basis.

Wardens Romero and Griffin exercised little control over these penitentiary administrators. "Romero didn't know about corrections," said a correctional officer, "so actually Bob Montoya was running the whole show down there." Inmates agreed, "Romero was just a figurehead, he didn't run nothing.... Griffin didn't have no voice here. Montoya ran this penitentiary." And, "The 'middle powers,' the captains, the deputy warden and all these people [were] pretty much running this penitentiary," said another inmate. A correctional officer said, "We couldn't rely on our warden...we relied on Montoya." And another correctional officer said, "The warden himself is just a figurehead. He's not anybody.... The deputy warden, the superintendent of correctional security [SCS] and your captains [run it]."

The day-to-day administration of PNM under these middle-level managers deteriorated. "After 1978, shift captains were virtually unsupervised by the Superintendent of Correctional Security (SCS) Manuel Koroneos and Deputy Warden Montoya" (Office of the Attorney General 1980b: 22). One of the captains who was in charge of PNM for his eight-hour shift every day said, "I didn't pay any attention to no wardens when I was there. Nobody really. I just ran things the way I wanted to, the way I felt was right." This lack of control over the shift captains led to growing inconsistencies in the prison's operation, dissatisfaction among line officers, increased incidents of harassment between inmates and COs, and the emergence of a coercive snitch system.

Growing inconsistencies in the operation of the prison

Inconsistencies among the various captains had been a complaint of inmates and COs since the early 1970s. Prior to 1971, there had been only one captain who oversaw supervision of the various shifts. This captain made frequent spot checks of all the shifts. Operations were considered by both inmates and COs to be very consistent at that time. "There was a lot of consistency. It was damn negative but there's some stability in knowing where the hell you are," said a former convict.

This captain was forced to leave the prison in 1971 after being indicted for allegedly beating an inmate following the October 1971 disturbance. Warden Rodriguez used the occasion of the captain's departure to create four captain's positions in order to build a promotional ladder among his disgruntled custodial staff. This was later increased to seven captain's positions. "The new captains expected to have the same power and autonomy that the one captain had under the old system" (Office of the Attorney General 1980b: 14). As the number of these supervisory positions grew, and as they were filled by long-time members of the custodial staff, the inconsistencies in prison operations tended to increase. Under Wardens Rodriguez, Aaron, and Malley, the captains and lieutenants who supervised the various shifts were under tighter control. "I'd say Malley, Aaron, Rodriguez knew what they wanted and if you didn't live up to it [as a correctional supervisor] you were out," reported a correctional officer. After Malley left, the tendency toward inconsistent operations, created by the large number of supervisory personnel, accelerated tremendously. "It seems like each individual [supervisor] was running different shifts.... There was no cooperation from anybody.... [When Malley left] the whole thing went downhill," said a correctional officer.

There were inconsistencies in both basic security and inmate discipline. Security grills in the main corridor separating the south and north wings from the central area of the prison were supposed to be locked at all times from 4:30 p.m. to 7:30 a.m. But COs reported that these corridor grills were rarely locked at night. A CO supervisor, who had worked at the prison since the 1950s, said, "Then of course these corridor grills.... I worked midnight shift a long time, many years. We used to leave them open because there's really no use of locking them at night time." And another CO said, "Security is obviously lax because the 'regs' were not being obeyed insofar as keeping those grills closed. This condition had prevailed so long, I'm talking about years, years, and years that it was practically a matter of standard operating procedure. The grills hadn't been closed in years." Only on occasion were the two corridor grills secured on the evening and night shifts. Spot checks by the SCS on the proper use of these corridor grills had not been made for years (Office of the Attorney General 1980a), so the locking of these grills was left up to the captain or lieutenant in charge of a particular shift.

Penitentiary procedures also required that, during counts and other activities when officers must enter a dormitory, one officer close and lock the door behind the other officers entering the dorm. The CO stationed outside the dorm entrance is to observe the dormitory through the locked door's small window. If any incident occurs, this officer is to leave the door locked and report the incident to his supervisor or the Control Center. But inmates and correctional officers reported that the proper procedure was not consistently followed. "Most of the time they had it locked. Once in a while they would have it open, the lieutenant would be standing inside the grill with the door standing open," said an inmate. Another inmate said, "I used to see occasions where two officers would go down there and count, especially on open dormitories where you've got sixty men living. I mean two officers are easy to overpower and they would come in here and they wouldn't even lock the door."

Some supervisors followed very closely the proper security procedures; others did not follow them at all. "The way it's run, there's no consistency, none whatsoever," said a correctional officer. "One day you're doing this one way and the next day it all changes…depending on the supervisor." Lax security, as was emphasized in earlier chapters, had long been a problem at PNM, especially during Rodriguez's wardenship in the early 1970s. The tendency toward greater inconsistency in security operations, however, worsened after 1978 when the various shift supervisors ran the prison at their own discretion.

The same inconsistent pattern was also evident in the discipline of inmates. "One captain comes in and says 'I want everybody single file,'" said a CO. "Another captain comes in and says, 'Walk the way you want.' So there is no continuity." Echoing these sentiments, an inmate said, "One captain will tell you 'you can do this' and the next day another captain will come along and say, 'No, what the hell are you doing? I'm going to give you a report.' So he gives you a report for something the other captain told you was right."

Consistency in operation and a set routine provides stability for an institution. "For an inmate, the best way to run an institution is routine," said a CO. "That's your biggest weapon." An inmate reinforced this idea by saying, "The thing that makes a convict do his time and do it in a way that is easier for him and easier for the guards is he gets his routine. You establish this routine where you're doing your time and all of a sudden they come and they disrupt it by moving you to another unit or lock you up [for bringing food] out of the kitchen." Under these circumstances it was difficult for inmates to calculate which behaviors would be punished or when they would be punished. Inmates were thus kept off balance. "There is no consistency," said an inmate. "One captain has a set of rules, another captain has his own set of rules. There is no set of rules that an inmate can go by. You never know where you're at. It's like everything around here is temporary."

This feeling of instability among inmates was understood by top corrections officials, one of whom quite eloquently pinpointed the problem:

> There was a feeling that there was nobody in charge, or that everybody was in charge...that you couldn't really get a consistency in your environment. Things were not reliable. Policies could be changed by the shift captain or lieutenant or line officer at his or her discretion, without any accountability. I think one of the things that all inmates look for is the rules and regulations. And they can choose to break them, but they want consistency. And there wasn't consistency here. There wasn't any sense of accountability, they knew that people could bend the rules or interpret them differently without having to worry about somebody getting on them about how they did it.

But there could not possibly be consistency in operations at PNM as long as the overall administration of New Mexico corrections was in disarray. With no strong leadership within the department, and with the political infighting between various bureaucratic camps, the middle-level administrators drifted in an inconsistent direction that was undermining both security and inmate discipline and ultimately control of the penitentiary. One of the most immediate effects of the inconsistent operation of PNM was growing dissatisfaction among correctional officers.

Correctional officer dissatisfaction and turnover

The turnover among officers reached its highest rate in PNM's history during this period. While no official data on turnover are available from the late 1960s, CO resignations reportedly increased during J.E. Baker's wardenship, creating, according to correctional officials from that period, a turnover rate that may have exceeded 40 percent. The turnover rate remained about 28 percent from 1970 through 1974, increasing to 44 percent in 1975 and 1976, 66 percent in 1977, 80 percent in 1978, and 76 percent in 1979 (Office of the Attorney General 1980b: H-1). After 1976, PNM had one of the highest turnover rates for correctional officers in the United States (Governor's Council on Criminal Justice Planning 1978c).

The dislocations within the department and the poor quality of supervision by the prison's middle-level administrators contributed to a deterioration of working conditions for correctional officers that drove many from their jobs. For the line officer the job had become an impossible task in just following the daily routines. A CO gives this account of some of the typical activities at his post overseeing dormitories in the south wing:

> You're all by yourself. [The shift captain announces mess] call, and you let [Dorm] A–1 out for chow. You open the door and let A–1 out. Right there you have got some sixty-five inmates going out for chow. Fifteen minutes later, you let [Dorm] F–1 [located across the main corridor from A–1] out for chow. At this time five guys from A–1 are coming back, so you have got to open that [entrance to their dormitory]. They call you again, "let another [dorm] out for chow."... You're running like a little rat up and down the stairs. You let people in, you go to the other side and you got fifteen to twenty inmates waiting to get into their dormitory.... I'd leave this grill open and I'd run to get the one across the [main corridor].... I would just leave it open.... Right there, they can just grab you,...there was no security at all.

Another correctional officer said, "[There was] an underlying panic to meet daily routine schedules, causing a tremendous compromise on security." The feeling that personal safety was constantly threatened during the conduct of routine activities led to an enormous level of stress on the job. And the routine activities could be overwhelming, especially with the number of inmates that each CO was charged with supervising. "They only had one guard for four units [two double-story dormitories].... All the guard is doing is standing in front of the grill," said a correctional officer. "That's his job, opening and shutting, opening and shutting the grill. That's what the guard is at the penitentiary." Another CO said, "It's hard. You had to be writing passes for anybody going anywhere. You spend at least an hour or two hours [every eight-hour shift] just writing passes...and you're working there [in charge of four dormitory floors] one guard for 300 inmates." And the hours were often very long. "State law says they can't work us over sixteen hours and by golly you'll work up to sixteen hours [go home for eight hours] and come back for the next shift," said a correctional officer.

These poor working conditions, especially the lack of personnel, had plagued the custodial staff for years. A veteran CO, who had worked at PNM since the mid-1960s, said:

> During the Rodriguez era [from 1970 to late 1975] we were very understaffed. I used to work four dorm [floors], hell, eight dorm [floors] by

myself. You'd have maybe two officers on the south side, two officers on the north side. They [the inmates] could have taken that institution anytime they wanted to. Anytime. We'd come on graveyard [shift] with nine officers [as compared to twenty-five officers on the graveyard shift the early morning of February 2, 1980].

Understaffing was not a new problem. What had changed was the quality of supervision and coordination of the custodial staff.

Formal guard training had always been a sporadic and unsuccessful exercise, and during 1978 and 1979 was in complete disarray because the legislature had "zero budgeted" the department's Technical Support Division which oversaw training. Few officers were getting the formal forty hours of training; of those COs employed in 1979, less than 30 percent had ever had any formal training (Office of the Attorney General 1980a: 16). Yet in the past, correctional officers had at least received fairly good informal instructions on their post duties from supervisors and more experienced COs. But by 1978 they were virtually on their own in figuring out how to perform at a particular post. A CO said, "I learned [how to be a correctional officer] on my own by asking around and finding out what's going on." Another correctional officer, echoing the experience of many new COs, reported, "[As a new CO], they put me on a unit by myself. They didn't instruct me at all. I worked towers for a night and then the next time they took me to A and F dormitories. And I had the keys; I didn't know what to do. They didn't instruct me.... They never made [my duties] clear." The lack of training was a primary source of frustration and high turnover among COs. "The main reason they have such a big turnover in guards is because they're not trained," said a CO. "They throw them in and they're not prepared."

The poor quality of supervision was a primary reason for the lack of even informal training. "[My supervisor] wouldn't say a word to me," said a CO. "He won't come up to me and say 'This is your job. You're supposed to do this.' He just let it happen. He's not really supervising." In addition to the lack of training, most COs felt that after Malley was removed as warden they had little support from the supervisors. "You could call for a captain to come down and help you, [but] you've got to push him, and it would take him three hours to get here," said a CO. "He probably gets tied up someplace else or he'd forgot about you.... You'd just have to rely on yourself or get another [CO] to help you."

The high turnover was related by many staff members to a lack of appreciation for the job the COs were trying to do. "I think the lack of recognition that they're doing their job by their bosses [is the reason for the high turnover]," said a caseworker. "The captains that they have there are incapable of doing that." And a CO said:

When you do something right, nobody remembers, but when you do something wrong, nobody forgets.... So instead of going to somebody and looking stupid by asking a question, they'd just say, "Forget it, this is the way we're going to do it.".... [There was] a feeling that your supervisor was under the same pressure you were and his supervisors also.... [We would] say "don't bother the supervisor, just do the best job possible and hope you make it through the day."

The supervisors not only ignored the needs of their subordinates, but also acted in ways that infuriated them. The scheduling of post and shift duties and promotions were perceived by most COs as unfair. "There's a clique in there. They play a lot of favoritism," said a CO. "And when you are on their shitlist, what they do is they stick you in the tower.... They feel that is discipline.... It's just tormenting the guy, trying to cause him some frustration." Another CO said, "[Promotions] are based on favoritism by the clique. I'd have to have an uncle [working at the prison]...to be a favorite, or do a lot of ass kissing."

Correctional officers also felt under constant harassment not only from inmates but from their supervisors. "We're getting it from the inmates and we're getting it from the lieutenants and the captains," said a CO. "We're getting hit from all directions." COs said: "There are some captains and lieutenants that the officers don't like at all because they try to treat them like inmates"; and "[The supervisors] come on with this real machismo [attitude]. Yell at people, scream at them, humiliate them. And not only inmates, their subordinates. They would do this to their own officers." An inmate agreed, "[COs] don't like the way the institution is running [or] the way they get treated.... The supervisors say, 'Hey, you don't have a kick-ass attitude, you're not with us.'"

The conditions of poor supervision, favoritism, and harassment that correctional officers were subjected to by the middle-level administrators at PNM were a primary reason for the high turnover and dissatisfaction among the custodial force. The turnover rate affected relations among COs. "[Correctional officers] couldn't feel part of a team because there are so many going in and out. You just couldn't form a group," said a CO. The custodial staff under the Deputy Warden, SCS, captains, and lieutenants was fragmented by a lack of communication, support, and respect. Under these conditions, the custodial force, like the upper levels of the department, was disorganized. Among the COs, "[there was] a feeling that the complex problems [of PNM] were bigger than anybody's ability to do anything about," a caseworker reported. A sense of embitterment set in between the line officers and the middle-level administrators. And apathy among the custodial staff became more widespread. As a CO explained:

You don't have communication between shifts. You don't have communication between officers. Nobody communicates because everybody is afraid of everybody else.... [At shift briefings] they'll just tell you that this guy was locked up for this reason or we had a shakedown here.... But they don't tell you that this light out in the fence is busted, or this door doesn't open right, or [about] tension in this unit. Nothing of that. They never told you anything like that.... They don't give a damn anymore. That's what it boils down to.

Under these conditions, new COs were entering an increasingly chaotic situation with little guidance or supervision. Formerly, new correctional officers were socialized by more experienced staff members into the subtle and delicate ways of defusing potential problems and dealing with both the day-to-day stress and verbal assaults from inmates. As a new "kick ass" attitude was emerging among correctional officers, including a number of correctional supervisors, these subtle, level-headed ways of dealing with inmates were no longer being communicated to younger COs. As a result, tension between the correctional force and inmates escalated as a game of mutual harassment came to dominate inmate-staff relations.

Harassment between inmates and custodial staff

Relations between inmates and COs, strained since the late 1960s, deteriorated into a pattern of mutual harassment. "Under [Warden Rodriguez] it seemed like you could do easier time," said an inmate. "I mean the guards were still there but it seemed like they didn't mess with you.... There wasn't the harassment.... It didn't seem like the harassment was as intense as under [wardens] Malley, Romero, and Griffin." Another inmate said, "Since I first got here it's always been convict against guard. They haven't ever really gotten along. It wasn't as bad till maybe a year, year and a half before the [February 1980] riot.... The guards had a tendency to overdo their authority and that created even a bigger barrier between us."

Many members of the custodial force became fixed in a game of harassment with inmates. The game proceeded through verbal exchanges that led to confrontations. An inmate said, "They would yell at us and they would cuss at us; that would lead us to cussing at them, so they'd take us and lock us up.... They never really approached you about something in the right manner." Another inmate said, "[The guards] can create a hassle out of just a little insignificant thing...[by] just say[ing] 'button your shirt' the wrong way.... the attitude is so wrong, so wrong that the guy responds to it negatively. Then words are exchanged and instead of just buttoning his shirt, he is liable to get a report for insolence." A CO agreed, "[Many COs] have no common sense.... They try to get [the inmates] angry.... They pick on a guy or try to get him angry and cause them to do something that'll lock him up.... About twenty-five percent [of the COs are like that]."

Largely due to the lack of supervision and guidance, younger, newly hired COs were especially prone to being caught up in this game of mutual harassment. New officers felt unnerved by the "catcalls" from inmates. They were given little guidance in dealing with this verbal abuse. The fear induced by these verbal taunts from inmates was often covered up by a "tough guy" image cultivated by a growing number of new officers. Said a veteran correctional officer:

> When inmates see a new correctional officer, they give him a hard time. They harass him to a certain extent, whistle at him, call him names.... And that right away makes a new officer nervous. He feels very uncomfortable because he's never had that happen to him before, or if he has, he's always been able to do something about it. In this situation, you can't do anything about it because they want you to react. They see what kind of reaction, and as soon as you react, they know which button to push the next time that they want to get you mad.

But many of the young COs were reacting by harassing inmates in return. An inmate said, "They were hiring more and more, I guess you might say, people on our own level. [Inmates] would think they were 'bad' and the guards would think *they* were 'bad.' So it would just cause a lot of conflict.... some of these guards were real young...and they're thinking they're the coolest things on earth; they've got a star on their chests and feel that they have command and can yell at you." A correctional officer agreed: "There's some officers that think they are 'bad' officers, think that they got power." And another inmate said, "These young guards, 18 to 21 years old, were harassing us in the hallway. I mean just getting up in your face and start hollering about 'get up against the wall' and 'single file' and 'tuck your shirt tail in.'" And a former CO said, "The new correctional officers, they're coming in with an attitude of all they want to do is kick ass. That's all they want to do."

But even veteran officers, including several of the supervisors, also got caught up in the taunting of inmates. An inmate said, "The harassment was really bad, even the lieutenants and captains were talking bad to us." Captains and lieutenants would verbally humiliate inmates. One lieutenant, who inmates had nicknamed "Green Eyes," was mentioned by several inmates and correctional officers as being particularly abusive:

> *Former inmate:* [There were] plenty of situations with Lt. "Green Eyes." He would let people walk by with their shirt out and all of a sudden pick one out and start swearing at him, cutting him up and down and getting

real close to him and looking like he was going to slug him or knock him down.... Sometimes I had the feeling that you had to take [Green Eyes] with a grain of salt, that he was all bark and no bite. But then sometimes, I've seen him go...off his rocker and start driving somebody up the corner and saying, "Hey, I told you this, you thought I was kidding did you? What the hell's the matter with you?" And you see him dragging somebody out of the mess hall.

Correctional Officer: ["Green Eyes"] would go out of his way to harass an inmate, he would see an inmate walk down the hall and for no reason he would point to the captain's office and sit down and chew him out for no reason at all. And if the inmate said anything at all, the inmate went to [disciplinary lockup] Cellblock 3.... He would just hope and pray that they would just open their mouth just to throw them in Cellblock 3.

"Green Eyes" was not the only supervisor involved in harassing inmates. An inmate said:

Two lieutenants would come into the unit and just verbally harass every individual in there. This one particular lieutenant [at the 10:30 p.m. count], his standard procedure was to come in and call everybody little girls and babies and mock them...saying "get your pants off and get in bed. What are you some little girl or a homosexual you don't want these men to see you taking your pants off with the lights on?" Just unnecessary harassment.... And then when an individual would stick up for his self-beliefs, he would be locked up.

A correctional officer agreed that inmates "had a hell of a time with custodial staff...harassing them...calling them girls." An inmate likened the harassment of inmates by these COs and supervisors to "baiting bears or poking dogs with a stick, agitating them, daring them to make their play."

The unsupervised captains, lieutenants, and COs were creating a situation in which the mutual harassment between staff and inmates was spilling over into incidents of violence. One of the captains was stabbed by an inmate in 1978, and several COs were physically attacked. Many of these incidents were an outgrowth of harassment in which COs and inmates were mutually provoked. That CO supervisors allowed such behavior to get out of hand, and that many of them personally participated in the harassment, reveals a breakdown in accountability and acceptable correctional practice. As experienced professional corrections personnel realize, such a social atmosphere created by ongoing incidents of harassment is potential dynamite. As an inmate said, "If you put a house cat inside of a cage...locked up for so many years and you constantly are teasing it, harassing it and you open that cage, that cat isn't going to be tame anymore...that cat's going to come out fighting."

Growth of the coercive "snitch system"

Related to the ongoing harassment of inmates by COs and middle-level administrators and to the predominance of a coercive control structure, was the growth of a coercive information gathering system. This system had its roots in the aftermath of the June 1976 inmate strike when staff members attempted to identify the strike leaders. This coercive snitch system contrasted radically with the informant system that had prevailed in the early 1970s, when informants volunteered information and certain COs and administrators had personal informants. A correctional officer said, "[Rodriguez, when warden in the early 1970s] was more secretive with inmates that came and told him things. Maybe he didn't go looking for information but inmates felt that they could give him a lot of information that wouldn't get out where they would get into trouble." A former convict agreed with this assessment:

> *Interviewer:* Were you ever aware of any direct solicitation of information, using threats or promises? Was that anything that was widespread [when you were incarcerated at PNM in the 1960s and early 1970s]?
> *Former convict:* Not in my experience. I never heard of anyone saying that they were promised anything for it.... I would say direct solicitation through that period didn't exist in any open way.

But after 1975, the custom of voluntary giving of information by inmates to staff diminished and was replaced by a system in which inmates were directly solicited for information. "Under Felix [Rodriguez] there was a lot of...personalized snitches," said a former inmate. "After Rodriguez was out, that broke up and the snitching [was solicited by] forcing people to snitch."

The breakdown of the old informant system was related to the curtailment of programs:

> *Caseworker:* When [former Deputy Warden] Herrera and [former Warden] Rodriguez and a lot of other people left [in 1975], the snitch system was left in a limbo situation. New people came in and they didn't have the information gathering techniques that other people had had before. And this crippled the administration....
> *Interviewer:* [Is it possible that] Aaron and Malley...by cutting out programs...may have tended to cut off a lot of the communication included in the [old informant] system?
> *Caseworker:* Yes. You're right. I'd say so strongly, yes.

By 1980, inmates were saying, "They never had snitches like they did now." According to inmates, by the late 1970s, "This penitentiary was run by a snitch system."

The breakdown of communication patterns between inmates and staff after 1975 created a situation in which the custodial force was under greater pressure to gather information, especially with more escapes and increasing incidents of violence. Since inmates were not forthcoming with voluntary information, many members of the custodial staff, especially some of the captains, began soliciting information through threats and promises. Inmates reported that they were promised early parole consideration, protection, and transfer to the minimum-security satellite institutions. They also reported that they were threatened with being locked up in disciplinary segregation or, in other cases, were refused protective custody if they did not inform. Among the reports given by inmates were the following:

> *Inmate 1:* They'd say we're going to give you more time if you don't tell us about certain things that we want to know that's going on in this cellblock or dormitory.... Some get paid parole and some get sent to the farm, better jobs, privileges.[1]

> *Inmate 2:* I saw plenty of use of informants by the captains. They'd promise them protection and that they'd be safe, and it would be kept confidential.... They use threats too. Like lockup. Take them down to the hole, strip them and leave them there for a while. And as soon as they'd cooperate, they'd let them out. Move them to a better cellblock or better dorm with promises of protection.

> *Inmate 3:* There was the old parole scheme. "If you don't tell us, when you go to the parole board we're gonna make sure you don't make it. We run this prison, they go by our word, if we tell them you can't go, that's it." And there's a lot of young dudes coming into this prison that want out, they're scared, so naturally they go for it.

Correctional officers confirmed these reports from inmates:

> *Correctional Officer 1:* I know they were telling them that they were going to take them to the [Honor] Farm.... That they would take them to the Farm if they would give them information.... I think that was the only way they were going to get it out of them, because they were already threatened and everything.

> *Interviewer:* Do correctional officers ever try to get information from inmates through the use of promises or threats?
> *Correctional Officer 2:* Yes, I guess that does happen a lot of times...I think they go more by promises than they go by threats. They say, you help me out on this and I'll send you to the Honor Farm or Sierra Blanca [two minimum-security facilities].

> *Interviewer:* Were you aware of any instances where an inmate would come and ask for protection and the administration would say, "Yes, if you give us information."?

Correctional Officer 3: I'd say that was policy…. If you had a guy come up to you and say [he needed protection, the captain would say], "Okay who hit you? If you don't tell us who hit you, we're not going to do anything, so either fork out the names or that's it."
Interviewer: And if they didn't talk, they didn't get protected?
Correctional Officer 3: That's right.

Correctional Officer 4: If something happened, they'd take them out alone and they'd tell them "you tell me what went on or you're going to get locked up and so much for your [parole] board." They were threatened that way. If a guy had a [parole] board coming up, they'd threaten him with his board.

Captains' informants, as a reward for snitching, were often immune from punishment for rule violations.

Correctional Officer: Now I have had instances where I would bring an inmate to the captain's office. Now this wasn't with all captains. And I thought [the violation] was bad enough to go ahead and write the report and lock him up in Cellblock 3. But he would just talk to him and send him back to the unit. So I finally got it through my head, well, I must have picked one of his snitches. So that made it a little awkward on the officer…because if you had a captain's snitch, the captain wasn't going to do anything to hurt his record for the parole board.

Inmate: There was this dude was always getting busted for sniffing [inhalants] and everybody knew he was a snitch, because they busted him with a rag in his mouth sniffing and they let him go…. This dude used to get off with a lot of things. He already knew that all he'd have to do is just snitch…. He's been busted five or six times for sniffing and he don't ever go to lockup.

Another coercive tactic was to intimidate an inmate by threatening to "hang a snitch jacket" on him. This tactic, which involved the threat of labeling an inmate a snitch (or informant) was used to solicit information. It was also used as a coercive means of control and as a means of retaliation against inmates by a few COs. Inmates reported the following:

Inmate 1: I seen guards put "jackets" on other inmates…[guard's name] put a jacket on an inmate, as a snitch…. He said it in front of other inmates like this, "If you don't start straightening up, I'm going to tell the inmates that you're a snitch." And other inmates heard it. "Wow this dude's a snitch!" So they started spreading the word around. But that guard knew what he was saying…. This dude had to go to protective custody.

Inmate 2: One of their favorite tricks…[was] if you wasn't a snitch, they would tell one of their snitches that, "Hey, he's a snitch." And they'd pass it around to somebody else…. "He's tellin' on us."… And you get your head caved in.

Interviewer: Why would they do that [i.e., label you as a "snitch"]?
Inmate 2: To get you to snitch.

Inmate 3: And then they threaten you with putting a "jacket" on you.... I had two friends, we were sitting up and talking, it was about 12 a.m. [Name of lieutenant] came in, he says, "I told you to go to bed." And he took them out here. When they came back I said, "What happened? What he tell you?" He says, "Man, that dude is too much.... He said if we didn't act right he was going to put a [snitch] jacket on us and that he could make it stick because he could write the papers out and everything."

Correctional officers also discussed the use of labeling inmates as informants as a coercive tactic:

Correctional Officer: If I was a guard and he was an inmate and I didn't like him, I'd punch it around and say, "Hey, man, let's put a snitch jacket on this guy." And another inmate come up right behind me and I'd say "Hey, man, this dude dropped a dime on this guy over here." They'll put a "jacket" on you and life expectancy with a "jacket" on you isn't too long. And that's what [gives names of several PNM administrators, captains, and lieutenants] all of them would do. If they didn't like you, they'd put a jacket on you, plain and simple.... I caught [name of CO] lying about another inmate to four or five inmates and the other inmates turned around and looked at him and said, "We'll take care of this."
Interviewer: What was the purpose of doing this?
Correctional Officer: To get even...if I was to walk up to an inmate and just started kicking the hell out of him, I would have a lawsuit on me, but what goes on behind closed doors, only the inmates know.

Inmates held informants in very low esteem. They were considered to be weak inmates who could not withstand the pressure put on them by other inmates and staff. They were also considered to be traitors in a situation that was increasingly defined by both inmates and COs as a "war." Some of the inmates' comments about informants included the following:

Interviewer: Tell me how most inmates viewed informants?
Former inmate: As a traitor.... It's like in a war.... It's us against them. And it's the same mentality down there. If you go across to the other side you're no more, no less than a traitor and a spy.

Inmate 1: There's people in this penitentiary that are going to hurt a snitch.... I'd say there's maybe ten percent of the people in this penitentiary that the police...actually caught [them] doing something wrong. The rest of the people are here behind a snitch some way or another. Somebody told on him and people don't like that.

Interviewer: Is there any consideration given to the fact that maybe they're forced into [giving information] by the administration?

Inmate 2: Nope. A rat's a rat regardless of how he gets that way.... They'll kill you once they find out who you are.

The growth of the coercive snitch system coincided with the rise in the number of inmates in protective custody. Prior to 1976, there was no special unit designated for protective custody. Those inmates needing protection were housed in a few of the cells in the Cellblock 3 disciplinary unit. "A couple of years before 1975,...we had only about fifteen guys [in Cellblock 3 for protective custody], but these people were snitches from the outside, people that testified against somebody [in court]," said a caseworker. A corrections official said, "[Rodriguez] had the protection and disciplinary units together...all in [Cellblock] 3.... It was the federal wardens [Aaron and Malley] that separated the two units."

In 1976, Cellblock 4 was designated protective custody to house inmates who, for one reason or another, could not live in the general prison population. These inmates may have been actually attacked or raped by other inmates or were young, physically weak inmates who feared for their safety. Some entered the prison with child murder or molestation convictions, and would for this reason be subject to attack by other inmates. Some may have been police informants on the outside. Others may have informed on the inside.

The number of inmates requiring protection skyrocketed after 1976. "We had just about everybody doubled up in there when I used to handle the [protective custody] unit," said a caseworker. "In 1977, we were just overloaded in there, everybody in the world was in there for protection." A New Mexico corrections official called the protective custody unit "the biggest disgrace in corrections in the country. It was double- and triple-bunked...as high as 200 [inmates]." In fact, Cellblock 4, with a designed capacity for 90 inmates, held 212 inmates at one point in 1978 (Office of the Attorney General 1980b: 27). Combining the number of inmates in the Cellblock 3 disciplinary unit (up to 200) and the Cellblock 4 protective custody unit (up to 212), nearly one-third of the total inmate population of PNM (reaching a high of 1,272 inmates) were locked down in some form of segregation during 1978. By contrast, in the early 1970s, less than 5 percent of the inmate population were in segregation status (Office of the Attorney General 1980b: 18). This gives a clear indication of the coercive nature of controls during the late 1970s.

Some of those locked in Cellblock 4 for protection were coerced into giving information in exchange for the protection. Their placement in protection, whether they actually informed on any inmates or not, stigmatized them as weak inmates and as snitches. A PNM staff member said, "Anybody who goes from population to [Cellblock] 4 was automatically labeled. He had the stigma of being an informant whether or not he was." Inmates agreed:

Inmate 1: So they put [this inmate] in Cellblock 4, all of a sudden he's a snitch. Never snitched on nobody, just came in here young and the Captain figured well if we put him out there, leave him in general population, he's gonna be in trouble. So he goes over there [to Cellblock 4] and all of a sudden he's [considered to be] a snitch.

Inmate 2: [Going to Cellblock 4] would put a label automatically as a snitch. [And] even worse, it would come out in the "change sheet," your name.... Any movement in the penitentiary it would say so [on the change sheet], you know from [Dorm] A1 to Cellblock 4. And everybody knew what Cellblock 4 was. [The "change sheet" was a daily listing of inmate transfers that was posted at the entrances of inmate living units, so that COs could keep track of inmates and see that they were moved as assigned. Inmates had very little problem getting a good look at the "change sheet."]

The coercive snitch system used by some of the middle-level administrators at PNM, besides producing notoriously unreliable information, affected social relations within the organization. Inmates and COs became even more socially distant:

Inmate: You can't get involved with a guard, [or] another [inmate] is going to put a bad jacket on you. You start talking to a guard, there's this guy that don't like you, he's going to run and tell his buddy that you snitched off this dude that just got busted, and you have nothing to do with it.

And the coercive snitch system also contributed to a growing sense of suspicion and mistrust among inmates. "Three-fourths of the inmates are snitching," said an inmate. "You can't hardly trust anybody. Seems like there are a lot more now than there was before...1976. Hell, you can't even trust your best friend anymore. They'll snitch on you." And another inmate said, "Hardly anybody trusted anyone.... It was because all that snitching that was going on in there."

The coercive tactics of the snitch system had the same effect as the other coercive controls instituted after 1976 of creating divisions among inmates. Many inmates recognized that these coercive tactics undermined their solidarity and allowed the administration to manipulate them. When asked why correctional staff members would "hang snitch jackets" on inmates, inmates said the following:

Inmate 1: So that the inmates would be fucking each other in here and they wouldn't fight against the guards...it would be more war of the inmates against each other.... While they're busy fighting against each other, they don't have time to get together and really try to straighten out the place and better it against the administration.

Inmate 2: The tactics used by [the captains] and [Deputy Warden] Montoya for five years is to keep us stirred among ourselves.... As long as they can keep us fighting each other, they can do anything with us they want.

Correctional officers also understood that infighting among inmates meant that they could not organize against the staff. "There are [inmate] groups that try to control it and there are other groups that are trying to [control] and they're fighting each other," said a CO, who added, "I'd say it has been to our benefit because it's kept them divided."

The late-1970s coercive regime, operated by middle-level administrators at PNM, effectively undermined inmate solidarity. But these tactics also led to increasing violence as inmate relations fragmented.

FRAGMENTATION AND VIOLENCE WITHIN THE INMATE SOCIAL STRUCTURE

The PNM administration's attempts to break up the organizational solidarity among inmates, beginning after the June 1976 inmate strike, were largely successful. The coercive disciplinary measures, increased use of segregation, the snitch system, and the transfer of inmate leaders and "trouble-makers" out of state decimated the organizational structure of the inmate society. These attempts to bring inmates under control through divide-and-conquer tactics created a vacuum of power among inmates, a vacuum that was filled increasingly through violence.

Breakdown of inmate solidarity and growing violence

The solidarity among inmates, and the control that inmate leaders had exercised over other inmates prior to 1976, had completely broken down by 1978. Contrasting pictures of the inmate social structure during the years of accommodation, under Rodriguez's wardenship, and the later period of fragmentation were reported by both inmates and staff members. Under former Warden Rodriguez "you had big cliques in the dormitories and cell blocks. If you weren't a member of that clique, you just couldn't live there," said an inmate. According to another inmate, these inmate cliques' leaders

> could counsel to act as a liaison between the administration and the inmates.... There was recognized cliques and [Warden Rodriguez] knew the names of the leaders of them cliques. Something got out of line, he would jump in.... He knew people here and he knew the cliques. *Interviewer:* They would keep the lid on the place?

Inmate: Exactly.
Interviewer: And somehow that's changed?
Inmate: Yes, it's lost.

A caseworker gives a similar assessment of the stabilizing influence before 1976 of inmate cliques, which by the late 1970s had been fractured:

> When I was first there in the [Warden] Rodriguez administration [prior to 1976], I could just about identify the different cliques and different powers, and there was an inmate code where inmates respected boundaries.... I could see the balance of power.... There was an intelligence behind it.... For example, a black inmate would go to the disciplinary committee and then they would try to assign him to a different unit. So the blacks began appealing it; it was going to upset the balance of power if they had [less than] ten blacks in a unit;...ten was the limit by which they could maintain peace. If you'd have one less than that, then guys would start taking their canteen and the fights would break out and upset the balance of power.... [But] the federal wardens [Aaron and Malley] had no respect for these inmate powers...had no respect for their ways. [Inmates] were trying to control their own environment and make it livable. [Aaron and Malley] had no respect for those kind of things, so they started breaking things left and right which created an imbalance.

After the inmate solidarity displayed during the June 1976 strike moved the prison administration to smash inmate organization and leadership, the inmate society became more fragmented. As a corrections official, referring to the late 1970s, said, "When you destroy cliques, you have the battle to take over." The segregation of inmate leaders removed inmates who had been troublesome to the administration, but also removed people from the inmate society who had provided stabilizing influences. "They had locked down almost all the instigators in that place," said a correctional supervisor. "[So for] leadership, they didn't have it." And an inmate said, "The leaders that could keep the lid on are locked down because they are a threat to this administration." The removal of these inmate leaders destroyed the mechanisms by which peace had been maintained among inmate groups.

> *Interviewer:* Did they lock up a lot of the inmates who had been real influential?
> *Inmate:* Yes they did.
> *Interviewer:* Would those be inmates who would normally kind of keep the lid on things in here?
> *Inmate:* I think so, usually.... There's white people that's been here for a long time and there's Chicano people that's been here for a long time.... [If there was potential trouble,] maybe six or seven white people would

go to the yard and we would talk to six or seven Chicano people that's got the say. We would get together and we'd talk it out.... These are the people that they'll lock up in a minute and they'll keep them locked up.

The strength of inmate groups deteriorated. The key problem facing the administration in 1976, a solidly organized inmate body in opposition to the administration, had been eliminated along with inmate groups organized around illicit activities such as drug trafficking. So, by the late 1970s, inmate groups were "not as strong as they used to be several years ago," said a CO, who related the decline of inmate groups to the administration's transfer of inmates out of state. "We found we had a program between other states...that we could transfer inmates out.... We got rid of our problem."

But actually, the prison administration traded one problem for another. Removing the immediate organizational contradiction of an organized inmate opposition, which emerged in 1976, gave rise to a new contradiction within the prison organization. The tactics employed to break up inmate solidarity led to a series of structural changes within the inmate society that spawned violence and disorder. This growing violence is tied to the removal of inmates who had provided the impetus for the solidarity and stable relations within the inmate society. As inmate groups broke down into small self-protective cliques, forces within the inmate society that formerly were capable of holding back disorder and violence among inmates diminished. By 1978, "there were cliques, but they weren't big enough to hold anything back if it turned up," said a former inmate, who added that inmate groups "were more powerful when I went in [in 1975] than what they were when I left [in 1978]." Other inmates concurred with this assessment.

> *Interviewer:* Were there inmates [during the six months before the 1980 riot] who were powerful enough to keep inmates from fighting each other?
> *Inmate 1:* Not really.... There are guys here from Albuquerque or Santa Fe, the biggest towns. Maybe there was eight of them that would hang around together, but they don't run anything.
>
> *Interviewer:* Before the [1980] riot there weren't that many inmates who could keep the lid on other inmates...?
> *Inmate 2:* No. It was kind of like everybody was looking out for themselves.

The lack of inmate leaders in the late 1970s meant that new inmates entering PNM were no longer under the restraints of an established order among inmates. Inmate leaders could no longer socialize new arrivals to this environment. A prisoner discusses inmate leaders:

Leader[s] are individuals that have respect amongst the other inmates.... It's more of a guidance type thing. You might have two or three young-sters that come in and they're real energetic and hyper and want to run crazy. And you have these older individuals that project themselves on these people and try to keep them in line, keep them from getting them-selves hurt and causing friction among everybody else. But as far as lead-ers [here at PNM in the late 1970s],...no, there's not.

New inmates arriving at PNM contributed to the breakdown of the inmate social order. "You didn't know who to trust anymore because they were coming in so new all the time," said an inmate. Some of these new inmates directly challenged the power and control exercised by older inmates who had not already been removed by the administration. A for-mer PNM caseworker said:

> Just before I left [in 1978] there was a new wave of upstarts coming in. And these new upstarts had no respect for the inmate code. They could care less about the tatoos and signs. They were just power hungry and wanted to coerce people...killing just for a small, little thing.... What they did is they began invading [territory].... Maybe they were first-timers to the penitentiary, but there was enough of them to be a force to reckon with, they would start invading territory and then..."Let's get it on," you know, pull out the lead pipes.... And all of a sudden this inmate that's never been challenged begins to have to cop out some of his territory.... I remember an old heavy, he was a big heavy when I went in there [in the early 1970s].... I saw his domain just diminish. They sliced it left and right to the point [that] just before I left [in 1978],...[this] old heavy, as a matter of fact, a number of the [old] heav-ies...ended up in protection.

While many observers relate the growing inmate violence to newly arriving inmates, it does not appear that the violent behavior was being imported from outside. Rather, new inmates, as never before, were enter-ing a disorganized social situation with undefined roles and lack of leader-ship. As they confronted, and were confronted by, this chaotic situation, many of the new inmates resorted to violence.

That the violence was not imported from outside is supported by data on inmates' convictions. In 1970, 45 percent of all crimes for which New Mexico prisoners were convicted were violent crimes. By 1975, the figure had dropped to 38 percent, and by 1979 it was 33 percent (Department of Corrections 1971, 1976, 1980).[2] Also, a profile of PNM inmates compiled in 1977 (when the inmate violence was increasing dramatically) by consul-tants for the New Mexico Master Plan showed that:

> in comparison to national averages, New Mexico's inmate population is *more* likely to have committed property, fraud and drug offenses, and

less likely to have been sentenced for murder, manslaughter and robbery.... [S]ignificant proportions of younger offenders are incarcerated for typically nonviolent offenses.... Certain significant characterizations appear appropriate regarding the criminal sophistication of New Mexico's inmate populations. The level of criminal sophistication is relatively low, more comparable to county jail populations in larger states...consisting of persons incarcerated for property crimes (Governor's Council on Criminal Justice Planning 1978b: 12).

These relatively nonviolent and unsophisticated inmates were entering an inmate social structure in which power was based more on violence than it had been in the past. Power in the early 1970s could be exercised through nonviolent means, so there was no need for violence and intimidation. The inmate social structure in the early 1970s was based on the nonviolent sources of power created by programs and illicit drug trafficking, the respective formal and informal mechanisms of remunerative control prevalent during the early 1970s. By 1978, however, the administration's coercive controls had inadvertently produced an inmate social structure in which, as one inmate said, "the stronger dominates...[through] physical violence." In the process, the traditional inmate code declined as an important feature of prisoner relations. As an inmate said, "It used to be where everybody would do their own time and that was it. Don't mess around with me and I won't mess around with you.... Now everybody has got the attitude where I'll mess with you before you mess with me."

The level of violence and disorder increased dramatically from the early 1970s to the late 1970s. From 1969 through 1975 there were no killings at PNM. From 1976 through 1979 there were six inmates killed by other inmates.[3] Assaults and fighting also increased dramatically. The following quotes attest to the dramatic increase in violence:

Interviewer: Have there been more fights after Rodriguez left [as warden in 1975]?
Inmate 1: Oh yeah. Before there wasn't. Sure there was a black eye here or a bloody nose, but nothing serious. But afterwards...they just started going wild.... People getting killed and stabbed.... This place is worse than the streets now.... every day you got to look out for your life.

Interviewer: What about the level of violence [from 1970 to 1980], was it high or low under Rodriguez [warden from 1970 to 1975] compared to the other wardens [in charge of the prison from 1975 to 1980]?
Inmate 2: I felt it was low compared to all those other wardens. Very low. I felt that there was hardly any violence that you could say, "Well, that was really bad." There was isolated incidents that got pretty bad. There was...a killing, once, in the yard [in 1968]. But it wasn't brutal.... He

was defending himself and just happened to kill the guy. But there wasn't rampant violence like where you could say, "yeah, this is a real bad situation."
Interviewer: What happened under [these later wardens after 1975]?
Inmate 2: ...there was just too much violence, you know in the dorms, in the units, all over.
Interviewer: It was getting worse?
Inmate 2: Yeah. Progressively worse.
Interviewer: So under each warden, it just...
Inmate 2: Just kept on increasing.

Inmate 3: Fists, that's all it was up under Mr. Rodriguez.... Your killing came up right here.... There was more killing in that penitentiary up under these [wardens, since 1976,] than I've seen now in about 25 years.

Correctional Officer: [Violence] has increased tremendously.... They're not there just to fight, they're out there to kill each other.

By 1978, violence had become a routine daily event at PNM. "A day didn't go by that somebody was fighting or wanting to stab somebody," said an inmate. Inmate fights occurred because of trivial disputes. "I've seen dudes get the hell beat out of them for a pack of cigarettes," reported an inmate. "It's very easy to make enemies here. Very easy. For any little reason," said another inmate.

While young Anglo inmates were attacked by Hispanic inmates, fighting generally did not appear to be primarily between members of different ethnic groups. "You'd have Chicanos beating up on Chicanos, and whites on whites, and blacks...on blacks," said a correctional officer supervisor.

Younger inmates, new to the prison, were especially subject to being attacked. An inmate said:

I hate young kids getting hurt, like getting raped, it's really against my principles, and this thing here is rampant.... [The administration] takes some young kid...and they throw him in a dormitory...and he doesn't have a chance .... The guy could scream his head off and the man [correctional officer] is not going to hear and even if he does hear, he'll come up and look, there is nothing he can do except call [for assistance]...by then it's over.... There's kids that get abused in other manners, not just rape. They get beat up, their commissary gets taken, they are taken advantage of one way or the other.

Inmates in the late 1970s tended to be younger. The average age of the inmate population dropped by three years, from 30 in the early 1970s to 27 in the late 1970s (Office of the Attorney General 1980b).

Some of these younger inmates were also a source of trouble in this disorganized and fragmented inmate social structure. "They have no idea of what prison life is like and they act like they ain't suppose to act, you know, too wild," said an older inmate. Another inmate said, of these younger inmates, "a lot of them are coming in thinking they're gonna run stuff, you know, they're 'bad.'" And another inmate said, "The youngsters that they're bringing in...they think when they get here that they've got to make their bones right away, that they've got to show something right away to be accepted. And this is where we have the most trouble." The socialization mechanisms of the inmate society that constrained and guided the behavior of younger, aggressive inmates in the past had broken down. Now, "a lot of these youngsters come in here and man, they get off in a wreak [creating havoc through their aggression]," said an inmate.

The aggressiveness of many of these younger inmates was elicited by the frightening level of violence they were confronting upon entering the prison. An older inmate sees this high level of inmate violence as a reaction to fear:

> *Interviewer:* Are the new inmates different?
> *Inmate:* I think they are different, younger as they're coming in. Now, I shouldn't be saying this, but as being younger, actually, they're more afraid in what they're doing.
> *Interviewer:* If they are more afraid, are they more likely to get picked on maybe?
> *Inmate:* No. I think they would be more inclined to pick on somebody just to show people that they're not afraid, while in turn they really are.... [Then] they get into trouble without thinking and they don't know how to get out of it.

These observations point to the underlying fear of these new, younger inmates. With a paucity of inmate leaders to guide and ease the transition for younger inmates, they were left to their own devices to deal with the fear. The fear of being assaulted, especially being sexually attacked, was a prevalent feature of inmate life, especially for younger inmates. "Homosexual attacks are so common and frequent as to be considered daily occurrences," said an inmate. In a 1979 newspaper interview, another PNM inmate said, "[T]here is at least one reported case [of rape] a day," and estimated that there may be "10 to 15 more non-reported cases daily" (*Albuquerque Journal* 9/16/79: B1).

Violence, the deadly dilemma, and emerging inmate roles

These new, younger inmates were faced with a deadly dilemma. The fear created by violent confrontations, or by the mere anticipation of them, produced inmates who either submitted to the exploitation of other inmates (became "punks"), sought protection from officials (became "snitches"), or fought (to prove themselves as "good people" to other inmates by developing a reputation as violent). Most inmates agreed that the only rational choice when faced with the irrational confrontation of a sexual assault was to fight viciously and develop a reputation as someone who others "did not mess with." "If he wants to keep his manhood," said an inmate, "he's going to have to fight." The other choices, submission or official protection, would lead to a prison experience of perpetual victimization. New inmates were thus advised by other inmates to fight or even kill if sexually assaulted. An inmate said he told an acquaintance from the street who had just arrived at the prison, "'Some people want your ass in here.' I told him, 'Here's a shank [homemade prison knife]. Man, I tell you, don't mess around.'" He advised the inmate to waste no time in attacking these other inmates. These sentiments were shared by many inmates, including one who said,

> If someone grabs your ass or makes an advance towards you or propositions you verbally, you do your level best to put that man away right there.... It's something that has to be done. If it's not done, you're doomed. You might as well just drop your pants and bend over because from then on your marked. Even if you don't kill the person, if you maim him or you disfigure him real bad, somebody else will respect that.

Inmates generally believed that they had to fight to ensure their long-term survival in the prison.

> *Inmate 1:* I seen sixteen guys take one guy one night.... It was the man's fault cause the man was afraid to fight.... I did [fight]. When I got whipped, I went to the hospital for awhile, but I healed up and I moved right back to that same dormitory.... It showed them that I wasn't scared of them.... I was doing an 11 to 55 year sentence; it was important to me.

> *Inmate 2:* I used to go down the hall, sometimes dudes would whistle at me and all that. Tell me "Hey mama." But I never put up with it. I'd go straight up to whoever it was and I'd tell them, "I got butt. You want it, take it." And that's why I'm still here [and not paroled], cause I never put up with it. I'd fight right away.... But some guys in here...they're scared. People can sit down and manipulate them. I seen it where they made guys cry.

These "ceremonies" of fear and confrontation consigned new inmates to the emerging roles of the new inmate social structure: the weak roles of punks and snitches, and the dominant roles of hardcore or "bad" convicts, who were defined by other convicts as "good people."

> *Inmate:* A lot of guys they get pushed a little bit and right away they show their weakness. You show your weakness if you let it. They want to find out what kind of dude you are...if you're a good person...or a snitch or if you're a homosexual.

A "good person" in this situation is someone who is not weak, does not give into pressure, refuses to be humiliated, and is not afraid to fight. He is a convict who has "proven himself" to be tough in an environment filled with rape, violence, and fear.

Rapes and assaults in prison are acts of degradation aimed at humiliating the victim and marking the perpetrator as powerful and dominant (Bowker 1980; Silberman 1978). In the late 1970s, such confrontational situations between inmates sharply increased, forcing more inmates into the deadly dilemma of choosing a course of action against the assaults. Some submitted and were marked as punks or homosexuals. This submission did not label them necessarily as sexual deviants but, more importantly, as "morally weak" individuals who would not stand up for themselves. (See Fleisher [1989] for a discussion of inmate roles.) They were then subject to perpetual attacks or to extortion by stronger inmates who forced them to pay for "protection" from attacks. Inmates who chose to seek protective custody, who in the inmates' vocabulary "pc'd up," were also seen as "weak" inmates who could not withstand the pressures of prison life. Added to being marked as weak was the stigma of being a snitch, since it was widely perceived among inmates that protective custody was a payoff for informing. Again, the key here, within the inmate social structure that was emerging in the late 1970s, was not so much the label of snitch implying an informant, but rather implying a weak individual. For "regular" inmates (i.e., the good people) who were "on line" standing up for themselves in the daily battles with other inmates and the prison staff, an inmate who gives into pressure from other inmates by not standing up for himself, and then gives into pressure from the administration by informing, was truly a person of weak moral character. A snitch label thus implies the weakest of inmates who were so low as to sell out their fellow inmates because of fear and intimidation. These inmates were allowing both other inmates and the administration to humiliate them. Succumbing to other people's attempts at humiliation is the worst possible fate for a convict (Abbott 1981). Thus the confrontations experienced by newly arriving inmates were in a sense situations in which an inmate's character was being tested. They were also situations in which reputations for violence were being built.

Reputations for violence as a source of protection and power

The fear of humiliation provoked by such confrontations is an important underlying impetus for creating an image as a "bad ass," someone who other people do not dare confront (Katz 1988). As inmates vied for such violent reputations, the number of confrontational incidents between inmates increased, especially among younger prisoners. This competition for violent reputations accelerated the cycle of confrontations and produced a growing number of both violence-prone inmates and those who were perceived as weak. Under these circumstances, the struggle involved in relegating inmates to the roles of victims or victimizers became a monotonous, horrifying, daily occurrence.

Developing a reputation for violence became a full-time activity as a growing number of inmates entered the competition for these victimizer, "badass" roles, a competition spurred by the fear of being assigned to a humiliated, victim role. Winners in this violent competition gained power in the emerging inmate social structure as force and coercion became the primary source of inmate power.

Inmates report that a premium was placed by prisoners on gaining a violent reputation. "The young ones, I don't know, I guess they're trying to think they are cool. They walk around pushing everybody around. They're just trying to get them a name, a reputation," said an inmate. "They want to be recognized as being real tough," added another. "This new generation is very aggressive.... They're all out to build a reputation here quick. As quick as possible.... They don't care if they leave or not," said a third inmate. One inmate, who was engaged in the building of a violent reputation, relates his fear of attack to his desire for such a reputation:

> I was little and considered by these inmates to be pretty fair game. So I was constantly being hassled.... Well, I had to build myself a reputation. And that's how come I got locked up [in disciplinary segregation] so quick...fighting all the time.... It took me a good two years to prove myself.... [If] the dude is real scared and still wants to prove himself, then he'll pick up a knife, run over, and stab a few of them.

A caseworker also attests to the growing significance within the inmate society of violent and rebellious reputations:

> *Caseworker:* Rebellion is almost the name of the game now for certain inmates.
> *Interviewer:* Do you think these inmates since they've been in the prison have built a reputation and their power through violence?
> *Caseworker:* Yes.
> *Interviewer:* And more violence is really okay because it increases their power?
> *Caseworker:* True, I would say so.
> *Interviewer:* And that's something that's really changed from the leaders of the old era?
> *Caseworker:* Yes.

Contradiction of coercive controls that promote violent reputations

As the building of these violent reputations among a significant core of inmates proceeded, the administration's coercive controls began to back-fire. The ultimate contradiction in the coercive control structure that emerged in the late 1970s was that for a significant number of inmates official punishment was becoming a reward within the context of the emerging inmate status system. One of the prerequisites for gaining a violent reputation was to be locked up in the disciplinary unit, Cellblock 3. A correctional officer said:

> [Gives name of an inmate, who developed a notoriously violent reputation] has been thrown out of Cellblock 3 numerous times. And he would screw up just to get back in there, because he's a "bad dude." He likes it. See, it's his reputation is what he's maintaining.... It require[d] four guards to get him out of his cell. And they had to clear the entire corridor, because he was so "bad." It was pathetic.... He figures it's a status symbol. Anybody who spends years in lockup has gotta be "bad."

Another correctional officer said, "Now, everybody's screwing up to go to [Cellblock] 3.... [It] was a punishment at one time, now it's a privilege." And, given the general violence and disorganization in the prison population, many inmates did not care if they were sent to disciplinary segregation, where life might be bleak but less chaotic. "In the last few years I've noticed the big majority of the people in the institution...don't care if they go to lockup," said an inmate. And another inmate said, "Those small reports, I can get a thousand of them and I don't give a shit because they don't mean nothing. They just keep you in [Cellblock] 3.... And even if you're stripped [in the hole], you're doing time anyway. To me it is [all the same] really."

The failure of the administration to take into account the dynamics of the inmate social structure led ultimately to a situation in which their attempts to control inmates coercively became mechanisms that fed into the competition for violent reputations. Within the context of the emerging inmate social structure, breaking the rules, creating disruptions, and, as a consequence, being locked up in disciplinary segregation became rewarding experiences for a significant number of inmates.

Growth of small, self-protection inmate cliques

As the PNM administration was losing control of the situation, inmates generally felt that they could not rely on the staff to protect them. To the extent that they could, inmates developed their own sources of protection against predatory inmates. The primary protection from assault was to combine with a small number of other inmates into self-protection cliques. "It's small cliques [of] three or four [inmates]," said an inmate. "It's usually among the young dudes." Another inmate said, "You've got to be in a clique to make it in here." If your small clique could develop a reputation for violence, then your sense of safety was further enhanced. As one inmate said,

> There's really no real organized tough cliques here like in other peniten-
> tiaries.... [There are] your half-ass young kids that need a group in
> order to protect themselves and they feel that by hurting somebody they
> cover themselves.

Having friends in the prison who were acquaintances on the outside provided a degree of protection for new inmates, especially inmates from the barrios of Albuquerque:

> *Interviewer:* Does being from Albuquerque help?
> *Inmate:* Very much.... I knew very many people before I got to the insti-
> tution.... So when I got here I started talking to the right guy. People see
> that.... They're not gonna try and bulldog you because they're gonna
> know this guy's from Albuquerque and he's got a lot of friends here.
> They are going to pick on somebody that doesn't have friends.... They
> can take from him because they know they ain't gonna get no kickback
> on somebody like that.

These cliques did not constitute the types of gang structures witnessed in other prisons (Irwin 1980; Jacobs 1977). "I know there were no gangs out there like the [Mexican] Mafia, the Family or the white Aryan [Brotherhood]," said a New Mexico corrections official. A CO supervisor agreed: "We never recognized the Aryan Brotherhood or the Black Guerrillas or the Mexican Mafia. It was not like in Arizona or California [prisons]. There was nothing like that over here." Inmates also agreed that organized gangs did not exist in the late 1970s. "There isn't any Aryan Brotherhood in here. There is no Mexican Mafia. There isn't that much organization in here," said an inmate, who added, "That's the problem!"

For the most part, these cliques were very loosely organized groupings that provided these inmates small, often temporary "ecological niches" (Hagel-Seymour 1988; Toch 1977) relatively free from the violence of the prison. These cliques tended to be ethnically homogeneous, though a few included both Anglo and Hispanic members. Most cliques broke down by ethnic groupings of "home boys" from cities and barrios in New Mexico:

> *Inmate:* The Blacks were a clique unto themselves and they were a weak
> clique.... Among the whites, not too much influence but say power.

They run protection rackets and gambling games.... The Chicanos are the strongest. Within the Chicanos [there are several] cliques. You have [Chicano cliques from the cities of] Albuquerque, Las Cruces, Espanola, Santa Fe, Gallup and so on. To break those down you have [cliques from various barrios] within Albuquerque.

Decline of organized inmate rackets

Inmate rackets were no longer the organized drug trafficking rings that had existed in 1975. By 1978, rackets revolved primarily around extortion and protection, both outgrowths of the growing violence of the late 1970s. Paying for protection was another way of creating a temporary safe "niche":

> *Inmate:* Once they do start getting protected by somebody, they gotta pay for the protection by buying a radio...watches, and weekly canteen. The guy [getting these items] will make sure nothing happens to that guy [paying for protection]. It goes on all over the institution. Some of its good for the inmates that need it.

> *Correctional Officer:* Let's say you're nineteen years old. They throw you in a dormitory and you don't want to get raped, you don't want anybody to knock the shit out of you, so what you do is pay for that kind of protection.... If I was going to be locked up, I'd probably be willing to pay for protection myself.

Drug trafficking had become a sporadic affair by the late 1970s. The administration was not tolerating the trafficking, though some COs, who were fired in 1979, were allegedly involved in bringing in small amounts of marijuana to individual inmates (*Albuquerque Journal* 4/6/79: A1). Other than this sporadic marijuana trafficking, very few drugs were entering the prison. Very little heroin was apparently available in the late 1970s. Ingredients for making alcoholic "home brew" could still be smuggled, as it had always been, from the prison's kitchen. And inhalants, such as paint, thinner, and glue, could be stolen from prison industries and the shoe repair and plumbing shops. Inhalant sniffing became a major activity for a large number of inmates, apparently replacing heroin use. As one corrections official stated, "When we had increased incidence of sniff...it usually was an indicator that the hard drugs were harder to get."

Organized rackets among inmates thus declined in the late 1970s and became a relatively minor source of power among inmate groups. Inmate cliques were not organized around the smuggling of contraband, as many of them had been in the early 1970s. "[Inmate groups] are not as strong as they used to be several years ago [when] we had a group that we considered Mexican Mafia," said a correctional officer, referring to the dominant drug-smuggling operations of the early 1970s. By 1978, cliques were organized primarily for self-protection.

Declining influence of nonviolent inmates and
growing influence of violent, hardcore cliques

Some inmate groups began to emerge as influential in 1978. The ACLU lawsuit against PNM (*Duran v. Apodaca*) gave a few Chicano inmates a limited leadership role within some inmate factions. These inmates were directly involved in negotiations for settlement of the lawsuit. But this leadership role was diminishing by late 1979 as inmates began to perceive little gain from the lawsuit:

> *Correctional Officer:* There are leaders in the Chicanos mainly because of this suit that was filed by the Durans.... Really made [Lonnie Duran] a power king. They were anticipating a lot more and they weren't getting as much as they wanted. So naturally, they started putting a lot of pressure on him. You could see it in Lonnie Duran that he was receiving a lot of pressure.

Other inmate cliques gained power in 1978 because of their violent reputations. In 1976 and 1977, Anglo convicts were very disorganized and were regularly attacked by Chicano inmates. Then, some strong Anglo cliques began to surface in 1977. "[It used to be that] the Anglo inmate didn't have a goddamn chance, because all the cliques were from Albuquerque.... The Chicano cliques were always fucking with them," said a PNM official. "So then they said, 'this isn't going to happen to the Anglo guys [anymore].'" And a CO said, "I noticed the white inmates...about three years ago [in 1977]...were waking up. They were weak, then all of a sudden they were more organized and more and more power." "But," he added, "its not a Mafia type [gang]."

One of the more notorious cliques was associated with three Anglo inmates who on April 16, 1978, beat another Anglo inmate to death with baseball bats for allegedly being a snitch (*Albuquerque Journal* 4/17/78). This incident first brought to public view the emergence of the violent, hardcore cliques that were setting a new direction toward disruptiveness within the prison. Two of the inmates convicted of this murder, William Jack Stephens and Michael Colby, came to be identified as leaders of one of the more violent cliques, made up mostly of Anglo convicts. The third inmate convicted of the murder, Michael Price, was also part of this clique. This clique emerged as an important power that struggled with other Anglo inmate cliques for dominance.

> *Correctional Officer:* We were having some problems among the whites. They were having internal problems amongst themselves.... We were gaining a lot of white inmates from California, and we have one from Walla Walla....

Interviewer: Somebody was tied to a certain leadership in the white faction?
Correctional Officer: I believe so.... Michael Colby and Jack Stephens.
They had nothing to lose any more.

The 1978 baseball bat murder, which resulted in life sentences, gave this
clique more status and power in the inmate society:

> *Caseworker:* I had them [Colby and Stephens] on my caseload for over a
> year after they [were convicted] for killing an inmate...with baseball
> bats. That one incident gave Mike Colby and Jack Stephens a raise in sta-
> tus as leaders. And the fact that the administration was more apt to be
> watching them closer also made them feel as having maintained a higher
> status, and this you heard from inmates and staff alike.

This clique was identified by PNM officials as a major force behind the
growing violence in the late 1970s.

> *Penitentiary official:* We had basically information that the driving force
> behind [much of the violence] was the white, Anglo supremacy group
> within the institution.... There was no name for it, I guess unofficially
> they were called the Aryan Brotherhood, but they didn't have an official
> organization.... The inmates that come to mind are Colby [and]
> Stephens in that group. We also had some others that were locked up in
> [Cellblock] 3.

An inmate who was associated with this clique said,

> There is no Aryan Brotherhood. They call us white supremacists. That's
> the administration. They are down on us white men.... There's about 12
> of us...in the same unit together.... I guess it could be considered a
> clique.... We have gone since about three years back [since 1977]....
> There's been a certain few of us white dudes and a certain few Chicanos,
> and we're all friends. We sleep in the same area and instead of keeping
> canteen in separate drawers, we keep it in one drawer so that everybody
> in our clique can use that one drawer. It's all shared equally.... When I
> first got here [in 1976] Colby was here and his cousins. I was just hang-
> ing around with them.... They just barely got here too.... We all proved
> ourselves to be good people.... It's just gotten to where we've all built a
> little bit of relationship with each other. It's just solid.

Of this clique, another long-term inmate said, "I had never seen such a hor-
rible white clique in all the years that I been in the institution like the one I
saw now." As this clique was forming, several other Anglo and Chicano
cliques were also organizing around their members' violent reputations.

Feeding this violent clique rivalry and formation was the entry of disruptive inmates from other prison systems. "You have inmates coming
from other institutions [in California and the state of Washington] that
are related to Aryan Brotherhood," said a CO. Also, the prison adminis-

tration began bringing federal and out-of-state transfers, the "troublemakers" shipped out under Malley's wardenship, back to the Penitentiary of New Mexico. A CO supervisor said, "Most of the guys that were either locked up or transferred out of state, once [Warden] Romero came in [during March 1978], they started letting these guys out and started bringing these guys back to the institution." Throwing these inmates back into the already violent and chaotic social situation merely made the struggle for dominance more volatile. These returning inmates, to the extent that they had been powerful before they were removed, found themselves having to struggle with a new generation of inmates who were seeking power. Now that nonviolent sources of power had been disrupted, this struggle could only proceed violently; and violent reputations, to the extent they could be established through action, became the basis for power among these competing cliques.

The inmates caught up in this competition for dominance and violent reputations composed PNM's hardcore cliques. Most of these cliques were housed in Cellblock 5, where several stabbing incidents occurred in 1978 and 1979 (Office of the Attorney General 1980b: 30). "I had been in charge of Cellblock 5," said a CO, "and the type of inmates I saw there were what you call a hardcore inmate." As an inmate correctly noted, "All the guys that get sent from Cellblock 3 [disciplinary unit] usually go to Cellblock 5." And another inmate said, "The strong cliques are always in Cellblock 5."

During 1978 and 1979, these cliques continued attacking weaker inmates, correctional officers, and each other. Discussing these violent cliques, the New Mexico Attorney General (Office of the Attorney General 1980b: 30) concluded:

> Because the power of the inmates in these cliques was based primarily on violence, their motives and behavior were inconsistent with maintaining order. With reputations for violence as the major source of power, these Cellblock 5 inmates now had a self-interest in creating disturbances to enhance their power and reputations with other inmates.

While the total number of inmates involved in these hardcore cliques was about 150 of the over 1,000 inmates in the prison, their behavior and disruptiveness set the tone for inmate social relations. The violence and fragmentation among these inmates affected virtually everyone within the prison. There were few safe ecological niches (Hagel-Seymour 1988; Toch 1977) remaining, and these safe niches were primarily created through the formation of cliques, some of which actively engaged in violence. These hardcore cliques, produced inadvertently by the administration's reliance on coercive controls, were leading the inmate social structure toward an implosion of violence.

In stark contrast to the early 1970s, when inmate leaders helped to keep the lid on potential inmate disturbances, inmate leadership, to the extent that it existed at all, fell by 1979 to these small cliques of inmates who actively engaged in violence and disruption. The leaders of these cliques "didn't so much keep them in line as much as they kept them out of line," said an inmate. By late 1979, "there [were] leaders out there… capable of starting to push [a] riot," said another inmate. "But this is the wrong type of leader." As 1980 began, PNM was on the brink of a complete breakdown of control both between the staff and inmates and among inmates themselves.

SUMMARY: BUILDUP TO AN EXPLOSION

In late 1979 and early 1980, PNM moved toward an open manifestation of the crisis that had been building for years. Coercive controls had created a confrontation between inmates and staff that soon deteriorated into daily incidents of mutual harassment. Ultimately, these coercive controls fragmented the inmate society, which became increasingly violent. The breakup of the inmate social structure mirrored the disorganization of the corrections administration. With leadership at the Department of Corrections in disarray, the prison was racing toward a disaster—a disaster that was precipitated by specific events that reflected continued fragmentation and the lack of a coherent policy of control.

First, during the summer of 1979, Warden Griffin began removing inmates from administrative segregation units (Cellblocks 3 and 4). This move addressed one of the major overcrowding issues of the ACLU lawsuit. However, this restriction on the use of administrative segregation, with no concomitant increase in positive incentives for order, merely removed a level of containment; and overcrowding was shifted to less secure dormitories.

Second, inmates became increasingly frustrated with the slow progress of the ACLU lawsuit. Major issues were bogged down in negotiation, and court-ordered implementation of changes in visiting and mailing privileges were simply ignored by PNM's middle-level administrators (Office of the Attorney General 1980b). Factions within the Department of Corrections were at odds over the substance and pace of the negotiations arising from the lawsuit. A major breakdown in negotiations occurred when Deputy Secretary Rodriguez dismissed federal mediators in October 1979 (Morris 1983). Growing frustration with the legal process prompted one inmate plaintiff to tell his lawyer in late November 1979 that he did not know how much longer he "could keep the heavies in line"

(Office of the Attorney General 1980a: 31). The inmates associated with the lawsuit were clearly losing their influence over other inmates. The struggle to keep alive a collective, nonviolent response to the administration's policies was rapidly eroding.

Third, in November 1979, the Department of Corrections eliminated one of the last remaining formal incentive controls, transfer to a minimum-security facility, after an inmate killed another inmate during an escape at Camp Sierra Blanca. All transfers from PNM were halted from November 1979 to mid-February 1980. Not only did this halt in transfers remove an important formal incentive for maintaining order, "it also contributed to a 20 percent rise in the prison's population from 957 to 1,157 in the three months before [February 2, 1980]" (Office of the Attorney General 1980b: 31).

Fourth, in the summer of 1979 a massive renovation project began at PNM. The renovation created constant noise, an unsettled physical setting, and a sense of uneasiness for both prisoners and staff. Renovation activities were not coordinated with the security needs of the prison. Tools and equipment, including hacksaws and acetylene torches, were left in areas that were accessible to inmates. Many COs told their supervisors that some of the renovations made the prison less secure. A particular concern expressed by COs was the placement in the Control Center of a large "shatterproof" glass bay window overlooking the main corridor. The lack of coordination between renovation activities and security needs at PNM reflected the overall administrative turmoil in the Department of Corrections.

Fifth, on December 9, 1979, eleven inmates escaped from PNM. Most escapees were identified as belonging to the violent, hardcore cliques. Except for one who was captured later, all escapees were apprehended and placed in Cellblock 3 prior to February 1, 1980. The escape was another episode of disruption that further enhanced these inmates' reputations. The escape also led to a sudden increase in shakedowns which inmates perceived as escalated harassment.

Sixth, in response to the embarrassment of the December 9th escape, Warden Griffin, in consultation with Deputy Secretary Rodriguez, decided to reorganize the PNM management. The reorganization was put in place and announced on January 15, 1980. The reorganization moved the intelligence division, educational services, psychological services, health services, and prison industries from under the supervision of deputy wardens to the direct supervision of Warden Griffin. The reorganization, especially the transfer of the intelligence division, represented a major loss in power for the middle-level administrators headed by Deputy Warden Montoya. At the same time as this internal reorganization was taking place at PNM, Secretary Charles Becknell, under increasing criticism from Corrections

Commission members and his political opponents in the state legislature for the December 9th escape and the earlier stabbing incident at Sierra Blanca, resigned. Leadership at the top and middle levels of the organization, already in disarray, was thus thrown into further turmoil in mid-January 1980.

Seventh, Cellblock 5, which housed the most disruptive, hardcore inmates when they were not housed in disciplinary segregation, was closed for renovation in November 1979. Many of these inmates had been leaders in the competition to develop violent and disruptive reputations. Most of these inmates were transferred to a less secure dormitory, Dorm E-2.

Eighth, there were a number of forewarnings that a major disturbance was imminent, yet no decisive actions were taken. On January 31, 1980, an intelligence meeting was held in Warden Griffin's office. Officials discussed rumors of escapes and possible hostage-taking. None of these warnings led to any enhanced security measures to forestall a disturbance. Forewarnings included a mix of rumors and intelligence, none of which could be confirmed. Officials had no way to distinguish reliable from unreliable information, a legacy of the coercive snitch system which often resulted in inmates telling officials anything to escape punishment or receive protection. As it turned out, among these rumors was one specific bit of intelligence, concerning a possible hostage-taking, that was an accurate forewarning.

The officers and supervisors who came to work for the night shift beginning at 11:30 p.m., February 1, 1980, had not heard about any of these warnings. These officers and the over 1,100 inmates housed at PNM that night were about to feel the full force of underlying organizational contradictions, which had been accumulating for years, exploding to the surface. The point had been reached in the organization's history when a significant number of inmates agreed with these sentiments, expressed by a PNM inmate:

> If you know that the institution is just here to fuck you over, what's the difference if you riot or not, they're going to fuck you over anyway. So go for it!

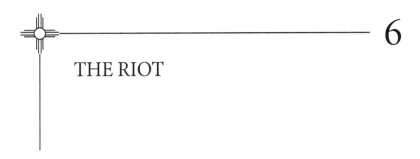

THE RIOT

6

At 11:45 p.m. on Friday, February 1, 1980, the morning shift that guards PNM from midnight to 8 a.m. received a routine briefing from the supervisor of the previous shift.[1] The briefing mentioned nothing about potential trouble or anything else out of the ordinary. Though correctional officers had been aware of several rumors about planned takeovers by inmates, their supervisors had issued no special instructions. COs, who are not armed while inside the prison (since inmates could overpower them and take their weapons), were merely told to "keep on your toes."

Shortly after midnight, the evening and morning shifts completed a count of inmates in the institution, which held 1157 inmates including 34 in a modular unit outside the main penitentiary building. All inmates were accounted for.

At about 1 a.m., on February 2, 1980, two groups composed of four COs each began a routine check of all cellhouses and dormitories in the south wing of the prison. [See diagram in Appendix B.] The check included a quick walk through each living unit, during which dayrooms were closed and locked. The first group checked and closed Cellhouses 1 and 2 and dormitories in the A and F wings. The second group, led by the morning shift captain, checked and secured dormitories in the B and D wings. No problems were encountered. The second group then entered Dorm E-2, the upstairs dormitory in the E wing.

During the previous month, some inmates in Dorm E-2 had smuggled into the unit yeast and raisins from the prison's kitchen. By the evening of Friday, February 1, they had concocted an intoxicating drink from these ingredients. Several inmates at about 8:30 p.m. began drinking this "home brew." By 10:30 p.m. some of these inmates were drunk, and they began to talk about starting an incident. According to other inmates in Dorm E-2 that night, these inmates by 11:00 p.m were quite loud and boisterous. But COs on the evening shift reported nothing unusual about Dorm E-2. Inmates in Dorm E-2, including some who were involved in the initial takeover, reported that at some point between 12:30 a.m. and 1:15 a.m. a plan was agreed upon to jump COs during the routine check and securing of dorms that always took place after 1 a.m. on weekend nights. It is not clear if the plan included an attempt to exit the dormitory. Hostages would be taken in the dormitory; and if the entry door could be successfully jumped, additional hostages would be taken in the south wing of the prison. Beyond the plan to take some COs hostage, the inmates had no idea what they would do next.

The inmates in Dorm E-2 had no contact with other inmates in the prison concerning their hostage-taking plan. As one Dorm E-2 inmate reported:

> No one knew it was coming down. I was up in the dormitory when it kicked off in E-2 and it all come down in a period of 15 minutes. People started talking about it and ribbing themselves into it and pretty soon there was about six people ribbed up so high that they couldn't back out. So they went with it.

In fact, a much more elaborate plan for a daytime takeover of the Psychological Unit, which was supposed to have occurred the following Monday, was the plan most inmates had thought would be followed. One inmate reported:

> There's been people planning a takeover to show the people [in the administration] something, for a long time, about a year and a half.... What a lot of inmates were talking about is taking over the Psychological Unit.

Several other rumors of takeover plans were also circulating among inmates, and some had been communicated to staff members.

The takeover in Dorm E-2 that did occur surprised inmates in the other parts of the prison, as well as many inmates in Dorm E-2. The inmates who initiated the takeover were members of the violent, hardcore inmate cliques that had been transferred from Cellblock 5 when it was closed for renovation. Among those later sentenced on kidnapping charges arising from the initial takeover was Michael Price (*New Mexican* 11/2/82), an inmate associated with the clique led by William Jack Stephens and Michael Colby, who were this night locked in Cellblock 3, having been placed there after their recapture from the December 9, 1979, mass escape.

The takeover did not involve a coordinated plan; it was hastily organized by a few inmates who, under the influence of alcohol, had "dared" each other to start an incident. The takeover of PNM by inmates proceeded through a series of opportunities, inadvertently given to inmates by the prison staff, that for the most part had not been anticipated by inmates. A Dorm E-2 inmate reported these observations:

> I don't think the riot was planned.... It just happened spontaneously. It just happened that the officers came by and...there was a little party going on and [the inmates] were boozed up. Its like somebody thought

about it and they said "why not?" Opportunity was there and so why not? Let's have fun. Nobody intended to escape from here [Dorm E-2] until that happened.

The line officer in charge of Dormitory E stood at the entrance of Dorm E-2 as the shift captain and one other CO entered. About thirty seconds later, another officer, the assistant shift supervisor, entered Dorm E-2. That both shift supervisors were in the same area of the prison, much less in the same dorm, is considered a poor security procedure. There was some speculation after the riot that the assistant shift supervisor entered Dorm E-2 because he had word of possible trouble brewing in the dorm. This supervisor later told investigators that he had no forewarning of trouble and merely entered the dorm to assist with closing it down. In fact, he would not have entered the dorm, he said, if he had thought there were going to be problems.

After all three officers were in the dormitory, the CO at the dorm entrance pushed the door to an almost closed position, leaving it unlocked. This was also contrary to the official procedure, which requires that these doors be completely closed and locked when other officers enter a dorm for any reason. Inmates in Dorm E-2, and in other living units, had observed that officers on post at these doors did not always push them completely shut or lock them on such occasions. The correct procedure was followed so inconsistently that inmates in Dorm E-2 correctly gambled that the door would not be closed or locked during the routine check in the early morning hours of Saturday, February 2.

At 1:40 a.m., the door and the three officers in Dorm E-2 were jumped simultaneously. Inmates quickly overpowered the CO at the door and the other officers inside the dormitory. The CO at the door had keys for Dorms E-2, E-1, B-1, and B-2. Four hostages were then under the control of these inmates, who now had access to the main corridor.

At 1:45 a.m., inmates from Dorm E-2 jumped the CO outside Dorm F-2, seized his keys to the A and F dormitories, and captured two additional COs who were just entering Dorm F-2 to close it down. A third CO, who had just entered this dorm, ran into the dayroom at the opposite end of the dorm; he was protected by some sympathetic Dorm F-2 inmates, who later helped him escape the prison. Total hostages were now eight, including the CO protected in the Dorm F-2 dayroom.

By this time hundreds of inmates were milling around the main corridor in the south wing of the institution. More than 500 inmates from Dorms A, B, F, and E-2 had access to the main corridor. Dorm E-1, a semiprotective custody unit, had been barricaded by its eighty-four inmates shortly after hearing the disturbance of the initial takeover upstairs in Dorm E-2.

At 1:57 a.m., two COs leaving the officers' mess hall, located in the central area of the institution next to the kitchen, saw inmates beating and dragging a naked man (who was later identified as one of the hostage COs captured in Dorm F-2) up the south corridor toward the grill that separated the south wing from the central area of the prison. They also noticed that this corridor grill was open, contrary to prison policy. The open south corridor grill, which rioting inmates had not anticipated, was a serious breach of security and a major factor that allowed the takeover to spread. The two COs judged that they could not reach the south corridor grill to close it before a group of inmates, who spotted them, could reach it. Instead, the two COs raced north up the main corridor away from the rioting inmates. As they passed the Control Center in the middle of the institution, they pounded on its window and shouted to the officer inside to electronically unlock the north corridor grill, which separates the north wing from the rest of the institution. The two COs entered the north wing, locking the north corridor grill behind them, seconds before a crowd of about seventy-five inmates reached the Control Center.

As the guard towers and the superintendent of correctional security, whose home was on the PNM reservation, were being informed over the telephone by the Control Center officer of the takeover, inmates in the main corridor congregated around the Control Center's recently installed glass bay window. A CO assigned to patrolling the prison's perimeter fence heard on his walkie-talkie the voices of inmates who had taken radio transmitting units from hostage COs. Realizing that the prison was being taken, this CO rushed to the Control Center to assist the officer on post there.

Inmates in the main corridor standing in front of the Control Center's window demanded that the officers inside open the set of grill gates leading to the front offices in the administration wing of the prison. The Control Center officer refused. These inmates began using pipes to beat a naked hostage who fell unconscious and was dragged away from the Control Center's window by other inmates. Inmates next began hitting the Control Center's window with pipes, which caused no damage. Then, inmates grabbed a metal-canister fire extinguisher from the main corridor wall across from the Control Center. The COs in the Control Center did not expect the glass in this window to break since it was supposed to be "shatterproof." It wasn't. The inmates' first and second blow to the glass with the fire extinguisher caused bits of glass to fall into the Control Center. The third blow produced a large crack down the middle of the window. As the two officers hastily ran from the Control Center, racing toward the front entrance of the prison, the glass shattered completely, allowing inmates to enter the Control Center. The two COs who had been in the Control Center managed to escape capture by inmates.

Further evidence of the unplanned nature of the takeover are the inmates' actions upon entering the Control Center. Instead of carefully identifying and finding keys to other parts of the prison, the inmates trashed the interior of the Control Center, sending keys flying from the board that provided key identification. The grills leading to the front offices and to the north wing, however, were not operated with keys; inmates merely had to press a few buttons to electronically open them. Thus, by 2:02 a.m., inmates had access to the entire main corridor and to the administration wing of the penitentiary. Access to specific cellblocks and to the rest of the institution was within reach as inmates began sorting through the keys on the Control Center floor.

Officers in the north wing of the prison, having been alerted to the takeover by the two COs who had just been chased by inmates into the north end of the main corridor, began to hide or barricade themselves from the rioting inmates. Two COs hid in a crawl space in the basement of Cellblock 5; they stayed hidden for the entire 36 hours of the riot, transmitting their location by telephone to the CO in Tower 3 before they took refuge. The hospital technician locked himself and seven inmate-patients into the upstairs floor of the Hospital Unit. Through telephone contact, he informed the CO in Tower 1 of their safe location. They remained there undetected until the riot was over. Three other COs who had locked themselves into Cellblock 3 were taken hostage about an hour later when inmates broke into the disciplinary unit.

The inmates who initiated the takeover in Dorm E-2 were delayed in their entry to Cellblock 3 because they could not initially find the keys to the unit. The shift captain was brought from Dorm E-2 to Cellblock 3. His life was threatened in an attempt to force the officers, who had locked themselves into Cellblock 3, to open the unit. The officers refused. Eventually, the inmates happened upon the key to the unit. They opened it and forced the shift captain to show them how to operate the mechanisms that unlocked the grill to the upper tiers and cells of the unit. Shortly after 3 a.m., inmates captured the three COs inside Cellblock 3 and began releasing inmates from the disciplinary unit. These three COs were locked into a cell in Cellblock 3. The shift supervisor was initially locked into another cell in Cellblock 3, but, under the control of some of the Dorm E-2 inmates who initiated the takeover, was later brought back to the south wing. Hostages now totaled eleven.

The first inmate killings during the riot occurred in Cellblock 3 immediately after the release of this cellblock's inmates. An inmate, shouting in Spanish, "No era yo. No lo hice." ("It wasn't me. I didn't do it."), was beaten, tortured, and mutilated. This inmate was assumed to have informed on other inmates who were also locked in the disciplinary unit. Another inmate, who was mentally disturbed and apparently kept other Cellblock 3 inmates awake at night with his screams, was shot in the head at close range with a canister fired from a tear-gas launcher taken from the Control Center. Like these two victims, many of the inmates murdered during the riot were perceived as "weak," "traitorous," or "insane." Murders of such inmates would not likely be avenged by other inmates. These were, therefore, safe targets for inmates engaged in building violent reputations.

At about the same time, another group of inmates had found keys to the prison pharmacy, located on the first floor of the Hospital Unit. The pharmacy contained narcotics, barbiturates, and sedatives, which were ingested in massive doses by inmates throughout the riot. The availability of these drugs did not contribute to the violence; if anything, these drugs tended to make inmates passive (*Albuquerque Journal* 2/18/80). As one inmate witness to the riot explained, "The people who were taking pills were so drunk, they wasn't doing no harm; they were just falling out left and right; and we was putting them on stretchers and getting them out of here." By the second day of the riot, overdoses of pharmacy drugs became the main medical problem for which inmates were being treated.

Other inmates in the early morning hours of the first day of the riot found keys to the basement area of the prison below the kitchen. This area contained the paint, shoe repair, and plumbing shops. An acetylene blowtorch was retrieved from the plumbing shop, and at 3:15 a.m. was used to open the far south corridor grill, leading to the Educational Unit and Dorm D-1, which contained eighty-six inmates and the twelfth (and last) CO to be taken hostage. This blowtorch was later taken to the other end of the penitentiary to open the far north corridor grill leading to Cellblock 5 and Cellblock 4. The far south and far north corridor grills were not electronically controlled and could only be opened with keys, which inmates could not locate. Cellblock 5, which was closed and empty due to renovation, was entered at about 5 a.m. using the blowtorch. Here two additional acetylene torches, which had been left by construction crews, were found by inmates. Later, these blowtorches would be used to enter Cellblock 4, the protective custody unit.

In the paint and shoe repair shops, other inmates found paint, paint thinner, and glue. These items were inhaled, or sniffed, for intoxication. In the main corridor, between 4 a.m. and 5 a.m., a number of inmates (some witnesses report as many as 150) began inhaling these substances from towels dipped in buckets. As one inmate witness observed:

When they got that "sniff"...people just went wild. That's when it really got out of hand and we couldn't do nothing...there was nobody listening to nobody. There was no unity at all. Nobody cared what anybody had to say; they were just doing their own things.

Many inmates claimed that the "sniff" contributed heavily to the violence, especially to the fights that began breaking out among inmates in the south wing.

In fact, the period between 3 a.m. and 7 a.m. was punctuated by the chaos, infighting, and violence that came to characterize this riot. There was no leadership throughout the riot. Inmates' actions were completely uncoordinated. Some inmates were setting fires in the administrative offices, others in the Psychological Unit. At certain points, inmates manning walkie-talkies radioed for firefighting crews to come into the prison; when firefighters approached the prison they were driven back by other inmates who threw debris at them. Other groups of inmates were raiding the pharmacy. Many were ingesting pills or inhaling paint fumes. Various inmates found keys to Cellhouses 1, 2, and 6 and Dorm C-1 and released inmates from these units. Other inmates were fighting, forming into small groups for self-protection, or hiding.

While all of these uncoordinated activities and fighting were going on during the early hours of the riot, a few inmates who had been released from Cellblock 3 and Cellhouse 6 discussed organizing the riot into a protest against the administration. These inmates included those involved in the ACLU lawsuit (*Duran v. Apodaca*), which was still under negotiation at the time of the riot. They managed in the early hours of the riot to get control of the three hostage COs captured in Cellblock 3. However, they were able to gain control of only one of the other nine hostages; and this hostage, who had been brought to Cellblock 3 with injuries, was released to authorities at 8:20 a.m., the first morning of the riot. The other hostages were being held by various groups in the south wing of the institution. Reportedly, the hostages held in the south wing changed captors on numerous occasions. The only clear exception was the shift captain, who was moved frequently but who apparently remained under the control of some of the inmates who had initiated the takeover in Dorm E-2. Unlike the three hostages being held in Cellblock 3, who were treated relatively well for the remainder of the riot, many of the hostages held in the south wing of the prison were beaten, stabbed, and sodomized.

The Cellblock 3 and Cellhouse 6 inmates who were attempting to organize the riot into a protest had little influence on the behavior of other rioting inmates. One inmate, who identified himself as a leader in this attempt to turn the riot into a protest against the administration, said:

> There were a few of us in here that were trying to freeze that [inmate-to-inmate violence] because it was wrong, it was dead wrong. Three hours after the riot started there was no stopping it. But there were a few of us that were saying, "Hey, if you want to burn it down, burn it down or tear it up or whatever you want, but quit killing people and don't turn this

thing against ourselves. If you got to fight somebody now, fight the Man, fight the administration."

But his and the other inmates' efforts to turn the riot into a protest were futile.

As fights began to break out in the south wing of the prison, injuries to inmates and killings began to increase. Many of the deaths that occurred in the south wing were the result of fights between small groups and between individuals. Fights over the hostages held in the south wing occurred. Many inmates, perceived as weak or defenseless, were attacked and raped; those offering resistance were beaten severely, a few were killed. Some of the assaults in the south wing appeared to be random. Inmates suffered injuries when they were hacked with meat cleavers, stabbed, or hit with pipes for no reasons apparent to the victims. A few of the killings in the south wing also appear to have been random. As an inmate said:

> I had three real tight partners that weren't snitches, weren't punks. They were damn good people. They got killed for no reason because they were in the wrong place at the wrong time when people were just killing people at random.

Of the thirty-three killings during the riot, seventeen occurred in the south wing of the prison, many in the early morning hours of the first day. Of the approximately 400 injuries and rapes, the vast majority also occurred in the south wing.

There is no doubt that the number of killings and injuries would have been much higher if the inmates of Dorm E-1, a semi-protection unit, had not successfully fought off an attempt by other inmates to enter this dorm. These inmates had barricaded the entrance to their dorm when they heard the disturbance of the initial takeover upstairs in Dorm E-2. Throughout the early morning hours, groups of inmates attempted to break into Dorm E-1 by tear-gassing and smoking the unit with fires set at its entrance. A sympathetic inmate, who had some friends in the unit, tossed a three-foot-long wrench through a hole in the wire mesh above the dormitory entrance door. This inmate was immediately jumped by other inmates in the main corridor who had observed his action; he was beaten to death. The Dorm E-1 inmates were able to use the wrench to knock bars out of a window in the rear of the dormitory. At 7 a.m., the inmates housed in Dorm E-1 escaped the penitentiary building and ran to the perimeter fence, surrendering to authorities for safety.

Law enforcement officers from the New Mexico State Police, Santa Fe City Police, and Santa Fe County Sheriff's Office began arriving at PNM at 2:15 a.m. and, along with PNM employees, surrounded the prison's double perimeter fence. Later, the National Guard, local firefighting units, and other law enforcement agents arrived. Their main duties were to secure the perimeter fence, guard and provide safety to surrendering inmates, and transport the injured to local hospitals.

Shortly after 2 a.m., about 30 minutes after the initial takeover, Warden Jerry Griffin joined Deputy Warden Robert Montoya and Superintendent of Correctional Security Emanuel Koroneos at the gatehouse beneath Tower 1. The debriefing of the two COs who had just moments before escaped from the Control Center convinced these PNM officials that, since the Control Center had been breached, the prison was under the complete control of inmates. These officials then began hearing radio transmissions from within the penitentiary. Inmates stated that if the prison was rushed, hostages would be killed. They demanded to speak to Governor King and to the news media. Throughout the riot, these warnings and demands would be repeated frequently. Griffin, Montoya, and Koroneos decided that they should attempt to negotiate the release of the hostages. Montoya contacted inmates by radio at about 2:30 a.m. to initiate negotiations. It was decided then that the prison would not be rushed as long as all the hostages remained alive.

Montoya's earliest contacts were with an inmate who had been involved with the initial takeover in Dorm E-2 and apparently had control of the shift captain throughout the riot. This inmate, who identified himself as "Chopper One," was soon joined on the airwaves by other inmates who had captured seven additional walkie-talkies and were broadcasting from several parts of the prison. All the hostages, these inmate voices said, would be traded for Montoya and for Lt. "Green Eyes," the correctional supervisor who was notorious for his harassment of inmates. Montoya refused these offers. Montoya's attempts to maintain a dialogue with only one inmate negotiator were hampered by repeated interruptions from other inmates who were vying for the role of spokesman. "Chopper One," in fact, became the broadcasting "handle" of several inmates. As Montoya established contact with one inmate, other inmates transmitted conflicting messages, contradicted other inmate "spokesmen," or argued among themselves over the airwaves. These confusing radio transmissions reflected the disorganization of the inmate social structure as well as the unplanned nature of the takeover.

Since hostages were not under the control of any one group, it was difficult to maintain a dialogue for negotiating their release. The faces and voices of inmate negotiators changed throughout the riot. The main inmate negotiators in the early part of the riot appear to have been a few inmates from Dorm E-2 who controlled the shift captain and possibly (at times) six other hostages captured in Dorms E-2 and F-2. As the riot progressed, some of these hostages came under the control of other inmates, some of whom actually helped hostages escape. Later in the riot, the inmates from Cellblock 3 and Cellhouse 6, who had been involved in the ACLU lawsuit negotiations and now controlled the three hostages captured in Cellblock 3, emerged as major negotiators.

Shortly after Deputy Secretary of Corrections Felix Rodriguez (the new Secretary of Corrections, Adolph Saenz, had not yet taken his post on the day of the takeover) joined Montoya in the gatehouse, it became clear to these officials that hostages were not under the control of any one group of inmates. At 5:25 a.m., the CO who had been protected by inmates in the dayroom of Dorm F-2 emerged from the penitentiary's main entrance, which faces Tower 1. The CO was aided in his escape from the prison by a group of inmates who disguised him as an inmate and escorted him out of Dorm F-2, up the main corridor, through the Control Center and the burning, smoke-filled administration wing, and out the front entrance. At about 7 a.m., a second hostage was released by the Dorm E-2 inmates who feared the hostage, who had been stabbed and badly beaten, would die in their custody. At 8:20 a.m., a third hostage, who had been captured in Dorm D-1 by a separate group of inmates and later brought to Cellblock 3 for medical attention from the hostage COs being held there, was released by the inmates who controlled the three Cellblock 3 hostages. None of these hostage releases came about as a result of negotiations. And all three of these released hostages had been under the control of different groups of inmates. Just after daylight on Saturday morning, nine hostages remained in the prison.

While these early negotiations were going on, other groups of inmates were busy using blowtorches to cut through the locked grill leading into Cellblock 4, the protective custody unit. No key could be found for this unit. Protective custody inmates locked in the south-facing cells of Cellblock 4 had seen, through barred windows and across the yard between Cellblock 4 and Cellblock 3, inmates being released around 3 a.m. from the disciplinary unit. Some also had heard the screams of the first inmates who were killed in Cellblock 3 shortly after it was taken by rioting inmates. Word of the takeover had quickly been passed through the vents to the inmates locked in the north-facing cells of Cellblock 4. At about 4 a.m., Cellblock 4 inmates began hearing the activities of rioters who were now at the entrance of Cellblock 4. At that point, these protective custody inmates knew their lives were in danger.

Cellblock 4, designated for protective custody in 1976, contained inmates who could not, for various reasons, live in the general prison population. Besides being perceived as weak, inmates living in Cellblock 4 were generally considered by most other inmates to be snitches, or prison informants who cooperated with the prison staff. While this characterization actually fit only a few Cellblock 4 inmates, the manner in which informants and protection cases were handled led to many inmates being labeled, often incorrectly, as snitches.

During the three hours from 4 a.m. to 7 a.m. that it took for rioting inmates to torch through the security grills leading into Cellblock 4, protective custody inmates barricaded their cells with metal bunks, attempted to tie their individual cell grills with towels or blankets, or jammed the locks to their cell grills with toothbrushes or other small items so that rioting inmates would not be able to unlock their cells. Cellblock 4 inmates locked into the north-facing cells attempted to yell for help and signal to law enforcement officers they could see standing just beyond the perimeter fence located outside this cellblock's windows. Even though there was an exterior door at the far west end of Cellblock 4, which can be entered from the outside, officials on the scene assumed that once the Control Center had been captured, inmates had control of the entire institution, including Cellblock 4. In addition, the decision not to rush the prison for fear of endangering hostages precluded a rescue attempt of Cellblock 4 inmates, since this action might be construed by those who held hostages as an attempt to retake the prison. The hostages' safety was the overriding concern of officials; inmates' safety was not a high priority.

As inmates at the entrance of Cellblock 4 were completing their cutting of the security grill, they began shouting the names of their intended victims who were inside the unit. Beginning at 7 a.m., small groups of inmates entered the protective custody unit. They torched open the metal encasement that held the control panels used to lock and unlock cells. Protective custody inmates who had not jammed the locks to their cell grills were fortunate. As rioting inmates operated the cell door locking controls on panels near the entrance of each tier, many of the Cellblock 4 inmates who had not jammed their locks were able to leave their cells. Wearing masks and "ponchos" they had fashioned out of blankets, they blended in with the rioters and left Cellblock 4.

Other Cellblock 4 inmates were not so fortunate. On the tiers where inmates had jammed the locks to their cell grills, the locking and unlocking mechanisms located on panels at the entrance of each tier would not operate. These inmates were trapped in their cells. Other inmates who had barricaded their cell entrances were also trapped. Using blowtorches, rioting inmates cut through the panels containing the unlocking devices in an attempt to bypass these mechanisms; others cut through the bars of entrance grills to the individual cells containing inmates. As the intended victims suffered through the agonizing wait while their cells were entered, they were taunted and told in vivid detail exactly how they would be tortured and killed.

These protective custody inmates were killed by four or five small groups, containing three to five inmates each. Some groups contained only Anglo inmates, others only Hispanic inmates; one or two groups were ethnically mixed with Anglo, Hispanic, and Black inmates. The groups appear to have acted independently in choosing victims and dealing out death. Inmates were tortured, stabbed, mutilated, burned, bludgeoned, hanged, and thrown off upper-tier catwalks into the basement. One inmate was decapitated; his head was later put on a pole, paraded through the main corridor and shown to the hostage COs held in Cellblock 3. One inmate, while reportedly still alive, had a steel rod hammered completely through his head. Another inmate was drenched with glue and set on fire. An inmate's genitals were hacked off with a shovel. In fact, there was an apparent competition between the groups in both the quantity and "quality" of their killings. In discussing the extreme brutality of the Cellblock 4 killings, an inmate (who was later charged by prosecutors with, but not convicted of, two of these murders) said in a 1988 PBS documentary on PNM, "Once they started killing then it got worse and worse and worse.... Finally there wasn't enough people to kill so they would have to do real crazy shit to the ones that they were killing" (Galan 1988).

There does not seem to be any motive, such as personal revenge, to account for these killings. No particular inmate killer among the suspects, for example, had apparently been "snitched off" by any of the victims. In fact, only a few of the inmates killed in Cellblock 4 were identified by staff and inmates as informants. These inmate victims were viewed as weak inmates and thus vulnerable targets of violence, whose deaths would not be avenged by other inmates. The fact that the victims were trapped in protective isolation not only increased the killers' sense of total domination but demonstrated the killers' "superiority" since they outsmarted the state authorities who were charged with protecting these inmate victims from such an action. For these perpetrators, this latter element enhanced the seductiveness of these killings.

As Jack Katz (1988) argues in his book, *Seductions of Crime*, such brutal, cold-blooded murders must be understood as primarily expressive acts, and only secondarily instrumental. Katz (1988: 305-306) notes the situational dynamics involved in the cold-blooded killings he discusses:

> In each of these cases, the movement of the protagonist into killing developed when actions by others [usually accomplices] brought into relief the question of whether the protagonist could sustain a posture of terrifying dominance.... [Such a killing is] a positive act of reclaiming status as an awesome deviant.

According to Katz, situations leading to cold-blooded murder often include the questioning by others of the killer's commitment to a deviant course of action, i.e., whether the perpetrator has only "a limited ability to embrace their project in deviance" (Katz 1988: 307). This group dynamic of proving one's commitment to a deviant project is amplified in a situation, such as the one in Cellblock 4 on the morning of February 2, in which small groups of inmates are competing for images as dominatingly "awesome" deviants. Each group feels compelled to outdo the other in its acts of violence. Thus the utterly senseless statement quoted earlier from an inmate witness, that "there wasn't enough people to kill so they would have to do real crazy shit to the ones they were killing," becomes comprehensible, though not rational from any instrumental or conventionally utilitarian viewpoint. These brutal acts eternally mark their victims as morally weak and their perpetrators as morally superior in the upside-down world that the inmate society had become. Inmates involved in these killings could count on gaining reputations as the most violent and feared inmates in the prison.

The Cellblock 4 killings were apparently over by 10 a.m. Twelve inmates in Cellblock 4 and three inmates in Cellblock 3 (including the two inmates who had been killed around 3 a.m.) were murdered in this brutal, cold-blooded fashion. In contrast to killings in the south wing, only one of the sixteen north-wing killings appears to have been the result of a fight, which apparently occurred in Cellblock 4 after 10 a.m. on Saturday.

More inmates would have undoubtedly died had they not been able to escape Cellblock 4. Besides those inmates who left their cells and escaped the protective custody unit when it was opened, other inmates living in this unit were rescued by sympathetic inmates. Some individual inmates entered Cellblock 4, found specific inmate friends, and sneaked them out of the unit. One contingent of about twenty Black inmates from Cellhouse 6 converged on Cellblock 4 about 7:30 a.m. to rescue one of their leaders, a Black Muslim minister, who had been locked in the protection unit. Upon his release, the Muslim minister told his followers to get as many protective custody inmates out of Cellblock 4 as possible. This group saved many of the intended victims (Black, Anglo, and Hispanic) from Cellblock 4. They brought these inmates to Cellhouse 6 where they combined forces for self-protection. About noon on Saturday these Black and protective custody inmates were able to fight their way to Dorm E-1 and escape through the window broken open earlier.

After 7 a.m., groups of inmates and individual inmates began leaving the prison through the window in Dorm E-1 and through the east end of Cellblock 5, via a metal door that had been cut open about 8:30 a.m. by an inmate using a blowtorch. Many of these inmates described to authorities scenes of torture, random violence, and death. A preliminary list of inmate victims was compiled along with lists of perpetrators. By 5 p.m. on Saturday, over 350 inmates had left the prison to surrender to authorities. Inmates would continue for the duration of the riot to escape the violence, mayhem, fires, and smoke through the exits cut in Dorm E-1 and Cellblock 5 and additional ones found at the rear of the kitchen and at the main entrance. By 1 p.m. on Sunday, the final day of the riot, only 100 of the prison's 1,157 inmates remained inside.

At about the time the killings of protective custody inmates in Cellblock 4 were taking place, another group of inmates reached Governor King over a field telephone given to them by officials. In an attempt to circumvent the confused messages coming over walkie-talkies, Deputy Warden Montoya and Deputy Secretary Rodriguez authorized the delivery to the front entrance of the prison of a field telephone to be used for negotiations. (Regular phone lines within the prison by this time had been destroyed.) At 8:30 a.m., inmates used the field phone to call a State Police district headquarters in Santa Fe. The Governor, who had just arrived at the headquarters, agreed to talk to the inmates. The inmates wanted a forum to be attended by the Governor, Montoya, Rodriguez, and the news media for airing their grievances. Governor King promised to set up a table in the prison yard in one hour for the conference. This conference never materialized, and inmates, who continued radio negotiations and at times face-to-face discussions with Montoya and Rodriguez, did not speak with members of the news media until after 7 p.m. on Saturday, the first day of the riot. As a result of this meeting between two news reporters and two Anglo inmates, who had been involved with the initial takeover of Dorm E-2, the now badly injured assistant shift supervisor was released at 8:22 p.m. At 10:45 p.m., Dorm E-2 inmates carried out a hostage tied to a chair; the hostage had been beaten just before his release. This hostage was released in anticipation of a camera crew entering the prison. When NBC cameraman Michael Shugrue entered the prison at midnight to record inmates' grievances, another hostage, after several minutes of arguing and fighting among his inmate captors, was carried from the prison to authorities on a stretcher. This hostage had also been severely beaten. Six hostages remained inside the prison.

Shugrue, standing in the visitors' room near the prison's main entrance, recorded a group of club-wielding inmates, many of whom were masked or wearing PNM's riot control gear, taken from the Control Center. The room was filled with smoke as inmates presented their grievances about poor food, nepotism, harassment, overcrowding, idleness, inadequate recreation facilities, and arbitrary disciplinary practices by the administration. They complained of "being treated like kids" by staff who "showed them no respect" and demeaned them on a daily basis. They demanded the resignation of Deputy Warden Montoya and other middle-level supervisors at PNM. Most of the grievances and demands were restatements of eleven demands contained in a written list handed to Montoya and Rodriguez at mid-afternoon on Saturday. Speaking of these eleven demands, two commentators correctly note that the demands "...proved to be relatively unimportant in the resolution of the riot" (Serrill and Katel 1980: 16).

Beyond the release of these three hostages, either in anticipation of or response to seeing the news media, negotiations with inmates had very little to do with the release of hostages or ending the riot. At 7:52 a.m. on Sunday morning, the second day of the riot, one of the hostages seized outside Dorm F-2 managed with the help of sympathetic inmates, to escape from the prison. At 8:15 a.m., in apparent anticipation of another news conference, the shift supervisor was released by the inmates holding him. Later, at 10:55 a.m., another hostage CO escaped with the help of inmates. At 11:50 a.m., the three COs captured in Cellblock 3, who had all been moved for their safety to Cellhouse 6 during the previous afternoon, were brought to the information booth just inside the main entrance of the prison. At 11:57 a.m., one of these hostages was released. Only two hostages remained in the prison by noon on Sunday, February 3.

These Sunday morning hostage releases occurred shortly after three Hispanic inmates (Lonnie Duran, Vincent Candelaria, and Kendrick Duran), who were among the few inmates who had been attempting unsuccessfully to organize the riot into a protest over prison conditions, ironed out an agreement with Montoya and Rodriguez during a meeting in the gatehouse beneath Tower 1. The agreement contained the following five points: 1) no retaliation against rioting inmates; 2) segregation policies be reviewed; 3) inmates be permitted to meet with members of the press; 4) no double-bunking of inmates in Cellblock 3; and 5) inmates be given water hoses to douse fires inside the prison. The Durans and Candelaria returned to the prison to seek approval from other inmates.

The final hours of the riot saw the setting of more fires, an increasingly larger stream of inmates leaving the prison to surrender to authorities, inmates being rushed to hospitals with injuries and pharmacy-drug overdoses, and bodies of inmates being deposited in the yard in front of the prison. A brief confrontation between Hispanic and Black inmates in the recreation yard behind the prison was broken up by police officers who separated the Blacks from other prisoners.

The Durans and Candelaria re-emerged from the prison shortly before noon for continued negotiations. These were witnessed by reporter Peter Katel who later, with co-author Michael Serrill, gave the following account of the last hours of the riot:

The two Durans and Candelaria emerged from the prison and announced that they had approval from other inmates to sign the agreement negotiated the night before.... Then negotiations became more complicated. Other inmates joined the Durans and Candelaria at the negotiating table. They haggled over exactly how the agreement was to be implemented by prison officials.... Officials were particularly worried about the presence of three new inmates, William Jack Stephens, Michael Colby and Michael Price, at the negotiations. Colby and Stephens escaped on Dec. 9 and were recaptured.... In 1978, they, together with Price, beat another inmate to death with baseball bats.... Their commitment to a peaceful resolution of the riot was considered dubious. Later, they were identified as prime suspects in some of the [riot] killings.... At about 12:30 p.m., Colby, Stephens and other inmates rejoined the talks and started making new demands.... Rodriguez says that at this point he began to worry that the Durans and Candelaria were losing control. He also began to wonder whether the majority of inmates inside were really aware of and had agreed to the five rather mild demands (Serrill and Katel 1980: 21).

Rodriguez, fearing that Colby and Stephens were gaining control of the situation, made a deal with them. He promised to transport them immediately to another prison out of state and told them to go back inside the prison to get their belongings. As soon as Colby and Stephens left, Rodriguez ordered Vincent Candelaria and Lonnie and Kendrick Duran (the inmates with whom he had been negotiating) to get the remaining two hostages, who were now seated blindfolded on the grass outside the main entrance. A few minutes later, at about 1:30 p.m., these last hostages were brought to Rodriguez. Immediately, police, National Guardsmen, and prison employees rushed the prison to retake it from the approximately 100 inmates still within. Authorities encountered no resistance from inmates during the retaking of the institution.

The February 2 and 3, 1980 riot caused $20 million in physical damage to the institution and over $200 million in riot-related expenses. Over 200 inmates and 7 of the 12 hostage COs suffered serious injuries. Thirty-three inmates were killed during the 36 hours of the riot. A 34th inmate died in October 1980 from injuries sustained during the riot (*Santa Fe Reporter* 9/3/81).

UNDERSTANDING
PRISON DISORDER

The 1980 riot was a dramatic and explosive episode in a continuing pattern of disorder which had its roots several years earlier. The social history presented in the preceding chapters documents the increasing crisis of control that emerged in the late 1970s. The riot was not an inevitable event; prison disorder could have continued to manifest itself in escapes and inmate-to-inmate violence. What happened at PNM, minus the riot, is happening at many maximum-security prisons. Perhaps the riot underscores the Penitentiary of New Mexico as a "worst case scenario" because total control was lost. But the uniqueness of the riot should not distract our attention from the more mundane levels of horror (the "riots in slow motion") that afflict prisons across North America and in Great Britain (*Washington Post* 4/10/90).

Two things stand out as characteristics of the 1980 riot at PNM: the almost total lack of organization by inmates and the inmate-to-inmate violence that punctuated the event. These two characteristics reflect the organizational changes documented in the preceding chapters. They also reflect the growing violence and social disorganization that has affected prisons throughout the U.S. during the late 1970s and 1980s (Bowker 1980; Haas and Alpert 1986; Irwin 1980; McVicar 1982; Olivero and Roberts 1987; Woldman 1987; Wooden and Parker 1982). As Stastny and Tynauer (1982: 5), commenting on the general state of U.S. prisons in the 1980s, wrote, "...today every prison is Santa Fe and Santa Fe is every prison. It is not a hopeful prospect."

Riots come in a variety of distinct forms and patterns (Useem and Kimball 1989). Any prison can experience a riot or major disturbance at any time. But when a riot begins, often because of immediate situational contingencies, the shape, direction, and tone of the event are affected by more long-term, underlying organizational trends. Previous state actions and bureaucratic decisions can set the stage upon which a riot event, should it occur, plays itself out. And, on even a broader scale, ideological, political, and economic trends in the larger society ultimately give shape to these events.

The 1980 riot at the Penitentiary of New Mexico stands in sharp contrast to the prison uprising that occurred in 1971 at Attica, New York

(Clark 1973; Hampton 1990; Wicker 1975). The Attica riot was character-ized by its very high level of organization among inmates. After an initial period of disorder immediately after the takeover, a group of inmates established leadership, enforced discipline over their fellow inmates, and created a strong sense of solidarity. Unlike the scene in 1980 at PNM, negotiations at Attica were a central and important event. Inmate-to-inmate violence was minimal. Though three inmates were apparently killed by other inmates during the early stages of the takeover, the vast majority of the forty-three inmate and hostage deaths were caused by law enforcement agents when they forcefully retook the prison (Bell 1985).

At Attica, a high level of political consciousness was expressed by inmate negotiators. As discussed in Chapter 2, this political consciousness was the culmination of a prisoner-based movement which had its origins in the radicalization of the poor inspired by earlier civil rights activities (Hampton 1990; Jackson 1970; Pallas and Barber 1972). Like the PNM riot, Attica reflected recent trends both in prisons and the larger society. By the time of the 1980 PNM riot, political mobilization within both impoverished urban areas and prisons had waned and was replaced with increasing disorganization and violence.

CLUES FOR UNDERSTANDING PRISON DISORDER

While the Penitentiary of New Mexico produced the most brutal and vio-lent riot in U.S. prison history, this prison, as we have seen, was not always violent. In fact, at the time of the Attica revolt, PNM was considered one of the most nonviolent prisons in the U.S. The inmate strike that took place at PNM shortly after the Attica uprising in 1971 involved some property damage and physical retaliation by COs upon inmates, but no assaults or violence among inmates occurred.

For a long period prior to 1976, the prison was orderly and nonvio-lent. From 1969 to late 1975, only three successful escapes and three unsuccessful escape attempts occurred. Violence between inmates was also minimal: there were no killings and only a few rare fistfights.

Beginning in October 1975, the level of disorder at PNM became worse. From late 1975 to 1980, there were thirty-six successful over-the-fence escapes and an additional eighteen unsuccessful escape attempts. Inmate violence became commonplace by the late 1970s.

Some of the immediate factors contributing to the 1980 riot certainly provide some clues for understanding this earlier shift from order to dis-order. These factors include the security lapses, complaints from inmates about prison conditions, overcrowding of the prison, and the presence of inmates who were prone to violence.

Prison disorder and security

First, the security lapses that caused the riot to spread could also have contributed to the growing disorder in the late 1970s. However, as is evident in the social history presented in previous chapters, lax security had been a nearly constant complaint of correctional staff since 1968, when many restrictions on inmates' movements were lifted. Custodial staff repeated often that the institution could be taken at anytime, in the late 1960s, early 1970s, and late 1970s. Expressing what many COs and inmates stated, one veteran CO said that "actually, the security portion of it has always been more or less the same." Another veteran CO, when asked to describe security before 1975 when the prison was relatively free of disorder, said: "security wasn't very tight, it was kind of loose." And, another CO agreed that security in the early 1970s "was loose" because inmates "had the run of the institution."

The highest marks for security enhancement were overwhelmingly given to Warden Malley in 1976 and 1977. Thus the first indications of disorder appear to correspond with tightened security, not a relaxation of security. After the disorder had increased at PNM, and after Warden Malley was forced to leave his post in early 1978, the middle-level managers of the prison enforced an increasingly inconsistent and generally ineffective routine of security. While not the cause of the disorder, this mismanagement in security from 1978 to the 1980 riot certainly reduced the level of containment of the disorder.

While the takeover could not have proceeded as it did on the morning of February 2, 1980 without the security lapses, many of these existed long before the riot. The opportunity to take the prison, or to escape or engage in violence, has always existed. While sound security procedures are an essential component in the improvement of prison management (DiIulio 1987), the existence of poor security by itself does not explain the disorder of the late 1970s and early 1980s at PNM.

In this context, it should also be noted that court-ordered reforms instituted after the 1980 riot included a substantial enhancement of security procedures and correctional officer training (Galan 1988). Yet the level of violence and disorder continued for several years after these enhanced security procedures were initiated (Galan 1988).

Prison disorder and living conditions

A second possible factor related to the increasing disorder in the late 1970s could be changing prison conditions. The important question is, which prison conditions changed significantly and which remained relatively constant between the periods of order in the early 1970s and disorder in the late 1970s? Inmate demands, formulated during the 1980 riot and expressed by inmates in its aftermath, included, among other items, complaints about food, recreation, and medical care. A deterioration of these basic services could have increased discontent and contributed to the greater disorder in the late 1970s. Yet inmates during the early 1970s also complained about the poor quality of some of these same services.

During the October 1971 strike, inmates' demands were very similar to those expressed during the 1980 riot. The inmates' list of demands, given to prison officials at the beginning of the 1971 strike, included better medical and dental care, better food, improved visiting accommodations, changes in parole policies, and the payment of 15 cents per hour for all inmate prison jobs (*New Mexican* 10/7/71). Reporting on individual grievances expressed by inmates following this incident, the officials at the time said, "Among the common grievances so far are food, medical service, harassment or mistreatment by guards, job pay, complaints against the parole board and not enough television time" (*New Mexican* 10/17/71: A5).

On August 30, 1972, there was a minor, isolated incident in the segregation unit (Cellblock 3), when thirty of its sixty-five inmates broke plumbing fixtures and started small fires in their individual, locked cells. No one was injured in the fracas. "The rampage by some inmates apparently erupted over complaints about food and medication" (*Albuquerque Journal* 10/12/72: F12).

During my first year working at PNM, beginning in January 1975, I heard repeated complaints from inmates about the food, medical services, and recreation, complaints that I would continue to hear until I left New Mexico corrections in 1978. Also, a former corrections official who observed the prison in 1975 and 1976 described the food services as "just deplorable" and warned a state legislative committee in 1975 that "the same thing that happened at McAlester, Oklahoma [a prison riot] is going to happen here [at PNM] if you don't improve that food services department." (Quote from 1980 interview conducted by New Mexico Attorney General's Office; see also *Albuquerque Journal* 12/13/75; *New Mexican* 12/14/75, 12/15/75.)

During the 1976 work strike inmates also voiced grievances similar to those voiced in 1971 and 1980. As one inmate wrote, concerning the buildup to the 1976 strike, "...the institution was infested with rats, the toilets didn't work and the food was, *as usual,* bad." (Stone 1982: 92, *emphasis added.*)

It does not appear that these specific elements of prison life (especially food and medical services) took a dramatic turn for the worse after 1975. They had always been poor. In fact, a full-time medical doctor was hired by the prison for the first time in 1978 in an attempt to improve medical services.

It should also be noted in this regard that food, recreation, and several other basic services were improved after the 1980 riot through court-ordered reforms (Useem 1985; Galan 1988). As is discussed in Chapter 8, disorder at the prison nonetheless continued for several years after the riot.

Other complaints expressed by inmates during and immediately after the 1980 riot do reflect important changes in prison conditions that correspond with the change from relative order in the early 1970s to disorder in the late 1970s. The shifts in these specific prison conditions are the focus of much of the discussion in Chapters 3 and 4 and in earlier articles on the New Mexico prison riot (Colvin 1982; Useem 1985). They are definitely tied to the shift from order to disorder. Of these changes in prison conditions, probably the most important was the dramatic drop after 1975 in inmate programs dealing with educational, occupational, and social skills. During the early 1970s these programs provided important incentives for order and significantly reduced the level of inmate idleness. Related to the 1976 shift in the administration's control structure, many of these programs were eliminated or greatly curtailed. Finally, many services (especially recreational opportunities) and the overall quality of prison life were under strain largely because of other deteriorating conditions in the prison. Namely, these were the escalation of harassment by many COs and the increasing levels of violence and overcrowding. The growth in prison population in the late 1970s was an especially aggravating factor (Useem and Kimball 1989).

Prison disorder and overcrowding

Overcrowding was a third factor present on the night of the riot. The actual capacity that night was 884 beds.[1] The number of inmates housed at PNM was 1,157; thus the prison was overcrowded by 273 inmates on the night of February 2, 1980. The overcrowding was most evident in the south-wing dormitories, designed to hold 50 inmates each. Many of these dorms held 80 or more inmates. (Dorm E-2, where the takeover was initiated, held 62 inmates on the night of the riot.) Except for the protective custody cellblock (Cellblock 4), which held six inmates above its 90 inmate capacity, none of the cellblocks or cellhouses were overcrowded. They each contained one man per cell.

The inmate population and the prison's inmate capacity have fluctuated greatly since PNM was opened in 1956 (Useem and Kimball 1989). During the late 1970s, the inmate population was generally at a higher level than in the early 1970s, corresponding to the shift from order to disorder

discussed earlier. In June 1972, the inmate population was 595. Throughout the early 1970s, it remained below the prison's designed capacity,
which at that time was 822 beds. But by June 1975, the inmate population
had suddenly surged to 991 inmates, 169 over capacity. The prison
remained orderly throughout the summer of 1975 as the population continued to increase. Then, on October 19, 1975 (three weeks after Warden
Aaron took over), the first signs of disorder began to appear when six
inmates escaped in what at that time was the "largest mass escape in
the...history of the prison" (*New Mexican* 10/22/75: A1). On November
15, 1975, the inmate population reached 1,018 inmates, 196 above capacity.[2] By December 31, 1975, overcrowding subsided as the inmate population dropped to its capacity of 822. Inmate disorder continued, however, as
more escapes and the first stabbing incidents occurred. The inmate population remained stable until late May 1976, when it grew to over 900. By June
30, 1976, the inmate population reached 913. After this point, prison disorder began to become more apparent, as the first inmate killing of the 1970s
occurred in August 1976 and the number of escapes rose. The reconversion
in 1977 of Dorms D-1 and C-1 from classroom and office space to living
units added 90 beds to the prison's capacity, raising it to 912. In 1977, however, the inmate population soared to 1150, setting the level of overcrowding at 238. On March 3, 1978, the prison was overcrowded by 360 inmates
when the population reached an all-time high of 1,272. The overcrowding
in 1977 and 1978 coincided with a dramatic increase in disorder. For much
of 1979, when the level of violence remained high, the inmate population
dropped to below 960. Thirty-two beds in a new modular unit and 28 beds
in the Annex Building, from which women prisoners had been moved,
became available in 1979, raising the prison's capacity during much of 1979
to 972. But in late 1979 and early 1980, the capacity of the prison was
reduced to 884 beds when Cellblock 5 was closed for renovation and the
Annex Building was once again slated as living space for women inmates.
This reduction in living space coincided with a rapid increase in inmate
population that produced the overcrowded conditions on the night of the
1980 riot. The inmate population thus fluctuated during the 1970s but was
above capacity during many points from late 1975 to 1980, corresponding
with the general rise in disorder.

Overcrowding definitely contributed to the level of tension already
present within the prison, especially with the "dramatic increase of 200
inmates in the three months prior to the riot [which] occurred because
transfers to satellite facilities ceased" (Office of the Attorney General
1980b: 8). But, by itself, overcrowding does not completely explain growing disorder. As Jonathan Freedman (1975) argues in *Crowding and
Behavior,* crowding does not produce stress or other forms of social

pathology unless accompanied by stress-producing conditions. Crowding can intensify stress or tension already present in a situation. PNM provides a clear example to support Freedman's arguments.

As discussed in Chapter 3, PNM was chronically overcrowded by about 115 inmates from 1960 through 1963, reaching a level that was 152 over capacity on December 22, 1962. Yet there was little disorder during this period. Also, the overcrowding in the summer of 1975, reported above, did not coincide with increasing disorder until after the administrative succession in top positions at the prison occurred in late September 1975. In fact, it was as this particular surge of overcrowding eased in early 1976 that the violence and disorder that would plague the prison throughout the late 1970s began to worsen. The stress, tension, and violence that exploded to the surface in 1977 and 1978 was certainly exacerbated by the extreme overcrowded conditions during those two years. But the other factors that produced stress in the late 1970s were apparently not present during the periods of overcrowding in the early 1960s and summer of 1975, since the overcrowding at those points did not correspond with increasing violence and disorder. Thus, a prison that is experiencing organizational disruption may move from a bad situation to a disaster if overcrowding also occurs. Without the other sources of organizational stress, however, a prison may ride out a period of overcrowding relatively unscathed.

Again, it should be noted in this context that crowded conditions at PNM have been entirely eliminated through court orders following the 1980 riot. The federal court in 1980 placed a cap of 800 on the inmate population in the main penitentiary building. And more cell space has been made available with the 1985 opening of the new North Facility, which has a capacity of 288 inmates and is located at the north end of the PNM reservation. However, high levels of violence, disorders, and escapes continued for several years into the 1980s.

Other prison studies give mixed findings on the link between overcrowding and prison disorder. Garson's (1972: 551) historical overview of prison riots finds little relationship between overcrowding and rioting. DiIulio's (1987: 74) comparative study of prisons also shows no relationship between overcrowding and prison violence. Ekland-Olsen, Barrick, and Cohen (1983) and Ekland-Olsen (1986) conclude from their analyses of Texas prisons that lowered average age of inmates, associated with overcrowding, was the cause of increases in inmate misconduct, not the overcrowding itself. Ellis (as reported in Gaes [1985]) points to the greater transiency of inmates during periods of overcrowding as the cause of increased disorder, not overcrowding per se. However, in a study by Gaes and McGuire (1985) of nineteen federal prisons, crowding did have an important independent effect upon assaults among prisoners. Thus research gives only mixed support for overcrowding as a direct cause of prison disorder.

It is thus possible to focus too much attention on overcrowding as *the* cause of growing disorder. But, as I wrote in an earlier article, "overcrowding cannot be completely discounted as a contributing factor" (Colvin 1982: 452). It certainly combines with other factors to contribute to growing disorder.

Prison disorder and violence-prone inmates

A fourth factor that may help us understand the growing disorder of the late 1970s is the possibility that a new type of disruptive inmate was emerging at PNM. The key question here is whether disruptive inmates are "imported" into the prison from the outside or whether they are "partly a prison product" (Toch 1978: 21). Many COs, inmates, and prison officials expressed the belief that a new type of inmate definitely was emerging in the prison. The exact characteristics of this new inmate were subjects of disagreement, except that most observers described him as "young." Also, the period when this new inmate began to be noticed is not entirely clear. There seem to be two distinct periods mentioned respectively by long-term staff members and by inmates and more short-term staff members. Veteran staff members, when asked whether new inmates are different than the old inmates who used to come into the prison, tend to point to a change they witnessed in the late 1960s when inmates started being more demanding, aware of their rights, disrespectful of authority, and inclined to use drugs. A veteran corrections official said:

> [Before the late 1960s,] inmates were a lot more law abiding, they were more acceptable of rules and regulations. It wasn't everybody saying "it's a violation of my constitutional rights." [Now] they're very confrontive. You give them an order and they want to know why in the hell you think you can give them an order.... We're dealing with an entirely different individual. He's younger; he's more demanding; he's more aware of the publicity that's given the inmate of his constitutional rights.... They're more critical of the slightest thing.

And a correctional officer said:

> When I first started here [in 1966] the inmates were passive. You tell them to "get in line," they'd get in line, "do this, do that," they'd do it.... Now (chuckle) it's different. Got a modern inmate. They want this, they want that. They see other places...[and] come in from the federal institutions, [and] say, "Oh, man, we had this, this and that." [And PNM's inmates say] "Yeah? That's good, let's do it here."

When asked to give time periods for the emergence of these inmates who were more confrontational, aware of their rights, and unwilling to follow the orders of COs, many observers placed the change in the late 1960s. "Let's say with the Beatles," said a veteran CO, who related the change in inmates with the counter-cultural movements of the late 1960s. "You know when the Beatles came through the whole world changed."

Clearly, this new inmate type emerged several years before PNM became violent and disorderly. Inmates demanding rights and questioning the staff's authority certainly posed a crisis for these administrators and COs. It is interesting that when asked to compare the old with the new inmates, the veteran COs tend to focus on the change they witnessed in the late 1960s when inmates became demanding. They do not focus on the period after 1975 when inmates became more violent, which was a separate change in inmate behavior from that discussed by these veteran corrections personnel. They saw the violence and the disrespect for authority as being of one piece. But, this disrespect began and continued during a period of relative order in the prison, the late 1960s and early 1970s. Increasing violence did not appear until 1976.

As discussed in Chapter 3, the movement toward inmate rights, which produced this new disrespectful inmate, was certainly an import from outside the prison, but it was accelerated at PNM by the "treatment regime" introduced by Warden Baker in 1968. Baker's appointment as warden undermined the old authoritarian regime which had produced the passive inmates fondly remembered by the veteran members of the custodial staff. The emergence of this new type of inmate, who was demanding and cognizant of his rights, is important for understanding a growing confrontational atmosphere between the custodial staff and inmates, which was expressed nonviolently in the early 1970s (except when some COs used physical retaliation after the 1971 strike) and began to be expressed through escalating harassment and violence in the late 1970s.

Other characteristics of inmates began to be observed in the mid-1970s that reflected the growing violence in the prison. Inmates, and correctional officers who had been employed by the prison after the early 1970s, focused on a change in inmates related to greater violence. As discussed in Chapter 5, a more violent inmate who no longer "did his own time," but "messed with" other inmates before they could "mess with" him, emerged after 1976.

While the growing awareness of inmates' rights in the late 1960s was clearly a phenomenon imported from outside the prison, the growing number of violence-prone inmates in the late 1970s was largely a product of the prison itself.[3] This is supported by information presented in Chapter 5: first, by the decreasing percentage of violent crimes for which inmates were being sent to the prison; and second, by the observations of Master Plan consultants, who in 1977 described the PNM inmate population as criminally unsophisticated and fitting more the profile of county jail rather than state penitentiary inmates. As a CO, who observed the rise in violence at PNM, expressed it:

> Actually the inmates are products of the prison system. You are going to have inmates come in that are nonviolent.... But working under those conditions [at PNM in the late 1970s], it forces a lot of good inmates to turn bad. You see inmates come in that you won't have any problems with; yet, you know that they're having problems.... [They] start acting a little crazy to make other inmates leave them alone.... So inmates are actually placed in a position, because of the type of prison that you have there, that they become violent. A nonviolent person can become violent just like a cat if it's cornered it can become violent. If you stand there and pose a threat to it, it'll attack, no matter how big or small it is, it will attack you. Human beings are the same way. If you place them in a position where they have to fight, they will fight.

This CO's observations about the prison producing violent inmates, rather than the entry of violence-prone individuals from outside as a cause of growing violence, is supported by prison studies that indicate a lack of correlation between prison violence and the entry of violence-prone inmates into prisons (Bennett 1976: 151; DiIulio 1987: 69-71; Ellis et al. 1974: 38; Garson 1972: 551; Jacobs 1977: 160). While it is clear that new types of inmates were emerging at PNM during the late 1970s, the fact of their appearance does not adequately explain the growing violence and disorder. The emergence itself of this new type of inmate who resorted more often to violence needs to be explained. The key to understanding the growing disorder is to understand exactly how violence-prone inmates were created by changes in the prison organization.

PRISON DISORDER, ORGANIZATIONAL CONTRADICTIONS, AND CHANGE

While all of the above factors (poor security, poor living conditions, overcrowding, and the presence of violence-prone inmates) contributed in varying degrees to growing disorder at PNM, these factors must be placed in the context of larger organizational and societal changes.

The disorder at the Penitentiary of New Mexico can be traced to the shift in the structure of control that began in late 1975. This shift, from a "remunerative compliance structure" to a "coercive compliance structure" (Etzioni 1970) created an immediate confrontation between inmates and staff because it undermined existing organizational accommodations. The "understandings" between inmates and staff that had prevailed since 1968 had given PNM a delicate balance of order. These accommodations, which included program participation, avenues for inmate power through inmate administrator positions, and, later, the toleration of drug trafficking, were important elements in the formal and informal systems of remunerative control that prevailed in the early 1970s. The almost complete and sudden dismantling of these accommodations in late 1975 and early 1976 led to organized inmate opposition to the administration. That inmates could organize themselves reflected a level of solidarity and leadership that had grown during the period of accommodation in the early 1970s. This inmate solidarity and leadership had contributed to low levels of violence. But by 1976 they presented an immediate threat to the rule of a new penitentiary administration.

This threat of an organized inmate opposition was crushed through a series of actions that created a new coercive control structure. This structure, while resembling in some ways the old authoritarian regime, with its emphasis on rigid discipline and the use of the "hole," differed from the authoritarian regime because it attempted to undermine any privileged positions for an inmate elite, i.e., those who held sensitive clerical positions prior to the late 1960s at PNM and in other prisons, such as Stateville (Jacobs 1977). Under the new coercive regime of the late 1970s, no accommodations were made to inmate power. And reliance on coercion during the late 1970s in many ways made this period even more repressive than the period prior to 1968, when the authoritarian regime had prevailed. As noted in Chapter 4, more inmates were placed in disciplinary lockup for relatively minor violations in the late 1970s than were placed there during the early 1960s' authoritarian regime, when minor violations were usually sanctioned with verbal reprimands.

The clear goal of the late 1970s coercive regime, with its increased use of segregation and transfer of instigators and troublemakers to prisons out of state, was to undermine inmate leaders' control and enhance the staff's authority by disrupting the solidarity among inmates. Such actions were aimed at creating a compliant group of inmates who would respect and follow the orders of the custodial force. But, in a contradictory fashion, these actions merely set into motion structural changes in inmate relations that created less compliance, more violence, and increasing disorder.

As inmate solidarity disintegrated, young inmates began entering a social situation that elicited violence from a growing number of inmates. With the loss of inmate leaders, and their sources of nonviolent power, new prisoners were no longer being guided and socialized into an established and stable inmate social structure. The vacuum of power created by

204 · THE PENITENTIARY IN CRISIS

the loss of inmate leaders produced a struggle for control among inmate cliques. As this violent struggle continued, a high premium for maintaining a reputation for violence emerged as a dominant force in inmate relations. Increasingly, new prisoners were confronted with this violence which forced them into choosing between being a victim (a punk who submits, or a snitch who seeks official protection) or a victimizer (an inmate who fights and develops a reputation for violence). As the inmate social structure at PNM increasingly broke down into small, isolated self-protective cliques, social control among inmates, to the extent that it existed at all, fell to a few of the most violent cliques that had emerged in the late 1970s. These cliques pushed the prison organization toward greater disruption and disorder. Once these disruptive cliques became a dominant force, the coercive means used by the custodial force to deal with their disorders were completely ineffective and may have actually played into the competition among these cliques for violent reputations.

The emergence of these violent inmate cliques was largely an organizational phenomenon. Its origin was the 1976 shift in the structure of control and the subsequent undermining of inmate solidarity. This important shift in the control structure has even wider origins in the political and ideological changes that were occurring in the larger society. In Chapter 2, these larger social trends were connected to changes in the organization of the prison. The long wave of optimism about offender rehabilitation finally arrived at PNM in 1968. However, the promising beginnings of inmate programs soon gave way to organizational apathy and corruption as programs ceased to expand in the early 1970s. Finally, the general consensus about rehabilitation died with the economic downturn of the mid-1970s. Though significant actors within the state government continued to promote the rehabilitative ideal, the reductions in inmate programs continued apace with a growing reliance upon coercive control of inmates.

A corrections administration torn by political and ideological strife in the late 1970s was incapable of arresting the drift, and later the surge, toward disorder. Coinciding with the 1976 shift in control structure at the prison was the beginning of a series of reorganizations emanating from the Governor's Office. These reorganizations not only made the lines of command within corrections unclear, they led to frequent turnover of top corrections and PNM administrators. These administrative successions led to a confused policy direction and allowed a middle-level clique of PNM administrators to run the prison in an inconsistent, incompetent, and often abusive and brutal manner. By 1978, the disorganization within the corrections administration paralleled the fragmentation within the inmate social structure. Concerted, effective administrative actions to deal with the growing disorder and violence became virtually impossible in this disorganized context.

The initiatives by the Governor's Office beginning in 1975 to bring PNM under greater executive control, and the initiatives by the warden beginning in 1976 to bring inmates under greater custodial control, both failed dismally. Each initiative was undermined by organizational contradictions that could not be eliminated by redrawing organizational charts or cracking down on organized inmate opposition. Instead, these governmental and administrative initiatives merely redirected the organizational contradictions toward creating a situation of increasing disorder, disorganization, and violence.

CONCLUSION:
CONTINUED CRISIS,
FUTURE PROSPECTS

Prison organizations are inherently contradictory. An underlying conflict between the keepers and captives defines all relations within prisons. This does not mean that prisons are inevitably in conflict or always violent. The underlying conflict is usually kept dormant in most prisons through an array of formal and informal structures of social control that offer inmates something to gain by conforming and something to lose by rebelling. To the extent that these social control mechanisms are viable, relative peace and order is maintained in a prison, and the inherent conflicts remain latent.

A good example of a prison that has maintained viable controls is discussed by Fleisher (1989). The Federal Penitentiary at Lompoc, California, houses some of the most violent and dangerous offenders in the U.S. Yet, as Fleisher documents, this prison has maintained an organizational climate that minimizes violence. An array of rewards and punishments constitutes a remunerative structure of control. A prisoner who engages in violence "pays a high price for losing self-control, and he pays immediately" (Fleisher 1989: 26). He loses income, earned from the relatively high-paying prison jobs and prison industries program, and "good-time," which is awarded to inmates for good behavior and can reduce the length of time before an inmate is paroled. He also risks an immediate transfer to a less desirable penitentiary that does not afford him the relative freedom of Lompoc. "The material and nonmaterial rewards and comforts that are available to inmates [at Lompoc] is the driving force of social control" (Fleisher 1989:27).

As discussed in Chapter 3, the Penitentiary of New Mexico prior to 1976 offers another example of prison control structures that keep the underlying conflict between keepers and captives dormant. As compared to federal prisons like Lompoc, however, PNM lacked the fiscal resources to maintain an expanding array of programs and other mechanisms that provide legitimate incentives for control. These limitations on expansion of such incentives led in the early 1970s to an internal contradiction within the organization. The growth of illegitimate incentives began to shape a social control structure that, while maintaining a nonviolent prison, was based on corruption. This internal contradiction (of good behavior being maintained through the tolerance of bad behavior) was greatly responsible for the breakdown of the remunerative system of control that had kept the underlying conflict within the organization inactive.

If viable control structures in prisons are disrupted through forces either internal or external to the prison organization, the restoration of effective means of control becomes extremely difficult. The ongoing "lockdown" at the Federal Penitentiary at Marion, Illinois, attests to the great difficulty in reestablishing control in a prison that has been through a period of violent disruptions (Breed and Ward 1984; *Newsweek* 1/15/90; Olivero and Roberts 1987). The murders, riots, and general disruption at Marion from February 1980 to October 1983 led the administration to institute a complete lockdown of the penitentiary. Inmates are kept isolated in their cells. When inmates are moved to a different cell, they frequently resist and fight with correctional officers. In a situation defined on both sides as "combat" and "war," resistance to any of the staff's attempts at control has become expected, normative behavior among Marion's inmates. Inmates at Marion are under the most coercive situation of control in any U.S. prison. Little else can be taken away from them, and they have nothing to lose. "Control" does not properly describe this situation. Instead, these inmates can be said to be "contained," like a dangerous explosive. Since the 1983 lockdown, Marion has experienced numerous killings and assaults of both staff and inmates. The underlying conflict between keepers and captives at Marion is seething immediately below the surface and is kept at bay only through a series of very expensive physical containments.

Most states cannot afford the elaborate system of containment in place at Marion. They cannot hold back the basic hostility with physical constraints alone. A viable structure of control has to be reestablished if order is to return. But such a restoration of effective structures of control is problematic.

PNM offers a striking example of how difficult it is to reestablish control at a state penitentiary. Following the 1976 disruption of incentive controls, coercive controls were relied upon to an ever-greater extent. To an increasing degree, inmates became alienated from this coercive system of control. And, as violence increased among inmates, inmate cohesiveness diminished; thus, the basis for reestablishing the intricate incentive controls dissolved.

Under the incentive-based, remunerative structure of control, inmate leaders and individual inmates generally perceived a self-interest in maintaining orderly behavior. Inmates were pulled by both the administration's controls and those exerted by other inmates toward behavior that maintained relative peace and order. As this remunerative control structure was both intentionally and inadvertently dismantled, and as coercive controls were brought more heavily into the situation, individual inmates became increasingly torn between the demands of the prison administration for compliance and the competing demands for noncompliance from a growing number of dominant inmates who no longer perceived a self-interest in maintaining order. In fact, these dominant inmates perceived a self-interest in creating disruptions. As cliques of disruptive inmates grew in power through intimidation and violence, their coercive controls over other inmates became more compelling than the coercive controls used by the administration. In this situation, defined by coercion on both sides, the inherent contradiction between the keepers and captives pulls the average inmate, who may be trying to serve out his sentence in a reasonable fashion, toward a frightening and deadly dilemma of choosing between competing demands upon his behavior and allegiances.

After the 1980 riot, PNM continued to experience disorder. Despite the 1980 settlement of the ACLU lawsuit through a series of federal consent decrees, which enhanced security, improved food, recreation and other living conditions, and eliminated inmate idleness and overcrowding, PNM remained for several years violent and disorderly (Galan 1988). The three-year period (1980–82) following the riot was especially disorderly: 7 inmates and 2 COs were killed, scores of inmates and COs were assaulted and injured, and 9 escapes and several disturbances occurred (*Albuquerque Journal* 1/28/90). The prison remained tense over the next seven years (1983–89) as 7 more inmates were killed, and 155 inmates and 125 staff members were officially counted as assault victims.[1] From 1984 through 1989, the combined rate per 100 inmate population of inmate-on-inmate and inmate-on-staff assaults averaged 4.3 annually, reaching a high of 6.0 in 1986 and a low of 3.0 in 1989.[2] These are comparatively high levels of assaults.[3] In addition, there were 29 escapes from 1983 through 1988. These included a 1987 mass escape of 7 inmates from the new "super-maximum-security" North Facility, during which a CO was shot, but not killed, by inmates (*Albuquerque Journal* 7/5/87; Galan 1988). A near riot, which was contained, was reported to have occurred after this mass escape (*New Mexican* 7/6/87). Thus, by 1988, order was still elusive at PNM.

Much of this continuing disorder was fed by the same underlying dynamics that led to violence during the late 1970s. In 1980, following the riot, the New Mexico Attorney General's investigative team, of which I was a member, pinpointed two essential measures that had to be taken to restore control and order at PNM: "Establish and fund an incentive-based inmate corrections policy; and hire and hold accountable stable, professional management to implement that policy" (Office of the Attorney

General 1980b: 33). Implementation of these measures has been greatly hampered by subsequent events and trends.

Concerning the first recommendation, the enhancement of incentive controls has been impeded by a new sentencing structure that undermines the incentive effect of increased programming. The federal court's consent decrees, signed by the State of New Mexico in 1980, provide inmates with a greater array of activities and programs and generally improve living conditions. While these program enhancements are essential for developing a viable control structure, the specific context in which they have been implemented greatly undermines their effectiveness for enhancing incentive controls. This context includes the loss of a parole mechanism which gives real force to any potential incentives connected to enhanced programming. Inmates began arriving at PNM in 1980 with fixed sentences mandated by New Mexico's determinate sentencing act, which went into effect in June 1979. After that point, program participation no longer led, as it did in the early 1970s, to early release on parole. Even with "good-time" provisions that shorten sentences, especially for those inmates who are able to participate in the prison industries program, the generally longer, fixed prison sentences mandated by the new law significantly reduce the incentive effect of programs. Sentence length has nearly doubled with the enactment of a number of legislatively mandated "sentence enhancements" that were added to the determinate sentencing law (*Albuquerque Journal* 4/19/78; Rhodes 1987). Determinate sentencing not only subverts control, it also undermines efforts at rehabilitation (Cullen and Gilbert 1982). This new sentencing scheme, still in effect in 1991, has removed a powerful incentive that can be used to induce both compliance and participation in rehabilitative treatment. Any incentive-based system of control established under determinate sentencing will be less effective, even with an array of programs and inmate activities. To be effective, these program opportunities have to become components in a system of control that provides meaningful rewards for positive behavior. The elimination of possible early release on parole removed the most meaningful of these rewards.

Also, in contrast to the early 1970s, program participation is not encouraged by significant members of the inmate leadership. They have no incentive to do so. Inmate leaders have not been groomed by program managers, as they were in the late 1960s, to support program participation. With the elimination of parole and the absence of inmate power and influence incorporated into these programs' designs, inmate leaders are not oriented toward these programs as they were in the early 1970s.

Instead, in the 1980s, inmate leaders continued to act at cross-purposes to the administration. Powerful rewards used to control other inmates became available to disruptive inmate cliques, which began in the mid-1980s to form into more structured, competing gangs. While not tolerated by the PNM administration, as it allegedly was in the early 1970s, drug trafficking in the late 1980s became, once again, a dominant activity (Galan 1988). Some of the disruptive cliques of the late 1970s were by 1987 organizing around and competing for control of these rackets. The rewards (such as access to drugs) and punishments (including death) under the control of these emerging inmate gangs overwhelmed the comparatively meager rewards and punishments used by the administration for compliance. As these cliques organized into competing gangs, violence and disruption continued, and the average inmate faced an ever-more fearful and deadly dilemma.

The federal court's consent decrees limit the prison administration in its attempts to segregate the leaders of these emerging gangs. The abuse of segregation by PNM administrators in the late 1970s properly led the State of New Mexico to consent to strict limitations on its use. Under these limitations, the administration has a more difficult task containing the activities of gang leaders. These consent decrees mandate that segregation cannot be used unless an inmate is proven to have been involved in an overt act of major misconduct. As George Sullivan, PNM warden from 1985 to 1987, said in a PBS documentary on PNM, "Gang leaders do not overtly involve themselves in major misconduct. They're puppeteers; they're behind the scenes" (Galan 1988). But, in the absence of meaningful positive incentives, segregation of gang leaders will produce, at best, only short-term containment. As long as the dynamics of violent competition among inmates remain, new gang leaders will keep emerging as old gang leaders are locked down. Thus, segregation is really no solution; it is merely a stopgap measure that will ultimately fail as long as the establishment of an effective incentive-based system of control is impeded.

The lack of an effective incentive-based control policy has left the prison administration at a huge disadvantage in its struggle with emerging inmate gangs. Meaningful rewards that might draw inmates away from gang activities have been greatly undermined by determinate sentencing.

Implementation of the second recommendation of the New Mexico Attorney General (to hire and hold accountable stable, professional management) has also been impeded. The series of administrative successions (five corrections secretaries and five PNM wardens from 1975 to 1980) are a primary reason for the disorganization of corrections prior to the 1980 riot. This rapid turnover of top administrators had a devastating impact on the policy direction and management at PNM. Between 1980 and 1987, this turnover continued with a succession of four corrections secretaries and five wardens.

The changeover in these corrections administrators is, as it was in the past, linked to the change in governors. Three different politicians held the Governor's chair between 1980 and 1990. Governor King, whose administration was rendered ineffective by continued press criticism of his handling of the prison (*Albuquerque Journal* 5/1/81, 9/9/81), left office in January 1983. A liberal Democrat, former Attorney General Toney Anaya, then became governor. He attempted to institute liberal reforms and rehabilitation programs in adult corrections. His efforts were hampered by the determinate sentencing act, the mid-1980 recession and oil price drop that reduced state revenues, and an obstinate state legislature that successfully resisted virtually every proposal put forward by Governor Anaya (*New York Times* 3/21/84). He also was heavily criticized by legislators and the press for his commutations of death sentences and pardoning of individual inmates. Anaya's attempts at liberal reforms, while good in theory, had the practical consequence of greater administrative confusion and political turmoil.

Anaya was replaced in January 1987 by Governor Garrey Carruthers, a conservative Republican. In 1987, Governor Carruthers and then newly elected Attorney General Hal Stratton began filing motions in federal court to reverse the consent decrees which the State of New Mexico had signed in 1980. This litigation threatened, once again, a drastic change in corrections policy. Governor Carruthers said in a PBS documentary, "It's not easy to overturn something that you have already agreed to.... One of the things that saves us, perhaps, is that we changed administrations. So, in changing administrations we at least can argue that we want something different [from the reforms in the consent decrees agreed to by previous governors]" (Rhodes 1987). Between 1987 and 1990, the State of New Mexico spent $4.4 million on litigation aimed at overturning the federal consent decrees (*Albuquerque Journal* 1/23/90). On January 22, 1990, the U.S. Supreme Court refused to hear the state's case and let stand a federal appeals court ruling that New Mexico must abide by the consent decrees. Thus, this latest attempt by a New Mexico governor to make a major change in corrections policies was thwarted by the courts.

In fact, the primary stabilizing influence on PNM during the 1980s and early 1990s has been the court orders which detail specific and consistent procedures for security, discipline, and staff training. Without these federal consent decrees, political influence on the management of PNM would have continued, and the disorder would have undoubtedly been worse.

Despite a 1990 inmate lawsuit that claims "prison conditions have considerably worsened in the past 2 years" (*Albuquerque Journal* 2/2/90: A1), the prison was beginning by 1990 to show some signs of stability: turnover of COs had been reduced to 30 percent (*New Mexican* 2/2/90), and violence and escapes were down significantly in 1989 and 1990. The combined rate of assaults against inmates and staff dropped from 4.5 per 100 in 1988 to 3.0 in 1989 and 2.9 in 1990. In 1989, for the first time since 1974, PNM experienced a year with no escapes; and none were reported during 1990. This recent lull in disorder may be the result of several factors.

First, given the reports of drug trafficking and the violent gang competition for its control in 1987 (Galan 1988), it is possible that one gang has emerged as dominant in the control of prison rackets. An inmate, who was identified as a major gang leader, was injured in a fight and segregated in January 1988 (Galan 1988). It was shortly after this incident that violence in the prison began to subside. The incident may have marked the end of the competition for control and the emergence of a more stable gang network, which may have the effect of reducing violence.

Second, stability in the operation of the prison also has contributed to this recent lull in disorder. As of 1991, one warden and one secretary of corrections had been in place since 1987. Following gubernatorial elections in 1990, a new governor took office in January 1991. Under new state constitutional provisions, this new governor, unlike his predecessors, will be allowed to seek a second, consecutive four-year term in 1994. Thus a particular source of instability in New Mexico state government has been removed. Of course, it is possible that a new corrections secretary, and possibly a new warden, will be named following the 1991 turnover in governors, especially since the new governor (Bruce King, who had been governor twice before) is from a different political party than his immediate predecessor. But the federal court orders have now been in place for over ten years, and the U.S. Supreme Court has made it clear that they will remain in effect no matter what a new governor or new prison administration may do. These court orders have ensured consistency and continuity of operations even in the context of further political, economic, and ideological shifts on the outside.[4]

This recent period of relative peace, however, is fragile. It is especially threatened by growing inmate populations and reduced government revenues. The state has attempted to stay ahead of inmate population growth by embarking on an expensive program of prison construction. In 1980, 1,477 inmates were housed at PNM and three minimum-security facilities. By 1990, 3,000 inmates were housed at the PNM complex and eight other corrections facilities located around the state (*New Mexican* 1/21/90). By 1993, the state projects an inmate population of 4,000 (*Albuquerque Journal* 1/28/90). This explosion of prison population undermines incentive controls, stability, and the state's revenue base, which increasingly has been diverted to prison construction. The growth in inmate population threatens to undo the progress that has been made in the last few years; it also draws state efforts and expenditures away from alternative measures that may in the long run be more effective in addressing overcrowding, prison control, and crime.

One alternative measure would be, in the words of Cullen and Gilbert (1982), to "reaffirm rehabilitation." The abandonment of rehabilitation in the mid-1970s as the goal of corrections has been devastating to American penology. Despite evidence that rehabilitation programs can work to reduce recidivism (Cullen and Gilbert 1982; Martinson 1979), we are still burdened with the "nothing works" attitude that justifies the warehousing of offenders (Johnson 1987). Warehousing criminals is not a means to any viable end. In addition, the incentive controls that I have highlighted as crucial for maintaining order in prisons only make sense in the context of the rehabilitative ideal. The funding for incentive-based programs will only come from legislators who see rehabilitation as the ultimate goal of corrections. The public, which in fact has consistently expressed support for rehabilitation (Cullen and Gilbert 1982: 257), must push their legislators in this direction.

As implied in the Chapter 2 discussion of external forces affecting prisons, even deeper changes in U.S. society must ultimately occur if we are to address the prison crisis. The 1980s and early 1990s have been economically devastating for the bottom one-fifth of the class structure: the undermining of the labor movement, rise of a low-wage service sector, declining real wages, and reductions in welfare spending significantly decreased the standard of living for impoverished groups (Katz 1989; Stuart 1990). At the same time, unbridled private investments of the wealthy during the 1980s have brought our nation to the brink of financial collapse, as capital has flowed into nonproductive mergers and wild speculation and generally out of the U.S. These trends must be reversed through a domestic "Marshall Plan" that directs investments toward job development, enhancement of human capital, the improvement of our productive capacity, and the rebuilding of our nation's declining cities and infrastructure (Colvin 1991). Additionally, we must promote a new definition of civil rights that includes "economic rights" (Adler 1987: 145–155), which should be reflected in legislation aimed at repairing and strengthening the position of organized labor. Economic restructuring must provide not only enhanced opportunities but also reduce the social disorganization and weak bonding that produce high crime in the poverty-stricken areas of our cities (Currie 1985; Walker 1989; Wilson 1987). The domestic Marshall Plan must therefore include a renewal of the community action spirit. As ever-greater tax dollars go to building prisons that do not rehabilitate but only brutalize, resources are diverted from education, job development, and the creation of viable communities that in the long run effectively prevent crime. In the process, we spend our scarce state revenues on mechanisms that only feed more crime back into society.

Crime-producing institutions, like PNM, must be transformed into places that promote rehabilitation and "mature coping" (Johnson 1987); this will only happen when effective incentive-based controls are established in prisons. Simultaneously, we must transform today's crime-producing neighborhoods into cohesive communities that prevent crime and offer viable alternatives to criminal activities for ex-offenders. If we do not take these essential steps, we will continue to create more crime and waste our scarce financial resources on maintaining and expanding violent prisons like the Penitentiary of New Mexico.

APPENDIX A

List of New Mexico State and Corrections Officials 1966–1980

GOVERNORS

Jack Campbell (Jan. 1965–Jan. 1967)

David Cargo (Jan. 1967–Jan. 1971)

Bruce King (Jan. 1971–Jan. 1975)

Jerry Apodaca (Jan. 1975–Jan. 1979)

Bruce King (Jan. 1979–Jan. 1983)

CORRECTIONS SECRETARIES AND DIRECTORS (none prior to 1969):

J. E. Baker (Acting Secretary of Corrections, July 1969–Feb. 1970)

John Salazar (Secretary of Corrections, Feb. 1970–Apr. 1970)

Howard Leach (Secretary of Corrections, Apr. 1970–Aug. 1975)

Mike Hanrahan (Secretary of Corrections, Aug. 1975–Feb. 1977)

Charles Becknell (Acting Secretary of Corrections, Feb. 1977–Apr. 1977)

Ed Mahr (Secretary of Corrections Apr. 1977–Mar. 1978; after reorganization, Director of Corrections Division, Apr. 1978–Apr. 1979)*

---

*Under 1978 reorganization, Secretary of Criminal Justice designated as top official in department; former Secretary of Corrections became Director of Corrections Division, which in Apr. 1979 was designated Deputy Secretary of Corrections. Secretary of Criminal Justice reverted back to Secretary of Corrections designation in Apr. 1979.

Charles Becknell (Secretary of Criminal Justice [Secretary of Corrections], Apr. 1978–Jan. 1980)*

Felix Rodriguez (Director of Corrections Division [Deputy Secretary of Corrections], Apr. 1979–May 1980)*

Adolph Saenz (Secretary of Corrections, Feb. 1980–June 1980)

WARDENS:

Harold Cox (June 1959–Oct. 1966)

Felix Rodriquez (Acting Warden, Oct. 1966–July 1967)

J. E. Baker (Aug. 1967–Feb. 1970)

Felix Rodriguez (Feb. 1970–Sept. 1975)

Ralph Lee Aaron (Sept. 1975–May 1976)

Clyde Malley (June 1976–Mar. 1978)

Levi Romero (Apr. 1978–Mar. 1979)

Jerry Griffin (Apr. 1979–May 1980)

DEPUTY WARDENS:

Felix Rodriguez (June 1959–Feb. 1970)

Horacio Herrera (Feb. 1970–Sept. 1975)

Clyde Malley (Oct. 1975–May 1976)

Robert Montoya (June 1976–July 1980)

APPENDIX B

Physical Layout
of PNM

Below is a description of the physical layout of PNM as it appeared from the late 1960s to 1980. Figure 1 contains a diagram of the PNM compound.

PNM sits on a 320-acre site located about 10 miles south of Santa Fe on State Highway 14. The main penitentiary building is surrounded by a double, chain-link fence. In 1976, circular rolls of razor-sharp "concertina" wire were placed between and on top of each fence. Placed along the double perimeter fence are four guard towers.

The main penitentiary building is laid out in a "telephone pole" design. The main corridor extends the entire 940 feet from the north to the south end of the prison. Living units intersect this main corridor "stem" like "crossbars" on a telephone pole. The penitentiary building is divided along its main corridor into a south wing, a central area, and a north wing.

The south wing of PNM houses dormitories, the Education Unit, and Cellhouses 1 and 2. In the late 1960s, four dormitory floors (D-1, D-2, C-1, and C-2) at the far south end of the penitentiary were converted from inmate living space to provide room for a growing number of education programs. In 1977, the bottom floor of one wing of this educational complex (Dorm D-1) was converted back to living quarters for inmates. The Education Unit and Dorm D-1 are separated from the rest of the prison by the "far south corridor grill gate," a barred grill that cuts across the main corridor.

The dormitories at PNM are considered medium security. Each floor of these two-story dormitories is self-contained. Thus in Dormitory E, the downstairs unit is designated Dorm E-1 and the upstairs unit is Dorm E-2. Each dormitory floor was designed to house fifty inmates. A typical dormitory is a large room containing four rows of beds; some rows, by the late 1970s, included bunk beds. At the opposite end of this room from the dorm entrance is a dayroom containing chairs, tables, and a television. At the entrance of the dorm is a "spring-lock" security door, which locks automatically when pushed completely shut. Between this door and the main corridor is a vestibule area containing showers, lavatories, and stairs to the other floor of the dormitory.

Diagram of the
Penitentiary of New Mexico (PNM) Compound
Late 1960s–1980

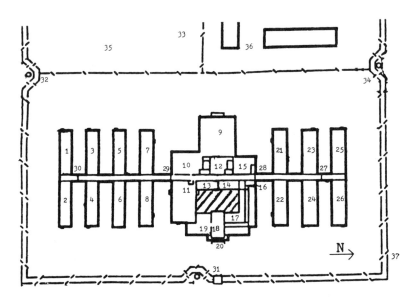

1. Dorm D-1 and Adult Basic Education
2. Education Unit (formerly Dormitory C)
3. Dormitory E
4. Dormitory B
5. Dormitory F
6. Dormitory A
7. Cellhouse 2
8. Cellhouse 1
9. Kitchen (basement shops)
10. Inmate Mess Hall
11. Gym/Auditorium (Captain's Office in Corridor)
12. Staff Mess Hall (adjacent to barber shop and canteen)
13. Catholic Chapel
14. Protestant Chapel
15. Library
16. Control Center
17. Visiting Room, Administrative Offices, Records
18. Main Lobby, Info. Booth
19. Warden's Office
20. Main Entrance
21. Hospital
22. Psychological Unit and Dorm C-1
23. Cellblock 3
24. Cellhouse 6
25. Cellblock 4
26. Cellblock 5
27. Far North Corridor Grill
28. North Corridor Grill
29. South Corridor Grill
30. Far South Corridor Grill
31. Tower 1, Gate House
32. Tower 2
33. Tower 3 (not shown; on west end of double fence)
34. Tower 4 and Sallyport for vehicle entrance
35. Recreation Yard
36. Prison Industries
37. Annex Building (not shown; north of double fence)

Dorms A, B, E, and F house inmates from the general prison population. The exception is the downstairs unit of Dorm E (E-1) which, in early 1979, was designated a "semiprotection" unit to house "weaker" inmates who for various reasons cannot mix with the "tougher" inmates in general population. Dorm E-1 was designated "semiprotection" in 1979 to relieve overcrowding in the main protective custody unit located in Cellblock 4 at the far north end of the prison.

The south wing also contains Cellhouses 1 and 2. These two cellhouses are considered medium security and designed to house, respectively, fifty-eight and sixty inmates, one to a cell. Individual cells are located along the outside walls of the cellhouses and open onto large common areas in the middle of these units. This is known as an "exterior cell" design. Doors to the cells are individually locked and unlocked with a key. There are two tiers of cells in each cellhouse. From the top tier inmates can look down to the first tier from a catwalk located in front of the individual cells. Showers and lavatories are next to the common area of the cellhouse near the cellhouse entrance. A dayroom is located at the far end of the unit opposite the cellhouse entrance. The cellhouse units are separated from the main corridor by two sliding barred grills. Between these two grills is a vestibule area containing a stairway, a closet, and an electronic control panel used to operate the entrance grills.

The south wing is separated from the central area of the prison by the "south corridor grill," a barred sliding grill that cuts across the main corridor just north of Cellhouses 1 and 2. The south corridor grill can only be unlocked with an electronic button housed in the Control Center, located up the main corridor at the other end of the central area from the south corridor grill. The grill locks automatically when slid completely shut.

The central area of the prison contains the main entrance, located on the east side of the building, the warden's office, visiting rooms, the records center, deputy warden's office, and other administrative offices. These constitute the "administrative wing" of the prison, which is separated from the rest of the central area by the Control Center.

The Control Center, located at the north end of the central area along the east side of the main corridor, houses keys to every part of the institution and contains electronic control panels to open the south corridor grill (leading into the south wing), the north corridor grill (leading into the north wing), and a set of barred grill gates leading from the main corridor to the administrative wing of the central area. Through small 6-inch by 9-inch panes of steel encased glass, officers within the Control Center can observe the main corridor of the prison. These small panes of steel encased glass were replaced in mid-January 1980 with a large 1 3/16 inch thick, "bullet resistant," one-way mirrored, glass bay window to improve the Control Center officers' view of the main corridor.

Also along the east side of the main corridor in the central area are the Protestant and Catholic chapels, the captain's office, and the gym. On the opposite side of the main corridor in the central area are the inmates' mess hall, the officers' mess hall, a barber shop, a canteen, the library, and the kitchen. Beneath the kitchen is a basement area containing laundry facilities and paint, shoe repair, plumbing, carpentry, and glass shops.

The "north corridor grill" separates the central area from the north wing of the prison. This sliding, barred grill that intersects the main corridor can only be unlocked by pushing an electronic button in the Control Center. It locks automatically when slid completely shut. The north wing contains the Hospital, the Psychological Unit, Cellhouse 6 and Cellblocks 3, 4 and 5.

The upstairs floor of the Hospital houses a small infirmary, which holds up to eight inmates. Clinics and a pharmacy are located on the lower floor of the Hospital.

The Psychological Unit was established in 1971 on the lower floor of a wing that had formerly housed a high school for inmates. In 1968, this high school became a federally funded Adult Basic Education program and was moved to the new Education Unit at the far south end of the prison. The Psychological Unit contains offices of psychologists who conduct counseling sessions and psychological testing. The upper floor of this unit prior to 1977 was office space for caseworkers. In 1977, it was converted to a dormitory space (Dorm C-1) for forty inmates.

Cellhouse 6 has an "exterior cell" design similar to that of Cellhouses 1 and 2, and is also considered medium security. It has a capacity of sixty-eight inmates, one to a cell. The north wing also contains three multiple-tier, maximum-security cellblocks (3, 4, and 5). Cellblocks have an "interior cell" design. On each cellblock tier, two rows of cells are aligned back-to-back in the center of the unit, which creates a large space between the front of each cell and the outside wall of the cellblock. Each cellblock has a grill at the main entrance and other grills at the entrances to each row of cells on each tier. These grills can be opened either electronically or manually with a key. In the cellblocks, individual cells can be opened from control panels encased in locked, metal boxes located on the walls of vestibule areas at the entrance of each tier of cells. These control panels include settings for "gang locking," which simultaneously locks or unlocks every cell on a tier.

Cellblock 3 contains three tiers of cells and is designed to house eighty-six inmates, one to a cell. From the top two tiers, there is a two-story and three-story drop to the basement off catwalks located immediately in front of these upper tier's cells. The catwalks in Cellblock 3 were completely fenced from floor to ceiling in 1976 to provide greater security.

Cellblock 3 is the segregation unit that houses inmates who have broken prison rules and are considered the most dangerous and disruptive inmates in the prison. In the basement of this disciplinary segregation unit are eleven maximum detention units (MDUs, or "the hole") that can be used for solitary confinement in "dark cells" devoid of light, beds, sinks, and toilets.

Both Cellblocks 4 and 5 are separated from the rest of the prison by the "far north corridor grill gate" that intersects the main corridor. This grill gate can only be unlocked with a key.

Cellblock 5 is a maximum-security unit composed of two tiers of cells and a basement. It has a capacity for sixty inmates, one to a cell. It normally houses inmates who are considered dangerous or escape risks but not currently being punished for prison rule violations. The basement of Cellblock 5 contains no cells; it houses the gas chamber, storage rooms, and crawl spaces between the basement and main floors of the prison.

Cellblock 4 is the third maximum-security unit. It has a capacity of ninety inmates, one inmate per cell. Prior to 1976, it was used primarily as an admissions and orientation unit for new inmates. In 1976, Cellblock 4 was designated as the segregation unit for protective custody. No unit prior to this time had ever been used exclusively for protection. As with all the cellblocks, it contains no dayroom, so recreational activities are greatly limited. Cellblock 4 has three tiers and resembles Cellblock 3. One difference, however, is that on the upper two tiers, no floor-to-ceiling fences were ever placed around the catwalks; only handrails prevent falls from the upper tiers to the basement.

Within the perimeter fence, outside the main penitentiary building, are a recreation yard and a small prison industries complex (opened in 1967) containing a sign and tag shop, a furniture shop, and a machine shop. Beyond the perimeter fence are warehouses, a small dairy, motor pool garage, power house, and the Annex Building, which for most of the period from 1956 to 1980 housed women prisoners.

NOTES

Chapter 1
INTRODUCTION

1. These interviews were especially important for determining the general levels of violence, use of disciplinary segregation, and other trends at PNM. Most of New Mexico's corrections records were stored in PNM's record office, which was completely destroyed by fire during the 1980 riot. Thus, for example, specific data on the number of assaults each year are unavailable since the records containing these data were destroyed. Only partial and incomplete records were recovered. Such trends in assaults had to be largely ascertained through respondents' impressions, which could not be as precise as official documents.

Chapter 2
THEORETICAL CONSIDERATIONS

1. Indeed, McElvaine (1984: 258) writes, "Only the need to regain the support of workers led [President Franklin D.] Roosevelt reluctantly and belatedly to endorse perhaps the most important law passed in the 1930s, the Wagner Act [which extended important rights to labor].... President Roosevelt...blocked the Wagner bill in 1934. It was reintroduced in 1935, and still the President wanted no part of it" until after it passed the Senate in response to popular social pressure. In addition, Lichtenstein (1982: 4) writes, "Although some well-known industrialists such as Gerard Swope and Henry Dennison encouraged the new industrial unions and supported the Wagner Act, the overwhelming majority of American businessmen fiercely resisted most New Deal reforms and fought the new CIO unions with virtually every political and economic weapon at their command." See also Skocpol (1980).

2. A central thesis of Rusche and Kirchheimer (1939) is "the principle of less eligibility," which I do *not* adopt in the present analysis. Melossi (1980: 18) summarizes Rusche and Kirchheimer's "less eligibility" thesis:

The central category [Rusche and Kirchheimer] employ in addressing the history of detention *within* this [the bourgeois or capitalist] epoch is the principle of *less eligibility*. Briefly, this principle functions in relation to the state of the labor market. It posits that the standard of living within prisons (as well as for those dependent upon the welfare apparatus) must be lower than that of the lowest stratum of the working class, so that, given the alternative, people will opt to work under these conditions, and so that punishment will serve as a deterrent. [Emphasis is Melossi's.]

While high unemployment often does result in deteriorating conditions for both the poor and the imprisoned, it generally has not been the case during the capitalist epoch that conditions for prisoners fall *below* those of the poorest stratum of the population outside prisons. Under certain historical conditions (i.e., when high unemployment coincides with low levels of unionization) there is a greater correspondence between the deterioration of living conditions for the poor and worsening prison conditions; but the latter, even under these conditions, rarely fall below the level of the former. Another problem with "the principle of less eligibility" is that it presents the teleological argument that prison conditions deteriorate *in order to produce* a deterrent effect. While deteriorating prison conditions may have this deterrent effect (though this is highly questionable), such a consequence cannot be posited as the force behind the worsening conditions. Rusche and Kirchheimer have also been correctly criticized for their almost exclusive focus on economic factors, which understates political and ideological influences on "penality" (Garland 1990). One can reject Rusche and Kirchheimer's "least eligibility" thesis while still drawing upon their pioneering insights about the connections between labor markets and imprisonment.

3. Also contributing to the decline of labor militancy was the "Red Scare" of the late 1940s and early 1950s, when labor militants, accused of communist sympathies, were run out of many unions.

4. Federal agencies indeed used "iron fist" tactics against militant organizing of the poor. The FBI's COINTELPRO campaign, aimed at Dr. Martin Luther King and other militants (like Fred Hampton) who struggled for civil and poor people's rights, was a coercive attempt to discredit, intimidate, divide, and undermine these movements (Hampton 1990; McCaghy and Cernkovich 1987; Wolfe 1978).

5. As Hodson and Kaufman (1982) argue, and as should be emphasized, not all monopolized industries in the core sector were compelled to grant concessions to organized labor. For this group of core industries, the labor market dynamics were still characterized by external competition

from domestic surplus populations. The barriers for entry into more technical jobs contained in these nonunionized core firms are largely educational. Higher wages for the skilled and more educated work force of such industries as chemical and oil refining are due largely to the smaller pool of potential job competitors who could replace such workers. Also, corporate, bureaucratic management models were introduced in these industries to forestall any incipient union organizing (Davis 1986; Edwards 1979).

6. An empirical connection between labor market dynamics and variations in correctional and welfare policies was found in a study of U.S. counties (Colvin 1990). Using a random sample of 184 urban counties in the U.S. and data from the late 1970s, counties were rated on the degree of unionization and other variables indicative of internal labor markets, which are less subject to external job competition from surplus populations. Using regression analysis, it was found that the greater the degree of unionization and internalization of county labor markets, the higher the rates of welfare recipients and welfare benefits and the lower the rates of commitments to state penal facilities. These relationships held when controlling for the degree of political liberalism, median income, level of government revenues, and rates of poverty, unemployment and crime in the sampled counties.

7. DiIulio's (1987) description and analysis of the patterns of control in Texas prisons greatly underplays the important role of informal controls in this prison system's compliance structure. DiIulio's brief against sociological interpretations of prison organization causes him to underestimate the impact of informal controls. Far from being the model system of inmate control DiIulio describes, the Texas prison system relied quite heavily on informal patterns of indulgence to gain cooperation from powerful prisoners (the "building tenders") who helped the prison staff induce and terrorize other inmates into compliance. Rather than being a "latent defect," as DiIulio would like to think of it, of the "model" system of control in Texas prisons, the "building tender" system, involving informal remunerative and informal coercive controls, was an important cornerstone to the entire system of control in these Texas prisons (Marquart and Crouch 1984, 1985; Martin and Ekland-Olson 1987; Crouch and Marquart 1989).

Chapter 3
YEARS OF ACCOMMODATION, 1968–1974

1. From 1956 until the early 1980s, PNM housed over 90 percent of New Mexico's prison inmates. When the prison was opened in 1956, the

design capacity was reported as "slightly more than 1,000" (*New Mexican* 8/15/56). Due to periodic renovation and redesignation of space, its inmate capacity has fluctuated over time: 1,022 from 1956 to 1968; 822 from 1968 to 1977; 912 in 1977 and 1978; 944 and 972 in 1979; and 884 near the beginning of 1980. During much of this period, the minimum-security Honor Farm at Los Lunas was the only other facility for adult men in the state's corrections system. The Honor Farm was filled only through transfers from PNM. Built in 1936, the Honor Farm had a capacity for 131 inmates; in 1976, this was increased through remodeling to 210. For a short period, 1964 to 1968, a forestry camp at Tierra Amarilla housed about 50 minimum-security inmates. In 1976, the minimum-security Camp Sierra Blanca at Capitan was converted from a juvenile facility to house 50 adult men. In 1978, a minimum-security correctional center at Roswell opened to house an additional 130 male inmates. In late 1980, a new medium-security institution with a capacity for 288 male inmates opened at Los Lunas. From 1956 to 1980, a small women's prison, designed to house 28 inmates, was located at the PNM compound's Annex Building, across the street from the main penitentiary for men. In late 1975, a women's honor dorm, housing 22 minimum-security inmates, was opened in Albuquerque. In December 1978, this women's honor unit was moved to a 40-bed facility in Radium Springs. Thus, for the period under study, the main penitentiary building at the PNM complex held the overwhelming proportion of the state's adult inmates.

2. These early-1960s inmate population figures differ from those which Hart (1976a) and I (Colvin 1982; Office of the Attorney General 1980b) report for PNM. These latter figures mistakenly include male inmates at the Los Lunas Honor Farm and women inmates housed in the Annex Building. The figures reported in the text of the current work correctly exclude these non-PNM inmates.

3. On average, the ethnic make-up of New Mexico's inmate population in the late 1960s was 49 percent Hispanic, 38 percent Anglo, 10 percent Black, and 3 percent Native American. These proportions remained roughly the same throughout the 1970s and early 1980s.

4. These coeducational classes continued until late 1975, when women's programming was moved to a new Women's Honor Unit in Albuquerque. Program opportunities for women deteriorated in the late 1970s, as the Women's Honor Unit was moved to a more remote location in Radium Springs. In the 1980s, a women's facility was opened in Grants, N.M., which, with its high unemployment and more rural location, offered virtually no opportunities for work or school release (*New Mexican* 8/24/82; Rhodes 1987).

5. Indeed, in 1973 an inmate on school release was found drunk on top of a building near the College of Santa Fe. For this individual's behavior, the entire school-release program was suspended for a semester. It was reinstituted in 1974 under tighter restrictions.

6. Drugs from the pharmacy were also given by staff directly to inmates as a means of control:

> *Correctional Officer:* I saw all kinds of tranquilizers for the inmates. They had inmates on Valiums; they had inmates on Librium; they had inmates on Equinal; they had inmates on Plasidil, Darvons. They just issue the pills to the inmates that were prescribed through the hospital.

> *Correctional Officer Supervisor:* Basically the way we controlled the institution was the drugs. Any time we had a problem with an inmate in Cellblock 3, we'd call the hospital and he was given drugs. . . . We had Darvons that were given out by the tons, I mean we gave everybody Darvons. And Chlorohydrate I think is what they were giving out at the time, and some of these little red pills that I don't even know what they were. We controlled the whole inmate population under Felix Rodriguez [when he was warden in the early 1970s] with drugs. And, it worked!... We had a lot of zombies in that place.

The practice of prescribing tranquilizers from the pharmacy for inmates apparently continued into the late 1970s. A top prison official said that the number of these prescriptions was reduced dramatically in 1978 with the hiring of a full-time doctor. However, the huge inventory of these drugs in the prison's pharmacy, discovered by inmates during the 1980 riot, suggests that tranquilizers were still being given to inmates in large quantities (*Albuquerque Journal* 2/18/80).

Chapter 4
YEARS OF CONFRONTATION, 1975–1977

1. The determinate sentencing act did not go into effect until July 1979. No prisoners sentenced under the new act actually arrived at PNM until after February 1980.

2. This dispute and struggle between the Governor's Office and the top corrections officials is recounted on the front pages of the *New Mexican* and *Albuquerque Journal* where it became a daily item from August through October 1975. A good summary of the dispute is found in Morris (1983) and Hart (1976a).

3. Montoya was hired by Warden Aaron in October 1975, upon the recommendation of Secretary of Corrections Mike Hanrahan, who was

concerned about affirmative action in the appointments being made at the prison. Montoya had worked six years as a caseworker in a juvenile institution in Arizona and then as an administrator in charge of adult training and security at the Fort Grant, Arizona, Penal Camp before becoming deputy warden at PNM (*Santa Fe Reporter* 3/19/81). Hanrahan had met Montoya at a Phoenix, Arizona, conference in September 1975.

4. In the early 1970s, under the wardenship of Felix Rodriguez, the maximum detention units, or "holes," were officially not in use. Inmates, however, reported that they were sporadically placed in the "hole" in the early 1970s, which was at that time an unauthorized sanction. This informal punishment was usually reserved for recalcitrant inmates housed in the upper tiers of Cellblock 3. "I was beat in 1973," reported an inmate. "I was beat in lockup and was beat from my cell to the 'hole.'"

5. Use of "*Inmate 1*," "*Inmate 2*," etc. in this and the next chapter is merely a convention to distinguish respondents in a series of quotes, not an identification of specific inmate respondents. Thus *Inmate 1* in this series of quotes is not necessarily the same *Inmate 1* in later series of quotes.

Chapter 5
YEARS OF FRAGMENTATION, 1978-1980

1. See Note 5 of Chapter 4 above.

2. Included in the category of violent crimes are homicides, kidnappings, rapes, assaults, and armed robberies. It should be stressed that this figure refers to crimes and not individuals. In addition, these figures refer to all New Mexico prisoners, including those in minimum security camps. The minimum security camps housed about 10 percent of all prisoners throughout the ten-year period from 1970 to 1980, and were filled only through transfer from PNM. The opening of the Roswell Camp in 1978 conceivably could have lowered the number of inmates with nonviolent offenses in the main prison. However, violent offenders, with the exception of sex offenders, were not excluded from transfers to minimum security camps. In addition, the trend toward less violent offenses was evident prior to the opening of Roswell, averaging 43 percent between 1970 and 1975 and 37 percent between 1975 and 1978.

3. This figure of six killings is derived from discussions with former PNM officials. Official records of killings during this period are not available.

Chapter 6
THE RIOT

1. The following account of the riot is based largely on the 169 interviews from the first phase of the New Mexico Attorney General's investigation, which also drew upon hundreds of other interviews conducted by the New Mexico State Police during and immediately after the riot. These interviews were the basis for the Attorney General's Part One Report (Office of the Attorney General 1980a).

Chapter 7
UNDERSTANDING PRISON DISORDER

1. This estimate differs from the 974 inmate capacity reported by the New Mexico Attorney General (Office of the Attorney General 1980a: C-1). The 884 capacity figure is based on 50, instead of 60, as the capacity for the open-bay dormitories. The figure of 50 was used by the federal courts in the negotiations of the ACLU suit against PNM, and apparently was the original design capacity of these dorms when the penitentiary was built in 1956. The dorm capacity of 60 is based on estimates given in the New Mexico Corrections Master Plan (Governor's Council on Criminal Justice Planning 1978a). Since the figure of 50 accords with the maximum capacity allowed under the American Correctional Association standards for these open-bay dorms, I have decided to use this lower figure for determining the prison's capacity at the different time periods discussed.

2. The 1,195 population figure for PNM reported for this date in the *Albuquerque Journal* (11/16/75) includes 131 inmates at the Los Lunas Honor Farm and 46 women inmates held in the PNM Annex Building and at the Women's Honor Unit in Albuquerque.

3. The literature on "importation" and "deprivation" models attempts to account for the rise of inmate roles within a prisoner subculture. The key argument between these two models is whether these roles emerge as a result of the deprivation under which inmates live (Sykes 1958) or are imported from criminal subcultures already in existence on the streets (Irwin 1970). This argument is especially pertinent for studying the apparent connections between prison gangs and street gangs. It is possible that in some states the street and the prison both shape the relationships and roles within gangs, and thus both contribute to the rise of violence in the streets as well as in prisons. Thus, violence may be imported into and exported out of prisons. In New Mexico, however, violent street gangs were not entering the prison from outside as they were in Illinois

(Jacobs 1977) and California (Irwin 1980). The violence at PNM at least in the late 1970s, appears to have been shaped primarily by internal organizational dynamics.

Chapter 8
CONCLUSION: CONTINUED CRISIS, FUTURE PROSPECTS

1. These figures are provided by the New Mexico Corrections Department through personal correspondence with Secretary of Corrections O.L. McCotter and PNM Warden Robert J. Tansy. Figures on the exact number of assaults of inmates and staff are not available for years prior to 1984. Thus assault rates for earlier years cannot be calculated.

2. These figures include assaults with and without weapons. These figures also include assaults in the main PNM building (housing 800 inmates) and the new North Facility (which houses 288 inmates and is under the control of the PNM warden). Thus the denominator used in calculating these assault rates is 1088: (155 inmates assaulted + 125 staff assaulted)/6 years = 46.7; 46.7 annual combined assaults/1,088 = .043 X 100 = 4.3 rate.

3. Since numbers of assaults at PNM for years prior to 1984 are unavailable, the best comparisons that can be made are with other prison systems. The rates for PNM from 1984–89 are: combined (inmate-on-inmate plus inmate-on-staff) 6-year average assault rate of 4.3, with a high of 6.0 in 1986; inmate-on-inmate 6-year average assault rate of 2.4, with a high of 2.9 in 1987; inmate-on-staff 6-year average assault rate of 1.9, with a high of 3.2 in 1986. These can be compared with figures from other studies. First, the following combined assault rates are computed for 1985 by Fleisher (1989: 25) for five maximum-security penitentiaries in the Federal Prison System: Lompoc, 1.5; Leavenworth, 1.6; Marion, 2.6; Terre Haute, 2.7; Lewisburg, 3.1; all Federal System facilities, 1.1. Second, DiIulio (1987: 54–56) gives assault figures for the three states he focused on in his comparative study, from which the following rates per 100 inmates can be calculated: California (1973–83), a combined 11-year average rate of 2.5, with a high of 3.8; Michigan (1977-83), a combined 7-year average rate of 4.6, with a high of 5.6; and Texas (1973–79) an inmate-on-inmate 7-year rate of 1.1, with a high of 1.6. The assault rate for Texas increased dramatically in the mid-1980s, possibly eclipsing somewhat those reported above for New Mexico (Crouch and Marquart 1989). While these comparisons are by no means exhaustive, they do indicate a comparatively high rate of assaults for PNM during the 1980s.

4. On June 17, 1991, the U.S. Supreme Court ruled in *Wilson v. Seiter* that inmates must prove "deliberate indifference" on the part of prison officials to overcrowding and other poor conditions which may constitute cruel and unusual punishment. This ruling runs counter to other court decisions since the 1960s concerning prison conditions and may portend the beginning of a return by the Court to the traditional "hands off" doctrine. It may also open for reconsideration court-ordered reforms in over 40 states, possibly including those in New Mexico. Indeed, "the Court has accepted a case involving circumstances under which prison officials can seek to get out from under the burden of such court orders" (*Washington Post* 6/18/91: A4). If the Court retreats from these reforms, increased instability in state prison systems is the likely result.

BIBLIOGRAPHY

Abbott, Jack Henry. 1981. *In the Belly of the Beast.* New York: Vintage.

Adamson, Christopher. 1984. "Toward a Marxian penology: Captive criminal populations as economic threats and resources." *Social Problems* 31: 435–458.

Adler, Mortimer J. 1987. *We Hold These Truths.* New York: Macmillan.

Albuquerque Journal. 10/7/71. "Inmates at state penitentiary go on sit-down strike, refuse to eat, no violence." Sec. A, p. 1.

———. 10/13/71. "State prison damage estimated at $65,000." Sec. A, p. 1.

———. 1/11/72. "Spokesman for 'concerned citizens' committee makes statement about dissolving 'administrative clique' at prison." Sec. A, p. 8.

———. 2/3/72. "Guards testify that climate of fear pervades prison, beatings ordered." Sec. A, p. 1.

———. 3/30/72. "Associate warden indicted on charges of battery against inmates." Sec. A, p. 1.

———. 10/12/72. "Penitentiary inmates voice complaints over conditions." Sec. F, p. 12.

———. 8/28/75. "Hanrahan gets Leach job nod." Sec. A, p. 1.

———. 9/22/75. "Warden given support." Sec. A, p.1.

———. 9/27/75. "Aaron: Prison depressing." Sec. B, p. 10.

———. 11/16/75. "Problems at prison continue to grow." Sec. A, p. 1.

———. 12/13/75. "Poor food cited." Sec. A, p. 12.

———. 2/10/76. "Program criticized." Sec. B, p. 6.

———. 5/29/76. "Warden attacks prison entities." Sec. A, p. 1.

———. 6/16/76. "Sit-down strike staged by 600 New Mexico inmates." Sec. A, p.2.

———. 6/17/76. "Prison dorm fight quelled by tear gas." Sec. A, p.1.

———. 6/26/77. "Penitentiary guards stop riot in block." Sec. A, p. 1.

———. 3/24/78. "Malley sees likelihood of rebellion at prison." Sec. A, p. 1.

———. 4/17/78. "Inmate beaten to death." Sec. A, p. 3.

———. 4/19/78. "Law on flat sentences will have sharp impact." Sec. A, p. 1.

———. 4/6/79. "2 ex-guards plead guilty in drug case." Sec. A, p. 1.

———. 9/16/79. "Prison sexual brutality changes inmate." Sec. B, p. 1.

———. 2/18/80. "Experts doubt drugs stoked violence at prison." Sec. A, p. 1.

———. 3/30/80. "Prison perspective." Sec. I, pp. 1–28.

———. 5/1/81. "Criticisms of pen worry aide Giron and Gov. King." Sec. F, p. 1.

———. 9/9/81. "King and Crist answer questions raised in PNM media probe." Sec. B, p. 2.

———. 7/5/87. "Guard shot as seven escape state pen." Sec. A, p. 1.

———. 1/23/90. "High court won't alter N.M. prison agreement." Sec. A, p. 1.

———. 1/28/90. "In bloody aftermath there was no way to go but up." Sec. C, p. 1.

———. 2/2/90. "Inmates take new legal action." Sec. A, p. 1.

American Correctional Association. 1983. *The American Prison: From the Beginning.* College Park, Md.: American Correctional Association.

Baker, J. E. 1964. "Inmate self-government." *Journal of Criminal Law, Criminology and Police Science.* 55: 39–47.

———. 1974. *The Right to Participate: Inmate Involvement in Prison Administration.* Metuchen, N.J.: Scarecrow Press.

———. 1985. *Prisoner Participation in Prison Power.* Metuchen, N.J.: Scarecrow Press.

Barrera, Mario. 1979. *Race and Class in the Southwest.* Notre Dame, Ind.: University of Notre Dame Press.

Bell, Malcolm. 1985. *The Turkey Shoot.* New York: Grove Press.

Bennett, Lawrence A. 1976. "The study of violence in California prisons: A review with policy implications." Pp. 149–168 in Albert K. Cohen, George F. Cole, and Robert G. Bailey (eds.), *Prison Violence.* Lexington, Mass.: D.C. Heath.

Berkowitz, Edward, and Kim McQuaid. 1980. *Creating the Welfare State.* New York: Praeger.

Blawis, Patricia Bell. 1971. *Tijerina and the Land Grants.* New York: International Publishers.

Bowker, Lee H. 1977. *Prisoner Subcultures.* Lexington, Mass.: D.C. Heath.

————. 1980. *Prison Victimization.* New York: Elsevier.

Box, Steven. 1987. *Recession, Crime and Punishment.* Totowa, N.J.: Barnes and Noble.

Braverman, Harry. 1974. *Labor and Monopoly Capital.* New York: Monthly Review Press.

Breed, Alan, and David Ward. 1984. *The United States Penitentiary Marion, Illinois: A Report to the Judiciary Committee, United States House of Representatives.* Washington, D.C.: U.S. Government Printing Office.

Brody, David. 1980. *Workers in Industrial America.* New York: Oxford.

Chafe, William H. 1986. *The Unfinished Journey.* New York: Oxford.

Clark, Richard X. 1973. *The Brothers of Attica.* New York: Links.

Clemmer, Donald. 1940. *The Prison Community.* Boston: Christopher.

Cloward, Richard A. 1960. "Social control in the prison." Pp.20–48 in Richard A. Cloward, Donald R. Cressey, George H. Grosser, Richard McCleery, Lloyd E. Ohlin, Gresham M. Sykes, and Sheldon L. Messinger (eds.), *Theoretical Studies in Social Organization of the Prison.* New York: Social Science Research Council.

Cloward, Richard A., and Lloyd E. Ohlin. 1960. *Delinquency and Opportunity.* New York: Free Press.

Colvin, Mark. 1981. "The contradictions of control: Prisons in class society." *The Insurgent Sociologist* 10: 33–45.

————. 1982. "The 1980 New Mexico prison riot." *Social Problems* 29: 449–463.

————. 1990. "Labor markets, industrial monopolization, welfare, and imprisonment: Evidence from a cross-section of U.S. counties." *The Sociological Quarterly* 31: 441–457.

————. 1991. "Crime and social reproduction: A response to the call for some 'outrageous' proposals." *Crime and Delinquency* 37: forthcoming (October).

Crouch, Ben M., and James W. Marquart. 1989. *An Appeal to Justice.* Austin, Tex.: University of Texas Press.

Cullen, Francis T. 1983. *Rethinking Crime and Deviance Theory.* Totowa, N.J.: Rowman and Allanheld.

Cullen, Francis T., and Karen E. Gilbert. 1982. *Reaffirming Rehabilitation.* Cincinnati, Ohio: Anderson.

Currie, Elliott. 1985. *Confronting Crime.* New York: Pantheon.

Davidson, R. Theodore. 1974. *Chicano Prisoners: The Key to San Quentin.* New York: Holt, Rinehart and Winston.

Davis, Mike. 1986. *Prisoners of the American Dream.* London: Verso.

———. 1988. "Los Angeles: Civil liberties between the hammer and the rock." *New Left Review* 170: 37–60.

Department of Corrections. 1971. *Annual Report.* Santa Fe: State of New Mexico.

———. 1972. *Annual Report.* Santa Fe: State of New Mexico.

———. 1976. *Annual Report.* Santa Fe: State of New Mexico.

———. 1980. *Annual Report.* Santa Fe: State of New Mexico.

DiIulio, John J. 1987. *Governing Prisons.* New York: Free Press.

Edwards, Richard C. 1979. *Contested Terrain.* New York: Basic.

Ekland-Olson, Sheldon. 1986. "Crowding, social control, and prison violence: Some evidence from the post-Ruiz years." *Law and Society Review* 20: 389–421.

Ekland-Olson, Sheldon, Dennis Barrick, and Lawrence Cohen. 1983. "Prison overcrowding and disciplinary problems: An analysis of the Texas prison system." *Journal of Applied Behavioral Science* 19: 163–176.

Ellis, Desmond, Harold G. Grasmick, and Bernard Gilman. 1974. "Violence in prisons: A sociological analysis." *American Journal of Sociology* 80: 16–43.

Etzioni, Amitai. 1970. "Compliance theory." Pp. 103–126 in Oscar Grusky and George A. Miller (eds.), *The Sociology of Organizations.* New York: Free Press.

Evans, Peter B., Dietrich Rueschemeyer, and Theda Skocpol (eds.). 1985. *Bringing the State Back In.* Cambridge: Cambridge University Press.

Feeley, Malcolm, and Austin D. Sarat. 1980. *The Policy Dilemma.* Minneapolis, Minn.: University of Minnesota Press.

Fleisher, Mark S. 1989. *Warehousing Violence.* Newbury Park, Calif.: Sage.

Fraser, Steve, and Gary Gerstle (eds.). 1989. *The Rise and Fall of the New Deal Order, 1930–1980.* Princeton, N.J.: Princeton University Press.

Freedman, Jonathan. 1975. *Crowding and Behavior.* New York: Viking.

Gaes, Gerald G. 1985. "The effects of overcrowding in prison." Pp. 95–146 in Michael Tonry and Norval Morris (eds.), *Crime and Justice,* Vol. 6. Chicago: University of Chicago Press.

Gaes, Gerald G., and William J. McGuire. 1985. "Prison violence: The contribution of crowding versus other determinants of prison assault rates." *Journal of Research in Crime and Delinquency* 22: 41–65.

Galan, Hector (producer). 1988. *Shakedown in Santa Fe.* Frontline (documentary).

Garland, David. 1990. *Punishment and Modern Society.* Chicago: University of Chicago Press.

Garson, G. David. 1972. "The disruption of prison administration: An investigation of alternative theories of the relationship among administrators, reformers, and involuntary social service clients." *Law and Society Review* 6: 531–561.

Gordon, David M., Richard C. Edwards, and Michael Reich. 1982. *Segmented Work, Divided Workers.* Cambridge: Cambridge University Press.

Gouldner, Alvin W. 1954. *Patterns of Industrial Bureaucracy.* New York: Free Press.

Governor's Council on Criminal Justice Planning. 1976. *New Mexico Standards and Goals.* Santa Fe: State of New Mexico.

———. 1978a. "Technical Report 3: Facilities Inventory." *Sourcebook for New Mexico Corrections Planning.* Santa Fe: State of New Mexico.

———. 1978b. "Technical Report 6: Inmate Profile." *Sourcebook for New Mexico Corrections Planning.* Santa Fe: State of New Mexico.

———. 1978c. "Technical Report 8: Department of Corrections—Personnel." *Sourcebook for New Mexico Corrections Planning.* Santa Fe: State of New Mexico.

Greenberg, David F. 1981. *Crime and Capitalism.* Palo Alto, Calif.: Mayfield.

Greenberg, David F., and Drew Humphries. 1980. "The cooptation of fixed sentencing reform." *Crime and Delinquency* 26: 206–225.

Greenberg, Edward S. 1979. *Understanding Modern Government.* New York: John Wiley.

Grusky, Oscar. 1968. "Role conflict in organizations: A study of prison camp officials." Pp. 455–476 in Lawrence Hazelrigg (ed.), *Prison Within Society.* Garden City, N.J.: Doubleday.

Haas, Kenneth C., and Geoffrey P. Alpert (eds.). 1986. *The Dilemmas of Punishment.* Prospect Hills, Ill.: Waveland.

Hagan, John. 1989. *Structural Criminology.* New Brunswick, N.J.: Rutgers.

Hagel-Seymour, John. 1988. "Environmental Sanctuaries for Susceptible Prisoners." Pp. 267–284 in Robert Johnson and Hans Toch (eds.), *The Pains of Imprisonment.* Prospect Heights, Ill.: Waveland.

Hampton, Henry (executive producer). 1990. *Eyes on the Prize II.* Blackside Productions (documentary).

Harrison, Bennett, and Barry Bluestone. 1988. *The Great U-Turn.* New York: Basic.

Hart, William. 1976a. "Profile: New Mexico." *Corrections Magazine* 2 (March): 27–36, 45–50.

———. 1976b. "Convicted murderer holds key position in prison administration." *Corrections Magazine* 2 (March): 30–31.

Hodgson, Godfrey. 1976. *America in Our Time.* New York: Vintage.

Hodson, Randy, and Robert L. Kaufman. 1982. "Economic dualism: A critical review." *American Sociological Review* 47: 727–739.

Institute for the Study of Labor and Economic Crisis. 1982. *The Iron Fist and the Velvet Glove.* San Francisco: Crime and Social Justice Associates.

Inverarity, James, and Daniel McCarthy. 1988. "Punishment and social structure revisited: Unemployment and imprisonment in the United States, 1948–1984." *The Sociological Quarterly* 29: 263–279.

Irwin, John. 1970. *The Felon.* Englewood Cliffs, N.J.: Prentice-Hall.

———. 1980. *Prisons in Turmoil.* Boston: Little, Brown.

Jackson, George. 1970. *Soledad Brother.* New York: Bantam.

Jacobs, James B. 1977. *Stateville: The Penitentiary in Mass Society.* Chicago: University of Chicago Press.

————. 1983. *New Perspectives on Prisons and Imprisonment.* Ithaca, N.Y.: Cornell University Press.

Jankovic, Ivan. 1980. "Labor market and imprisonment." Pp. 93–104 in Tony Platt and Paul Takagi (eds.), *Punishment and Penal Discipline.* Berkeley, Calif.: Crime and Social Justice Associates.

Janowitz, Morris. 1969. "Patterns of collective racial violence." Pp. 317–339 in Hugh Davis Graham and Ted Robert Gurr (eds.), *Violence in America.* Washington, D.C.: U.S. Government Printing Office.

Johnson, Robert. 1987. *Hard Time.* Montery, Calif.: Brooks-Cole.

Kalinich, David B. 1980. *The Inmate Economy.* Lexington, Mass.: D.C. Heath.

Katz, Jack. 1988. *Seductions of Crime.* New York: Basic.

Katz, Michael B. 1986. *In the Shadow of the Poorhouse.* New York: Basic.

————. 1989. *The Undeserving Poor: From the War on Poverty to the War on Welfare.* New York: Pantheon.

Lemann, Nicholas. 1988. "The unfinished war" (Part 1). *The Atlantic* 262 (December): 37–56.

————. 1989. "The unfinished war" (Part 2). *The Atlantic* 263 (January): 52–68.

Lichtenstein, Nelson. 1982. *Labor's War at Home.* Cambridge, Eng.: University of Cambridge Press.

Lynch, Michael J. 1988. "The extraction of surplus value, crime and punishment." *Contemporary Crises* 12: 329–344.

Lynch, Michael J. and W. Byron Groves. 1989. *A Primer in Radical Criminology.* New York: Harrow and Heston.

Mandel, Ernest. 1978. *Late Capitalism.* London: Verso.

Marquart, James W. 1986. "Prison guards and the use of physical coercion as a mechanism of prisoner control." *Criminology* 24: 347–366.

Marquart, James W., and Ben M. Crouch. 1984. "Coopting the kept: Using inmates for social control in a southern prison." *Justice Quarterly* 1: 491–509.

————. 1985. "Judicial reform and prisoner control: The impact of *Ruiz v. Estelle* on a Texas penitentiary." *Law and Society Review* 19: 557–586.

Martin, Steve J., and Sheldon Ekland-Olson. 1987. *Texas Prisons.* Austin: Texas Monthly Press.

Martinson, Robert. 1974. "What works?—questions and answers about prison reform." *Public Interest* 35: 22–54.

———. 1979. "New findings, new views: A note of caution regarding sentencing reform." *Hofstra Law Review* 7: 244–252.

McCaghy, Charles H., and Stephen A. Cernkovich. 1987. *Crime in American Society*. New York: MacMillan.

McCleery, Richard. 1968. "Correctional administration and political change." Pp. 113–149 in Lawrence Hazelrigg (ed.), *Prison Within Society*. Garden City, N.Y.: Doubleday.

McElvaine, Robert S. 1984. *The Great Depression*. New York: Times Books.

McVicar, John. 1982. "Violence in prisons." Pp. 200–214 in Peter Marsh and Anne Campbell (eds.), *Aggression and Violence*. New York: St Martin's.

Melossi, Dario. 1980. "Punishment and Social Structure." Pp. 17–27 in Tony Platt and Paul Takagi (eds.), *Punishment and Penal Discipline*. Berkeley, Calif.: Crime and Social Justice Associates.

Milovanovic, Dragan. 1983. "Weber and Marx on law: Demystifying ideology and law—toward an emancipatory political practice." *Contemporary Crises* 7: 353–370.

Morris, Roger. 1983. *The Devil's Butcher Shop*. New York: Franklin Watts.

New Mexican. 6/16/53. "A new pen—now!" Sec. A, p. 1.

———. 7/22/56. "New prison a big hit." Sec. A, p. 1.

———. 8/15/56. "Last convicts moved from prison." Sec. A, p. 1.

———. 2/4/70. "Baker ok suggests clash of legislature and Cargo." Sec. A, p. 3.

———. 2/11/70. "Baker tenure lies in 'positions law.'" Sec. A, p. 1.

———. 2/18/70. "Approval of Baker fails in rules vote." Sec. A, p.1.

———. 2/19/70. "Baker resignation throws penal system into confusion." Sec. A, p. 1.

———. 4/30/70. "Corrections chief resigns, claiming Governor welshed." Sec. A, p.1.

———. 10/7/71. "N.M. prisoners continue strike." Sec. A, p. 1.

———. 10/8/71. "Seven injured in disturbance." Sec. A, p. 1.

———. 10/10/71. "N.M. prison: 14 years of peace." Sec. A, p. 3.

———. 10/12/71. "Damage to pen set at $65,000." Sec. A, p. 1.

———. 10/17/71. "Newsmen tour N.M. pen, security tight." Sec. A, p. 5.

———. 8/28/75. "Hanrahan: Gov.'s choice for Leach job." Sec. A, p. 1.

———. 9/14/75. "NM's secretary of corrections." Sec. A, p.1.

———. 9/25/75. "Warden transfer 'virtually certain.'" Sec. A, p. 1.

———. 10/3/75. "DA, AG argue to grand jury." Sec. A, p. 1.

———. 10/20/75. "Six inmates flee N.M. prison." Sec. A, p. 1.

———. 10/22/75. "Trusty flees penitentiary." Sec. A, p. 1.

———. 12/14/75. "Prison dining hall described as smelly." Sec. A, p. 2.

———. 12/15/75. "Prison need appraisal draws support." Sec. A, p. 9.

———. 6/16/76. "Inmates back at work." Sec. A, p. 1.

———. 8/17/76. "Six inmates suspected in N.M. prison killing." Sec. A, p. 1.

———. 2/6/79. "Becknell confirmation faces challenge today." Sec. A, p. 1.

———. 2/7/79. "Senate confirms Becknell." Sec. A, p. 1.

———. 8/24/82. "Women inmates again sue over program." Sec. A, p. 2.

———. 11/2/82. "No contest pleas entered on kidnapping charges." Sec. A, p. 2.

———. 7/6/87. "Escapees still at large." Sec. A, p. 2.

———. 1/21/90. "Corrections faces overcrowding again." Sec. B, p. 1.

———. 2/2/90. "Heed lessons from 1980 prison riot." Sec. A, p. 5.

New Mexico Penitentiary. 1969. *Annual Report.* Santa Fe: State of New Mexico.

Newsweek. 1/15/90. "A new home for Noriega?: The federal prison in Marion, Ill., the nation's most secure pen, holds hard men doing hard time." Pp. 66–69.

New York Times. 3/21/84. "Legislative resistance to Gov. Anaya's bold social programs." Sec. I, p. 16.

Office of the Attorney General. 1975. *Penitentiary Investigation.* Santa Fe: State of New Mexico.

————. 1980a. *Report of the Attorney General on the February 2 and 3, 1980 Riot at the Penitentiary of New Mexico, Part One.* Santa Fe: State of New Mexico.

————. 1980b. *Report of the Attorney General on the February 2 and 3, 1980 Riot at the Penitentiary of New Mexico, Part Two.* Santa Fe: State of New Mexico.

Olivero, J. Michael, and James B. Roberts. 1987. "Marion Federal Penitentiary and the 22-month lockdown: The crisis continues." *Crime and Social Justice* 27–28: 234–255.

Pallas, John, and Bob Barber. 1972. "From riot to revolution." *Issues in Criminology* 7: 1–19.

Palmer, Ted. 1975. "Martinson revisited." *Journal of Research in Crime and Delinquency* 12: 133–152.

Piven, Frances Fox, and Richard A. Cloward. 1971. *Regulating the Poor.* New York: Vintage.

————. 1977. *Poor People's Movements.* New York: Vintage.

————. 1982. *The New Class War.* New York: Pantheon.

President's Commission on Law Enforcement and the Administration of Justice. 1967. *The Challenge of Crime in a Free Society.* Washington, D.C.: U.S. Government Printing Office.

Reagen, Michael V., and Donald M. Stoughton. 1976. *School Behind Bars: A Descriptive Overview of Correctional Education in the American Prison System.* Metuchen, N.J.: Scarecrow Press.

Rhodes, Hal (senior producer). 1987. *America's Prison Crisis: Monuments to Failure.* KNME–TV (documentary).

Rose, Stephen M. 1972. *The Betrayal of the Poor: Transformation of Community Action.* Cambridge, Mass.: Schenkman.

Rusche, Georg, and Otto Kirchheimer. 1939. *Punishment and Social Structure.* New York: Columbia University Press.

Santa Fe Reporter. 6/10/76. "McClendon: Mellowed macho." Pp. 3–7.

————. 4/12/79. "Acting corrections head ousted in '75." P. 3.

————. 3/19/81. "Accused deputy warden promoted." Pp. 3, 6.

————. 9/3/81. "Hell on earth: The Penitentiary of New Mexico; a special report." Pp. 1–14.

Serrill, Michael S., and Peter Katel. 1980. "New Mexico: The anatomy of a riot." *Corrections Magazine* 6 (April): 6–24.

Shils, Edward. 1975. *Center and Periphery*. Chicago: University of Chicago Press.

Shover, Neal, and Werner J. Einstadter. 1988. *Analyzing American Corrections*. Belmont, Calif.: Wadsworth.

Silberman, Charles E. 1978. *Criminal Violence, Criminal Justice*. New York: Random House.

Skocpol, Theda. 1980. "Political response to capitalist crisis: Neo-Marxist theories of the state and the case of the New Deal." *Politics and Society* 10: 155–201.

Spitzer, Steven. 1975. "Toward a Marxian theory of deviance." *Social Problems* 22: 638–651.

Stastny, Charles, and Gabrielle Tyrnauer. 1982. *Who Rules the Joint?*. Lexington, Mass.: D.C. Heath.

Stone, W. G. 1982. *The Hate Factory*. Agoura, Calif.: Paisano.

Stuart, Charles (producer). 1990. *Hunger in America*. Stuart Television Productions (documentary).

Sykes, Gresham M. 1958. *The Society of Captives*. Princeton, N.J.: Princeton University Press.

Thomas, Charles W., and David M. Petersen. 1977. *Prison Organization and Inmate Subcultures*. Indianapolis, Ind.: Bobbs-Merrill.

Toch, Hans. 1977. *Living in Prison: The Ecology of Survival*. New York: Free Press.

———. 1978. "Social climate and prison violence." *Federal Probation* 42: 21–25.

Useem, Bert. 1985. "Disorganization and the New Mexico prison riot of 1980." *American Sociological Review* 50: 677–688.

Useem, Bert, and Peter A. Kimball. 1989. *States of Siege*. New York: Oxford.

Van den Haag, Ernest. 1975. *Punishing Criminals*. New York: Basic.

Walker, Samuel. 1989. *Sense and Nonsense about Crime*. Pacific Grove, Calif.: Brooks-Cole.

Washington Post. 9/11/89. "Prison population up 7.3% in six months: A record." Sec. A, p. 16.

————. 4/10/90. "Violence in 19 prisons rocks Britain." Sec. A, p. 19.

————. 6/18/91. "Court raises burden in prison lawsuits." Sec. A, p. 4.

Wicker, Tom. 1975. *A Time to Die.* New York: Ballantine.

Wilsnack, Richard W. 1976. "Explaining collective violence in prisons: Problems and possibilities." Pp. 61–78 in Albert K. Cohen, George F. Cole, and Robert G. Bailey (eds.), *Prison Violence.* Lexington, Mass.: D.C. Heath.

Wilson, James Q. 1975. *Thinking about Crime.* New York: Basic.

Wilson, William J. 1987. *The Truly Disadvantaged: The Inner City, the Underclass, and Public Policy.* Chicago: University of Chicago Press.

Woldman, William. 1987. *Prison Conditions: The Congressional Response.* Washington, D.C.: U.S. Government Printing Office.

Wolfe, Alan. 1978. *The Seamy Side of Democracy: Repression in America.* New York: Longman.

Wooden, Wayne S., and Jay Parker. 1982. *Men Behind Bars: Sexual Exploitation in Prison.* New York: De Capo.

Wright, Erik Olin. 1973. *The Politics of Punishment.* New York: Harper Colophon Books.

INDEX

Aaron, Ralph Lee, 102, 123, 198; and Apodaca, 97, 119; background and orientation of, 97–98; and drug trafficking, 100; escapes under, 117; and Hanrahan, 104; and inmate social structure, 158; and Malley, 98; and McClendon, 98–99; and middle-level administrators, 101, 142; and Montoya, 141, 229 n .3; observations about PNM, 98; opposition to, 103–4; and organizational changes at PNM, 99; and policy vacuum, 103; and rehabilitation programs, 99–100; resignation of, 104; term as PNM warden, 218
ACLU lawsuit (*Duran v. Apodaca*), 117–19, 125, 138, 170, 183; consent decrees of, 126, 209; and Master Plan and Standards and Goals, 119, 121, 123; negotiations of, 126, 129, 173
Adamson, Christopher, 6, 23–24
administrative confusion in New Mexico corrections, 131–39, 212
Administrative Services Division (Criminal Justice Department), 126, 127, 135–37
administrative succession, 3; control structures, effect upon, 39–40, 99–103; and inmate expectations, 95–99; in New Mexico corrections, 95–103, 139, 211; and prison disorder, 199, 204
Adult Basic Education Program (ABE), 55–57
Albuquerque Journal, 229 n. 2
Alianza, 49, 90
alienative involvement, 36

alternatives to increasing use of prisons, 213–14
American Civil Liberties Union (ACLU). *See* ACLU lawsuit
Anaya, Toney: as attorney general, 65, 81, 83, 93, 104, 138; as governor, 212
Apodaca, Jerry (governor), 92, 103, 125, 132, 134, 139, 217; and Aaron, 97, 104; and Becknell, 127, 128; contradictory appointments by, 119, 127; and Gov. King, 137; and Leach, 93–94; and Malley, 128; and reorganization, 4, 7, 92 124, 125, 126, 133; and Rodriguez, 93–95, 126
Approach Associates, 123
Aragon, Manny, 9
Aryan Brotherhood, 168, 171
Attica prison riot, 47, 194
authoritarian regime: compared to coercive regime, 203; at PNM, 2, 43–46, 52–55; at Stateville, 14, 42–43

Baker, J. E.: background of, 53–54; and correctional officers, 55, 69–70, 144; and inmates, 61, 64–66, 201; and rehabilitation programs, 54, 56, 58, 59; and remunerative controls, 70; security and discipline under, 54–55, 69–70; term as acting secretary of corrections, 217; term as PNM warden, 71, 218
Barefield, Shirley, 56
Barrick, Dennis, 199
baseball bat murder, 170–71, 192

Hart, William, 228 n. 2, 229 n. 2
Herrera, Horacio (deputy warden), 72, 74, 94, 218
Herrera, Jerrie, 9
Hodson, Randy, 226 n. 5
"hole" (maximum detention unit): closing of in 1968, 54–55; reopening of in 1976, 109, 111; use of before 1968, 44–45; use of in early 1970s, 87, 230 n. 4
honor units at PNM, 59
Hopkins, Alfred, 42

importation model, 231 n. 3
imprisonment: growth in rates of in New Mexico, 89; growth in rates of in U.S., 30
inconsistencies in operation of PNM, 142–44
indulgency pattern, 37–39
informal controls of prisoners, 37–38, 83–86, 112, 114, 227 n. 7
informant system. See "snitch" system
inhalant sniffing, 169, 182
inmate administrators: and inmate strike of 1971, 76–77; and inmate strike of 1976, 106; and low levels of violence, 86; power sources of, 63–64; problems associated with, 62–63; and inmate programs, 61, 63–64; removal of in 1976, 98–99, 102; and remunerative control at PNM, 60–66
inmate clerks, 65–66, 86
inmate code, 158, 161
inmate council, 65
inmate demands: during riot of 1980, 185, 190–91; during strike of 1971, 196; during strike of 1976, 106
inmate expectations about change: and ACLU lawsuit, 118–19, 173; and expanded programs, 75; and administrative succession, 95–96, 99
inmate idleness, 42, 45, 118, 197, 209

inmate leaders, 203, 208, 210; demise of in late 1970s, 115, 138, 157, 163, 173; during early 1970s, 63–64, 157, 173; ineffective during 1980 riot, 183; and PNM administration, 105–07, 109; segregation and transfer of, 110, 157, 158; and socialization of new inmates, 159; and strike of 1976, 109; and strike of 1971, 76–77; and violence, 86, 171
inmate participation in prison administration, 54–55, 61, 122
inmate rights, 120, 122, 126, 200–01
inmate social structure, 10, 38; contrast of between early and late 1970s, 157–60, 203; and disciplinary segregation, 167; and drug trafficking, 84–85; and hardcore cliques, 170–73; ethnic composition of, 168–70, 228 n. 3; fragmentation of in late 1970s, 115, 157–73; and inmate administrators, 60–65; and new inmates, 160, 163, 200–01, 204; and prison disorder, 39–40; during riot of 1980, 185, 189; and strike of 1971, 76–77; and strike of 1976, 109
inmate strikes: in 1971, 75–78, 194, 196; in 1976, 106–09, 196
inmates: age of, 160, 162, 200–01; beatings of by staff, 38, 78, 108–9, 112–13, 118, 142; and correctional officers, 68–70; fear of humiliation among, 165–66; and hardcore cliques, 172; and inconsistencies in prison operation, 143; population levels of, 89, 213; race and ethnic relations among, 189, 191, 228 n. 3; rackets among, 80–83, 169; segregation of, 155; and "snitch" system, 154–56, 165; sources of power among, 63–64, 161, 166, 169, 172; violence among, 160–61, 164–66, 200–02, 230 n. 3
Intensive Classification Center (ICC), 123–25
Inverarity, James, 23

confusion in corrections, 125, 129, 131, 133, 139; Apodaca's plan for, 92; compromises for legislative passage of, 132–33; dismantling of, 134–35, 137; Governor's Council lead role in, 120; and (Gov.) King, 134, 137; and Master Plan recommendations, 124; and prison disorder, 204; resistance to, 93–94; and Standards and Goals, 122, 124
Richards, Bud (corrections commission chairman), 125
Richards, Ken, 9
riot of 1980 at PNM: Attica riot, contrasts with, 193; breaching of control center during, 180–81; breaking into prison pharmacy during, 182; characteristics of, 193; demands by inmates during, 185, 190–91; entry of Cellblock 3 during, 181; entry of Cellblock 4 during, 186–87; events preceding, 173–75; forewarnings of, 175; hostages taken during, 179, 181–83, 186, 190–92; inhalant sniffing during, 182; initial takeover of, 177–79; injuries during, 184, 186, 192; inmate leadership, lack of during, 183; killings during, 181, 184, 188–89, 192; negotiations during, 185, 190–91; and overcrowded conditions, 198; physical damage and expenses caused by, 192; rescue of inmates by other inmates during, 189; retaking of prison at end of, 192; securing of perimeter fence during, 185; security lapses during, 179–80; sequence of events of, 177–92
Rodriguez, Felix: and ACLU lawsuit, 138, 173; as acting warden, 52–53; and Apodaca, 93–95; balancing act of, 53, 70–75, 89; banned from PNM, 103, 94–95, 126; and Becknell, 136; correctional officers opinions of, 78; and Criminal Justice Department, 126; as deputy secretary of corrections, 136–37, 218; as deputy warden to Cox, 52, 218; as deputy warden to Baker, 54, 71, 218; disciplinary segregation during wardenship of, 114–15, 230 n. 4; drugs during wardenship of, 81; early career experiences of, 52; and factions at PNM, 74; and Griffin, 140; harassment levels during wardenship of, 148; and honor units, 58; and inconsistencies in prison operation, 142; informants during wardenship of, 151; inmate discipline during wardenship of, 79; inmate social structure during wardenship of, 66, 157–58; and inmate strike of 1971, 75; and King, 73, 136–37; and Leach, 72; and Mahr, 136; and middle-level administrators, 52, 73, 142, 174; protective custody during wardenship of, 155; and reassertion of control, 74–75; and rehabilitation programs at PNM, 55, 58–60, 78; and riot of 1980, 186, 190–92; and Salazar, 72; security during wardenship of, 79; understaffing during wardenship of, 145; as warden of PNM, 71, 94, 218
Romero, Levi (warden), 140–41, 148, 218
Roosevelt, Franklin D. (president), 225 n.1
Roswell Correctional Center, 128, 140, 228 n. 1
Rusche, Georg, 22–23, 225 n. 2

Saenz, Adolph (secretary of corrections), 186, 218
Safe Streets and Crime Control Act of 1968, 28
Salazar, John (secretary of corrections), 71–73, 217
Santa Fe County Sheriff's Office, 184
Santa Fe City Police, 184

School Release Program at PNM, 56,
91, 96
security: and Aaron, 98, 102; under
Baker, 69–70; comparisons of
between early and late 1970s, 195;
inconsistencies in, 142–43; and
Malley, 101; and prison disorder at
PNM, 195; and renovations before
1980 riot, 174; riot of 1980, lapses
during, 179–80; after riot of 1980,
209; under Rodriguez's wardenship,
79
Seductions of Crime, 188
segregation. *See* disciplinary segregation and *see* protective custody
Serrill, Michael, 191
Shils, Edward, 14, 16, 26
Shugrue, Michael, 190
Skocpol, Theda, 225 n. 1
Slade, Florence, 120
"snitch" system, 151–54, 156–57, 175
social class differences among staff and
inmates, 68
social movements: affecting PNM in
late 1960s, 46–52; waning of in
mid-1970s, 90
Spitzer, Steven, 22
Standards and Goals. *See* New Mexico
Standards and Goals
Stastny, Charles, 193
State Police Division of Criminal Justice Department, 126
Stateville, 14
Stateville Penitentiary, 2, 11, 14, 42
step system, 42, 59, 86, 111, 113
Stephens, William Jack, 170–71, 178,
192
Stone, W. G., 44
Stratton, Hal (attorney general), 212
structuring variables, 5
Sullivan, George (warden), 211
surplus labor, 18
surplus population, 20–21, 32; in core
and periphery sectors, 27, 227 n. 5;
growth of in 1974–75, 89; and
imprisonment, 23–24; in non-

union labor markets, 22, 25, 30; as a
"problem population," 22, 26; in
unionized labor markets, 25–27, 29
surplus value, 18
Swenson, H. R. (warden), 42
Swope, Gerard, 225 n. 1
Sykes, Gresham M., 20, 34, 37, 40, 83,
107

Tansy, Robert J. (warden), 232 n. 1
Technical Support Division of Criminal Justice Department, 126, 135,
146
Texas prisons, 38, 199, 227 n. 7
The Right to Participate, 54
Tierra Amarilla (prison) Forestry
Camp, 228 n. 1
Tijerina, Reies Lopez, 49–50, 90
toleration of drug trafficking. *See* drug
trafficking and *see* informal controls
of prisoners
Towers, Sharon, 118
transfer of inmates: out of state, 110,
159, 172; to minimum security
facilities, 152–53, 174
treatment staff at PNM, 66–67, 120–21
treatment regime at PNM, 52–55, 201
Treaty of Guadalupe Hidalgo, 48
Tynauer, Gabrielle, 193

U.S. Federal Penitentiary at Lewisburg,
Pa., 42
U.S. Federal Penitentiary at Lompoc,
Calif., 207
U.S. Federal Penitentiary at Marion,
Ill., 97, 208
U.S. Federal Penitentiary at Terre
Haute, Ind., 54
U.S. Forest Service, 48, 50
U.S. Supreme Court, 212–13, 233 n. 4
unemployed. *See* surplus population
unemployment, 30, 89. *See also* surplus
population